HIGHLIFE
& my other lives

HIGHLIFE
& my other lives

Richard Walker

First published in Great Britain by Amaurea Press 2025
Amaurea Press is an imprint of Amaurea Creative Productions Ltd.
www.amaureapress.com

Copyright © Richard Walker 2025

The right of Richard Walker to be identified as the author of this work has been asserted in accordance with the Copyright, Designs and Patents Act 1988

All rights reserved. Apart from any fair dealing for the purposes of criticism or review, as permitted under the Copyright Acts, no part of this book may be reproduced, copied or transmitted in any form or by any electronic or mechanical means, including information storage and retrieval systems, without permission in writing from the publisher.

ISBN 9781914278761 (hardback)
ISBN 9781914278778 (eBook)

British Library Catalogue in Publishing Data
A catalogue record for this book is available from the British Library.

Book design and typesetting by Albarrojo
Cover design by Albarrojo & Li Qinyuan
Author photo © Ian Cook
Other photos in the book are from the author's personal collection
Turtle glyph © Adobe Stock/Ann

Printed and bound by CPI Group (UK) Ltd., Croydon, CR0 4YY

For Lauren
1955 – 2016

One of Lauren's favourite photos. En route to Cyprus. French Alps. 2005.

Prologue
The Voyage Out
9

Act 1
The Poor Man's Eton and The Poet
33

Act 2
Fledglings
93

Act 3
Merry Go Round
119

Act 4
Eleftheria i Thanatos
(Freedom or Death)
171

Act 5
Last Dance
245

Epilogue
289

Prologue

The Voyage Out

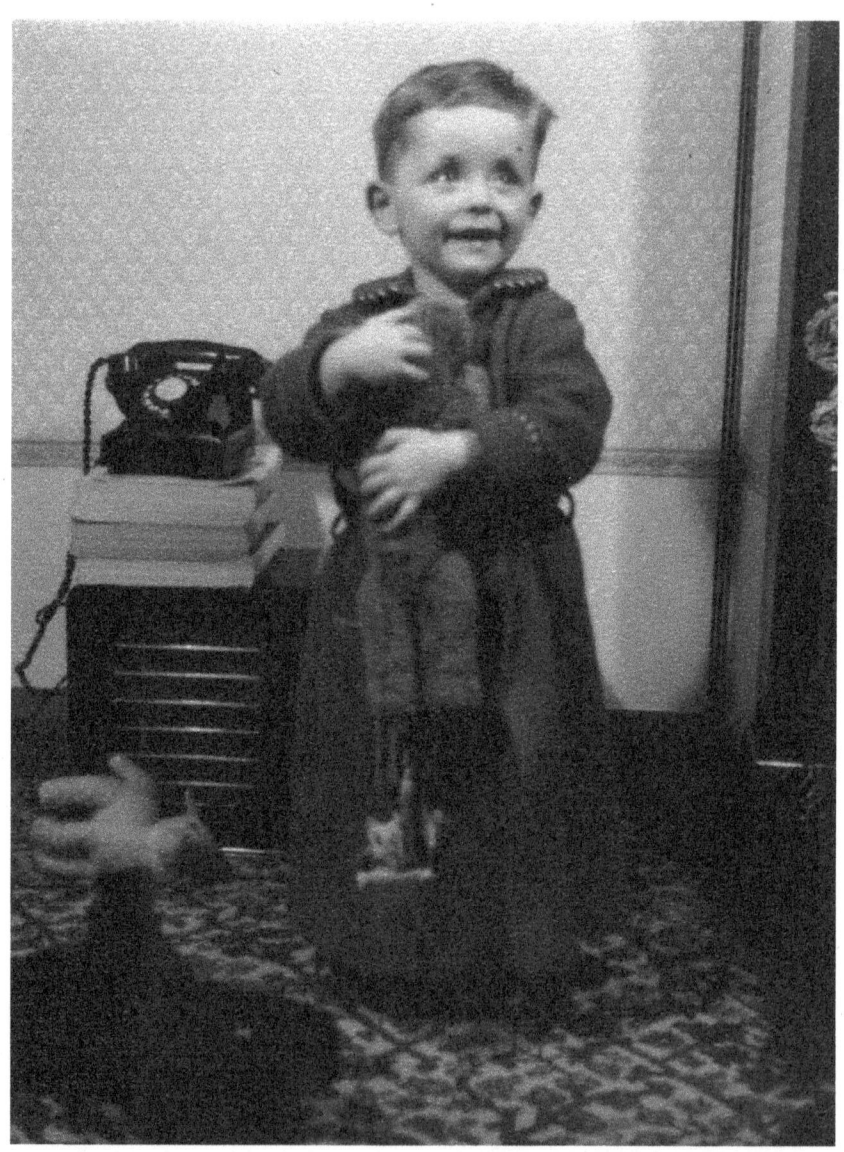
Richard and teddy. Probably late-1955, on the cusp of Wokingham/Guildford.

I'M STANDING UNDER and behind a high counter. I can reach the top but I can't see over it. Men's voices talking loudly and laughing hover in the air. On a far wall away from the counter there's a semicircle with red, green and black portions of colour separated by wire. Sometimes a dart thuds into the board, and I can see the back of a man's head and his hand pulling the dart from the board. Once three darts land tightly clustered in one of the fenced off portions and a loud cheer bounces off the walls and ceiling.

The weather, the sky, the sodden bark of trees, leaf mulch, the windowpanes, the smoke from the chimney weaving upwards, my socks and shoes, my shirt, pullover and flannel shorts, which bulge and drop down my right leg with the weight and gravity of coppers, sausages, gravy, roast dinner, the vegetable garden beds, everything, all of it, my life is in shades of grey, brown, khaki, beige, black. There are few splashes of colour.

My Mum pushes me to nursery school. From our house it's up and halfway down Shepherd's Hill. She's friends with the lady in charge. They chat about when my Mum's going to pick me up. The lady in charge says, 'Don't worry Gwen, he'll be fine. He and Andrew keep each other busy.' Andrew's my friend who's mum is the lady in charge.

My father has a black car. Inside it's all brown – leather, I think.

I like it when we're going to turn a corner. Then an orange tongue flicks out of the side of the car behind his head to show we're going to turn. There's one on each side. The colour of the tongue reminds me of Noddy and Big Ears, who vibrate in books with bold colours, though my father's car is much darker than Noddy's.

On the way home from school I stop at Lewis's the newsagent and buy a Barratt's Sherbet fountain in a bright yellow tube with red lettering and a liquorice stick. I don't know why they call it a fountain. It doesn't fountain like a volcano does. You have to suck the sherbet up through the liquorice tube, which is sticky and the sherbet gets clogged in it. Or, if I have enough coppers, I buy a quarter of Bassett's sherbet lemons weighed out with a scoop in a silver bowl. I'm absorbed by the intense, acid yellow of these hard-boiled sweets, their tartness on my tongue and whether I can pass the fish and chip shop and reach the big corner house, where I turn left then right towards my own much smaller house; whether I can reach that corner house before my sucking on the outer casing explodes the shattered sweet with sherbet fizzing on my tongue. If I suck on more than two in a row, the roof of my mouth grows sore and I spend the time at home probing it with my tongue.

On the common behind the house we carry jam jars to the pond. We scoop jellied frogspawn, tadpoles, sometimes a newt. The black water has a dark green slime and is ringed with bulrushes whose dark chocolate seed heads are like sausages on green sticks.

Once I climb a tree in Peter's garden. He lives up the hill in our close. When I fall and hit the ground with my back there's a sack of air expelled from my lungs and a searing pain. This is death I know. Then the air flows in and the pain is a sharp ache. I manage to stand up and tell Peter I'm going home. Mum tells me I've been 'winded', and the pain will stop soon.

It's my sixth birthday and I'm allowed to invite four friends from school home for tea. Mum asks if there's something special I'd like for my birthday tea. Tomato sandwiches, I say. She tells me I have those all the time. They're not special. But I tell her they're my favourite and I want a big plate piled high with tomato sandwiches all for me. Can she please make a separate plate for others who might want tomato sandwiches?

The washing machine is pulled out from a cupboard next to the sink. It's filled with hot water and detergent, sheets are pushed in and pressed down with a large wooden spoon into the belly of the machine. The metal lid is put on and screwed round to tighten it like the lid of a jar of jam. The metal vat vibrates through the kitchen, when it reaches its maximum speed and tries to dance around the kitchen Mum has to lean on it with all her weight to stop it crashing into the cupboards. Then the mangle is attached to the top of the washing machine, she feeds in the sheets and I use all my strength to turn the handle, slowly squeezing the last of the soapy water from the sheets.

I'M IN A darkened room and a woman with a white coat is on the other side of some complicated apparatus. She asks me to sit on the stool on my side and she sits on the other. She tells me please to put my chin on a hard plastic rest scooped to hold it comfortably. Then she leans across and guides my right hand, 'You're right-handed, aren't you?' she confirms. 'Mmnh, mmnh,' I nod in agreement.

'Please put your hand on this handle and move it around slowly then stop when you see something.'

'I'm doing it.' I stop. 'It's the tail of an animal,' I say, not sure.

'Good. See if you can move the handle so you find the whole animal.'

I'm moving it too quickly. The head of an animal flashes by, then its paws. I slow down. Now I have it! 'It's a *tiger!*' I cry out.

'Great!' she says. 'Now I'm going to introduce another picture. Don't move the tiger.'

I nod on the chin rest, anxious not to make a mistake. Some black bars appear. Is it a cage? I wonder.

'That's right. Just move the tiger in the cage now please.'

I hesitate. I don't want to put the tiger in the cage. She senses my hesitation.

'It's just a game. We can get the tiger out of the cage before we finish.'

We play games like this for some weeks along with more serious ones where I have to tell her what letters in a light box at a distance I can see. The big ones at the top are easy. Lower down it gets more difficult, especially when it's a 'c' that might be an 'o', or a 'u' that might be a 'v.'

Dad and Mum take me to see the surgeon. 'He's the doctor who's going to operate on your eye, the left one that isn't so strong,' says Dad.

'We haven't agreed yet,' says Mum.

'It'll be alright, he'll be fine,' says Dad.

Mum says nothing.

When I wake, I can't see anything but I know I'm in bed. A woman's voice, not Mum's, says everything has gone very well and this afternoon they'll be taking the bandage off my right eye, my better one, and then Dad and Mum will come and see me. And tomorrow they'll come back and I'll try on the glasses. 'Just for reading,' she says. 'You won't have to wear them all the time.'

The next day I try the glasses and they feel like little claws round my ears. The light hurts a bit but I can see the shapes of letters and words clearly. The surgeon appears and stands at the end of the bed talking quietly with Dad and Mum. I hear him say 'Today', and 'One month, then six months, then one year.'

When he's gone Dad says, 'If you do well, he said you can stop wearing them before you to go to secondary school.'

Mum gives me a cuddle and says nothing, but I can see the tears in her eyes more clearly than I've ever seen them.

WE'RE ON HOLIDAY in one of the brewery workers' cottages in Kimmeridge Bay, Dorset. Dad knows the family which owns the brewery. There are outside toilets and a cobwebby shed where we sleep in bunks with Jane, my younger sister, and my friend

Peter from the same street. His mum's German. It's a thank-you present from the brewing family for allowing their son to lodge with us sometimes while he's learning the brewing business at the Friary Meux Brewery in Guildford. They draw the water from the River Wey in the valley at the bottom of the cobbled High Street. On brewing days a brown, sticky fug covers the town and we go to see the cows auctioned in the cattle market by the river. Their mooing echoes round the sheds and their giant, smelly pats splatter on the concrete floor.

Andrew and I have a gang. The Black Hand Gang. Sometimes he comes over and we go on to the common behind my house. In summer we build dens from bracken. His garden has a big walnut tree at the bottom and we spend hours climbing it trying to see how high we can get. We like to crack open the brown, dark wrinkled walnuts between two bricks without smashing the edible nuts to smithereens. Rarely, we get a perfect hit and the nut cracks open to reveal its two halves; it's like what I imagine it would be if we were on a desert island and picking the brain out of a tiny monkey's skull. Once Andrew falls from near the top of the tree crashing through the branches to the ground where the inside of his knee smashes onto one of the bricks. Then I see the white bone of his knee through the torn flesh and blood. I run inside to fetch someone, his older sister or one of his parents, and he has to go to hospital.

One day I come home from school and both Mum and Dad are there, which isn't normal. Dad doesn't usually get back from work until later. He says, 'Richard, please go and sit in the dining room. We have something important to tell you.'

I'M STANDING ON the station platform in Guildford with Mum and my little sister, Jane. There's a lot of luggage, brown suitcases piled up, which the porter has helped us bring from outside the station where the taxi dropped us. We board the train to Waterloo Station in South London. I get a smut in my eye from the coal dust. We cross London in a taxi to catch another steam train to Liverpool, where we board the Elder Dempster Line boat, the SS Apapa. We're making the journey to Africa in reverse from Liverpool – later, I learn it was the leading city in Europe for the slave trade. A wobbly but immaculately scrubbed, polished and roped gangway leads up to the white, elephantine vessel with a brown funnel. I'm super excited.

Las Palmas in the Canaries is the first place we step on which isn't British. Panniers on donkeys are stacked high with hands of green bananas. Bathurst, now Banjul, in The Gambia and Freetown in Sierra Leone are the first two African cities we see. Canoes paddle out to our steamer; baskets are lowered and loaded with unfamiliar mangoes and pineapples, then hauled on board. I've never seen such fruit 'live'. Until then, I've eaten only tinned and never seen a fresh pineapple, let alone a fresh mango. I love them both, savouring their distinctive juices.

I'm quickly good at deck quoits and compete with adults who now, I realise, were being indulgent. There's a cricket net too. Not much ball swing in the air – but plenty of movement off the deck to bamboozle you. The biggest thrill onboard is the saltwater swimming pool. It's more of a plunge pool cut out of the top deck, about eight metres square with an exhilarating depth of two metres. In a heavy, listing sea, the water in the pool swings crazily, swirling from side to side, sometimes revealing the bottom of the pool, then it turns back and smashes against the other side in an impressive arc of seawater. The first time this happens, I'm in the pool, and the swell is only enough to spray a few adults seated in their deck chairs around the poolside. There's good-natured shrieking and laughter, what a jolly bit of fun, to entertain and cool us down on a hot day! The second time, the adults in their deck chairs are soaked, their card games swept aside, their newspapers or books sodden, their drinks spilt, and their glasses washed along the deck. Most thrilling is a girl in the pool, who's flung out by the seawater wave, tossed into the air, and crashes into the deckchairs. This time the adult screams and shouts are genuine shock and fear. I'm jealous of the girl and wish it'd been me. I want to be embraced by the power of the sea and to be swept up in the air and thrown aside. I spend the rest of the voyage manoeuvring myself into a position to make this happen. But I never achieve the heights of being cast aside by a giant wave.

Sometime after five o'clock, Jane and I have high tea with the other children in the dining room: fish paste sandwiches, biscuits with a hole with red jam in the middle, strawberry jelly, sponge cake, jugs of orange squash. Then we go to the cabin we all share. I have the top bunk, Jane the bottom one. Mum has a separate bed underneath the porthole window. I love the sense of miniature mountaineering climbing up to my bunk. While we get undressed, pull on pyjamas, and clean our teeth, Mum gets ready to go out to dinner. A heady fountain of perfume swamps the cabin announcing the advanced stages of her preparation. Elizabeth Arden's Blue Grass. That all-encompassing, pungent chemical wave was what perfume meant to me for years. It was only later as an adult that I smelled other more subtle perfumes with their complex range of notes and melodies. Blue Grass was a full-on brass solo. Later perfumes were string quartets or Chopin Études. Mum, her name is Gwen, only ever wears perfume in the evening. To wear it at any other time, she thinks is 'frivolous'. She has to explain the word to me.

Gwen, when a child, fell from an upstairs window of their London house onto the railings below. I don't know how old she was when it happened or how seriously she'd been injured, I suppose she must have been lucky to survive. She never wanted to talk about it. Later she had a prematurely, slightly curved spine, which I assumed was related to the accident. I so much wished I'd asked her about it and much more. She was the eldest of three children, and when their mother died young, her father, a publican, expected her to leave school to look after him and her brother, Arthur, and her sister, Connie. It must have been an enormous frustration and quiet disappointment in her life to have to assume the role of housewife and mother when she was still a teenager. But like so many women in the interwar generation, she assumed the duties expected of her. I think she recognised that sense of responsibility in Queen Elizabeth II. She identified with it firmly, becoming a lifelong devotee of the monarch who outlived her. I wish I'd found a way to explore it all with her: the accident, being her father's housekeeper and siblings' mother, and her frustrated ambitions for her own education. We weren't expected or encouraged as 1950s children, certainly in my family, to explore the prior and private worlds of our parents' lives before they were our parents. By the time I was old enough to understand this, I realised she had an aspiration and curiosity for learning and books which no one else in her or my father's family shared. She lived through it and learned as she went along. When I was fifteen years old, she was the only parent in our modest cul-de-sac who'd heard of Samuel Beckett. She bought us both tickets to see *Waiting for Godot* at the Yvonne Arnaud Theatre in Guildford. It was funny and strange in parts. I'm sorry that I wasn't brave enough to break the conventions that her world and she herself had set: keeping silent about challenging personal things that became 'Private, No Entry'.

She lived through the Blitz working at the premier international music publishers Boosey and Hawkes and the Performing Arts Society. After Dad, George, died, she started regularly going to the Royal Festival and Wigmore Halls in London with women friends or alone. She'd endured an unhappy, childless first marriage before she met Dad relatively late in both their lives. I regret I know no more about her first marriage. I regret even more that I learned and know so little about both Dad and Mum's interior lives.

Contemplating some of these moments in her life, I consider how glamorous and special it must have felt to be on a liner with her young children sailing to an unknown place but safely comforted by all those then middle-class rituals like dressing for dinner.

Sometime later – it seems like the middle of the night, but it's probably ten o'clock – she appears with a plate of sandwiches. She's filched the sandwiches laid out for supper when there's a break from the dancing; half-awake we have what she calls 'a midnight feast'. She usually stays with us, but occasionally returns to continue the onboard, nightly party. It takes thirteen nights before we dock at Takoradi, west along the coast from Accra. Dad's on the dockside dressed in khaki: a short-sleeved tunic, capacious and ironed shorts, both garments stiff from excessive starching. He wears off-white socks to the knee and brown highly polished shoes. Behind him are an electric blue Renault Ondine saloon, his personal car, and a jungle green jeep for our luggage with a driver, a corporal with two stripes. Dad holds out his arms to hug Mum, Jane and me. We drive the five hours from the dockside to our new home: No.23 Burma Villas.

One of the twists of the British Empire is you steam thousands of miles south to West Africa and end up living in *Burma* Villas. The Royal West Africa Frontier Force, including an estimated 65,000 Gold Coast troops, fought against the Japanese as part of the Allied front on the Bengal-Burmese borderlands in the Second World War. Their overland journey from northern Ghana to the troop carriers on the Gold Coast passed through the forests where I soon see golden cocoa pods glowing in the dark.

DAD, A CAREER military man, has flown to Ghana some months ahead of us to start his new role as an adviser and trainer to Nkrumah's post-independence Ghanaian army. In 1960, he was already semi-retired from the British military and running the Territorial Army base in Guildford. When he got the invitation, he must have thought his boat had come in. A colonial-style bungalow with a veranda and staff quarters in a separate block at the back; what seemed unlimited duty-free booze and fags – he was partial to both – and an unexpected boost to income and pension for what his friends would have called 'a cushy number'. It was a desk job for someone who had served pre-War in the cantonment in Shanghai. My earliest photos of him are in rickshaws enjoying a day out with his mates. He'd been at Dunkirk and spent a good chunk of his war in North Africa and later was amused to see me puffing, for a season, Camel cigarettes, their packets branded with ochre pictures of camels, pyramids and palm trees. We were in a pub on Guildford High Street; he was on his second pint of Courage Director's bitter when he saw the packet and casually alluded to smoking hashish in Cairo during the War. It was a rare glimpse of another life before me, before his wife, my Mum, Gwen.

He helped deliver the post-war rebuilding of Germany based in Luneburg Heath near Hamburg. It was where he met Gwen on the same mission, she through the Women's Royal Voluntary Service. After he died, Mum told me they did some of their 'courting' in the Four Seasons Hotel in Hamburg. And she remembers finding herself on the floor under her bar stool after Dad had ordered a third cocktail and turned to talk to the man on his other side. Later, when I ran a literature festival in Hamburg, I went to look at the hotel. It was impressive. I'd worked out that I might have been conceived there. But the hotel refused to reveal any of its secrets about Mum and Dad's past.

What *is* sure about their 'courting days' are the pictures of them now on my sitting room wall in the snow outside a wooden chalet, Pension Villa Buchenhain. It's in the village of Ehrwald, Austria, about 80 kilometres north-west of Innsbruck, which is where you'd fly today to reach it. Though I imagine they went there from northern Germany by train. There they are dressed in boots, heavy socks, corduroys, Fair Isle sweaters, for my mother a headscarf against the cold and both are on wooden skis. The contrast between this snowy setting before I arrived in their lives and my early memories of them in humid, tropical Ghana couldn't be greater. Villa Buchenhain is still operating, though George and Gwen wouldn't recognise its indoor swimming pool or the wellness centre. The magnificent views of the Zugspitze remain the same, while there's now a shorter season with less snow.

I'M WITH MUM, Dad and Jane watching polo: beach chairs, cool boxes with green bottles of black Star beer, a tartan rug, my parents' friends, Ghanaian and international, in conversation and laughing, with the polo match a backdrop to their noisy party. I hear the thwack of the polo stick on the ball and see fetlocks protected with buckled khaki protectors like miniature cricket pads.

Dad and Mum must have driven us past the original, undamaged statue of Kwame standing outside Parliament House hundreds of times. I remember asking about the two-storey, white, red-tiled roof, and open balconied colonial building. It seemed, even then to me as a child, remarkably unspectacular for a Parliament House.

IN NOVEMBER 1961, I've just turned nine years old and we're in Independence Square during the state visit to Ghana by Queen Elizabeth II. It's early evening after sunset and we're seated in metal chairs with Dad and Mum just behind the dignitaries. There's a military parade, though I've already sat through several and am not impressed by it or the speeches. What I like are the fireworks.

After what seems an eternity of rockets firing hundreds of feet into the night sky in loops and criss-cross patterns, huge wheels whizzing fiercely, fountains of light cascading bigger than a house, the climax of the show flares into life. The heads of the two Heads of State – President Kwame Nkrumah and Her Majesty Queen Elizabeth II – in multicoloured fireworks blaze out their portraits in silhouette. They face each other illuminating a perfect unison, two heads of state still doubly incandescent in my memory. We are allowed to stay up late that evening even though we have school the next day. Before I go to sleep, I slip out of bed and pull back the curtains to look at the paw-paw trees silhouetted against the night sky above the apex of our bungalow roof.

I can hear laughter and the chinking of glasses from the small party Dad and Mum are having in the sitting room.

For weeks I've been looking forward to playing for the school cricket team against the Royal Yacht Britannia due to dock on the state visit. I relentlessly practise my forward defensive and off-drive with a tennis ball. We arrive in the Renault in good time at the cricket ground with its small pavilion. When we get out and it's quiet no one is immediately alarmed. But it soon becomes clear that somehow Dad has got the wrong day. Unbelievable for a military man! The cricket game had taken place the day before. I stand on the coconut matting which forms the wicket and cry. It's the first time I ever feel Dad and Mum have let me down. There's a reception onboard the Britannia early that evening. There are no other children there. I wonder if Dad has got special permission to bring me as compensation for missing the cricket match. The decks are scrubbed almost white, the brass gleams, the dark teak or mahogany of cabin doors show a reflection as you walk by. The navy uniforms are white as ice in the humidity, some braided with gold and blue. Adult talk and laughter. The tinkle of glasses. But I am still miserable about the missed game. One of the crew tries to cheer me up by showing me some of the grand rooms below deck. I want to show my appreciation, but I'm desolate inside.

THE GHANA ARMED Forces Primary and Junior High School Jane and I attend has a breeze block wall, its lower half is smartly painted in sea blue with its upper half in sky blue. It carries a pink shield with a yellow circle in its centre and a deep blue Ashanti character, which symbolises the Supremacy of God. The motto, on the lower half of the shield, is: 'Except the Lord,' referencing Psalm 127 in the King James Version: 'Except the Lord build the house, they labour in vain that build it.'

In the colonial period it had been for the sons and daughters of white British army officers with no Ghanaian children. Post independence all the boys and girls are Ghanaian, except a handful of white children like Jane and me whose fathers are now honorary Ghanaian officers. All the teachers are still white British, including the Headmaster, Mr Atherton, who wears a civilian version of my father's uniform with baggy shorts, white knee socks and highly polished shoes. I still have a framed, advanced swimming certificate signed by Kenneth R. Atherton, in copperplate handwriting, August 1962. But Mr Orchard is my favourite teacher and wears long dark trousers, colourful Ghanaian shirts and sandals. Muttering from some parents, 'Sandals without socks!' I hear Mum at some social occasion discussing Mr Orchard's 'racy wife' who's 'gone off with another chap.' I never learn whether this is a temporary or lasting situation nor whether Mr Orchard's boozing – which sparks the comments about his wife – is short-lived or prolonged.

IN OUR BURMA Camp sitting room Dad has installed a vast combined wireless and record player encased in a wooden cabinet that's much taller than me. His regular early evening begins just before 6pm; he sits opposite this wooden pulpit as if for a sermon. No-one can talk or disturb him at this time . . . 'because your father wants to know what's happening in the world.' Reuben brings the large Gordon's gin and tonic which Dad has taught him to make. Sometimes he jumps up, fiddling with the dials on the wireless trying to reduce the hiss and static. Some sibilance or interference usually remains. Then the intermittently sonorous resonance of the BBC World Service booms out . . . 'This is London calling . . . London calling . . .,' reverberating and rattling through the rattan front of the cabinet like a medium summoning a spirit from another world. Which, in its way, it is.

On one occasion, Dad lets out a loud 'Ssshush,' and calls out, 'Gwen, Gwen, come!' She dashes into the room, worried, 'What is it, George?' Dad points at the cabinet and then puts an index finger to his lips to signal silence. I'm sitting quietly in a corner recalling the wave on the beach that afternoon that had rolled me over at least half a dozen times.

I know something is important because he's called Mum, and they exchange words that are anxious and agitated. I've never seen him call her when listening to the World Service news. After the bulletin finishes, Dad turns off the wireless. They continue whispering for a while, then sit quietly, unspeaking until they rise to get washed and dressed for dinner. I too head for my shower at the other end of the bungalow. Over dinner my father sometimes asks what we've done at school that day and what we've done after school before he arrives home. This time he tells Jane and me there is something important we should know. He's just heard on the news that the President of the United States has been assassinated. He doesn't know yet whether our school will be closed as a security precaution. It doesn't, but I hear the teachers and other adults talking about it in the following days.

Dad and Mum also listen through the cabinet to their modest vinyl collection, including the American crooner, Jim Reeves, with his Nashville country sound. Other favourites are Dean Martin and Frank Sinatra. It's singers like these which give me an aversion to sentimental vocalists with syrupy lyrics about love, loss and heartbreak. Mum endlessly, it seems, plays the soundtrack from South Pacific – 'I'm gonna wash that man right out of my hair' – which sticks like chewing gum, producing in me an equal disdain for Hollywood musicals. Dad's also a fan of the Cretan-Greek singer Nana Mouskouri. I don't understand the attraction, as the picture on the record cover is a prim looking woman wearing horn-rimmed glasses, her hair stiff with sprayed lacquer. Like many things you're exposed to when younger, you either embrace them passionately – mine was sport and exercise of all kinds – or loathe them fiercely. Later in life, I've come to appreciate the vocal qualities of those singers, if not their lyrics. I can enjoy a musical now at the right time in the right company. And I've learned to love some opera.

THESE MIDDLEBROW WESTERN singers are in complete contrast to the music I most enjoy. Saturday evenings, once or more a month, are a special occasion that always excites me. We know we have to be showered and in our best clothes – still shorts for me – by 6pm Reuben has washed and polished the electric blue Renault. Jane and I sit in the back, me with my foot tapping, while my father drives us all to the Ambassador Hotel. We were on our way to listen to Highlife music live. Dad circles round the hotel driveway and pulls up by the front door under an awning. Four bellboys open all its doors simultaneously, and we step out like minor film stars with Dad handing over car keys and going round to offer his arm to Mum. The band is already in full swing. We walk under the purple bougainvillaea spilling down the steps and head for the music. Some of my parents' Ghanaian and international friends are already seated at round tables with clusters of ice buckets holding green bottles of Star beer. They shout, wave and laugh, 'George you brought the piccaninnies!' Another roar of laughter explodes. My sister and I are the 'piccaninnies'. From the Portuguese *pequeno*. It's Pidgin English usually used about Ghanaian children. This term is now a racial slur.

But the Ghanaian officer using the term to a white friend, Dad, about his children is a sign of belonging and inclusion. A kind of, 'I have piccaninnies, you have piccaninnies, we all have piccaninnies.'

The band plays on ignoring their raucous laughter and the other noisy parties. With its many guitars and jazzy horns playing driving Akan rhythms, it's loud and brassy. I love the sound, the mix of melody, tone and pace. Sometimes there are vocals, and I like the pitch and incantation, though I rarely get more than a snatch of the lyrics. It doesn't matter. Its fusion holds me, captures me in its beat. I love, too, the rush of the first ice-cold Coca-Cola and the adults talking loudly and laughing. Some of the Ghanaian men in multi-coloured shirts are already on their feet swaying and shuffling in time to the beat of the music. In the warm, breezeless night air, cigarette smoke hangs and wreathes in misty circles which adds to the air of mystery and excitement.

Highlife emerged first in Ghana in the 1920s using a combination of Ghanaian rhythms and western instruments. It borrowed from other genres such as calypso and the foxtrot. Consensus has it that it was first called Highlife by Ghanaians who loved the music but who were too poor to access the exclusive clubs where it was played. The initial audiences had to pay seven shillings and sixpence and to wear evening dress. This limited attendance to the wealthy Gold Coast aristocracy with a sprinkling of foreigners. Following the Second World War, it democratised to an extent, particularly in urban centres like Accra. In 1956, the year before Gold Coast became Ghana, the leading Highlife musician of the day, E. T. Mensah, played a filmed concert with Louis Armstrong as part of his tour of Ghana. The timing of the Armstrong visit, the year before independence, was perfect. Highlife music had taken its place fully on the international stage announcing the emergence of a nation about to become independent of its colonial master. In one concert the footage cuts away as Louis introduces the next number, while he says, 'This song is for the Prime Minister,' and there is Kwame Nkrumah dignified and handsome sitting in front of a white couple, Sir Charles Aden-Clarke, then the Governor General, and his wife. Louis sings 'Black and Blue' with the searing line, 'My only sin is in my skin.'

But it's the music itself that draws me in along with the excitement of the venue and party atmosphere in which it's played. It influences my listening and later preferred taste for jazz, rock, blues, funk and its offshoots into my teenage years and much later. Fela Kuti, the great Nigerian musician, was influenced by a visit to Ghana and experience of Highlife in the late 1960s. And out of which he coined the term 'Afrobeat'. It's unsurprising that my early exposure to Highlife, its environment, its subliminal social and political impetus, meant that later at my boarding school I found classical music lessons stilted and remote.

ONE DAY AFTER school, when we don't go to the beach, I'm alone in the shade of a mango tree. I'm sitting on the red clay topsoil called 'laterite', which is common in West Africa and is sometimes used for constructing buildings. I'm playing with my Dinky Toy soldiers: their lorries, jeeps, tanks, armoured cars and, with a bucket of water, building from the laterite a model encampment of the one in which I live with roads, bungalows and barracks. I spot a snake in the lime-green hedge. It's a vivid, bright green, slender and long. It pauses low in the hedge in my eye line and darting its head holds my gaze for a long while. I sit there wondering what to do. I do nothing but stare back. Then it's gone swiftly, just as it appeared. I don't tell my parents. That would put an end to my afternoon play when my mother dozes on her bed after lunch.

It was a western green mamba – probably a young one – native to West Africa. The average length of adults is four to seven feet! Contact with humans is rare, but when it does bite, most recorded bites have been fatal. It's comparable to many species of cobra, but its bite is more severe and life-threatening within a shorter period. Victims have been known to suffocate within thirty minutes of being bitten due to paralysis of the respiratory muscles. Probably less for a skinny boy of nine. The scientific name for mamba is *Dendroaspis*, which my basic Greek tells me is 'tree snake'. Which means it had probably slithered down the mango tree under which I'd been sitting. Playing with my toy soldiers had been so nearly so fatal.

Once I find a huge python curled up asleep in the storm drain outside our bungalow. I run inside. Dad's at work and Mum's asleep. I tell Reuben. He goes out the back and returns with a machete. 'No, no! Not that!' I cry. I lead him to where the python's still sleeping. 'He just eat. He will sleep long time,' says Reuben. 'Wait till Mastah come home.' That evening I hear Dad telling Reuben to find two more houseboys in the street and get rid of the python. 'Will they kill it?' I ask Dad. He doesn't reply. I go to bed sad. It's my fault if they kill the python. Then I know they'll kill it. And I'm sad, feeling guilty for two days.

Mum directs the garden planting through our part-time gardener. He wears a torn, muddy white vest and ragged shorts with an African spade which he uses like a cross between a pickaxe and a hoe. Mum ensures we have tomatoes and potatoes. We also have several clumps of maize, taller than adults, which is a novelty as human food. At this time in Britain, it's only animal fodder. Its tall yellow-green bamboo-like leafy shafts provide excellent coverage for hiding from my sister. In addition to mango trees, we have rows of pineapples growing from their clumps of vicious spikes which fan out from the base, circles of barbed wire guarding the succulent, golden fruit at their heart. From my bedroom, at the back of the house, I lie on my bed and gaze through the mosquito netting at the small forest of spindly, single-stemmed papaya or pawpaw trees. These grow to the height of the bungalow and taller. All the large, lobed leaves cluster at the top of the tree along with clumps of elongated, oval fruit. They hang pointing downwards like the breasts of the naked women I see by the roadside cradling children on their hips. Over weeks, I watch the fruit enlarge and ripen from deep tropical green, slowly becoming tinged with yellow-orange until the entire fruit glows amber in the dark.

About a hundred yards away in the scrub across the road by the perimeter fence are groves of cashew nut trees. I go scrumping cashews there with my Anglo-German friend Dirk. We pick some of the large pods each of which contains a single cashew seed or nut. That's why they're so labour-intensive to harvest and expensive. What we don't know is that the nut is protected by anacardic acid, which irritates the skin – severely in the case of children. That evening my arms swell up with bumpy red blotches. We have to go to the army hospital to find something to soothe them and help me sleep.

The second time I'm in an Accra hospital, a civilian one in the city, is when we return from three months' leave in Europe.

Mum is out of the routine of beach life. She always insists on a meticulous lathering of suntan cream. Our first time by the sea following a European winter, she forgets, and I have a day on the beach in and out of the water like a scrawny puppy. That evening my skin begins to prickle then turns to a low heat bubbling up and coming to the boil sometime before midnight. I'm in agony. I have to stay in the city hospital overnight. A nurse takes a transparent papyrus of skin from the corner of each shoulder and peels it all the way down my back. She repeats this action four times. At home on the following nights, I have to sleep on my side or front and even then my sleep is broken. Mum is mortified and, for the rest of our 'tour', the sun lotion discipline at the beach or pool is strictly enforced.

One day we go to a different beach where the waves are so wild it's difficult – 'dangerous,' Mum says – to go into the water. We are with some friends of theirs who have no children. Dad and the man are setting up a barbeque, drinking beers and laughing. Mum and Olive are sitting on a fallen coconut tree trunk chatting quietly. Jane is digging in the sand nearby. I'm bored and wander off into the coconut groves. I become aware of something in one of the taller trees ahead. It's a boy, not much older than me, shinning up the tree trunk to reach the coconuts. He has a leather strap round his waist and the trunk and is leaning backwards to keep the strap tight. When he reaches the top his machete slices into the growth that attaches the coconuts to the tree. They tumble down in ones, twos and threes thudding in the sand in front of me. A storm of coconuts, more than a dozen, in a sudden, quick explosion. Then it's quiet and the boy shins down the tree. He smiles but doesn't speak, slicing the top off one he passes it to me to drink the water. I take it, drink half and hand it back. 'For you,' I say. He smiles and drains it. Then he's collecting the coconuts in two sacks and disappears into the grove with the coconuts over his shoulders.

Further on there's a small clearing in the dense grove with a patch of sunlight and in the middle a dark shadow. As I get nearer, I see the shadow is alive. It's a turtle on its back, each of its legs tied to a rope with a stake in the ground. It struggles now and then trying to roll off it's back, but it's clearly exhausted and each effort seems weaker than the last. I'm horrified and terrified. I want to release it but I'm afraid to. Then I'm running back in the direction of Dad and Mum. When I see them I start shouting, 'Come! Come quickly! There's a turtle. It's dying. We need to let it go.'

Dad is the first to react, following me back to where the turtle is staked out. As we arrive, the turtle is struggling feebly rocking from side to side. Dad shakes his head slowly. 'I'm sorry. We can't do anything Richard.'

'But it's cruel! It's going to die!'

'We can't interfere. It's not ours.'

'It's not theirs either. It's not fair.'

'It's more theirs than ours,' says Dad, and puts his arm round my shoulders to lead me away. My eyes are full of tears. Mum is blurred. My shoulders shake. I fall against her and sob. And sob. Not fair. Cruel.

DESPITE ALL THE outdoor activity and sport in Ghana and later, I never suffer a broken bone. Nor am I at all sickly – though sometimes I suffer from night-time asthma with quite fierce bouts. Mum brings me from my bed and sits me in a recliner on the veranda until the cooler, fresher air of the small hours leads to sleep. I love waking at dawn still on the veranda by a mango tree, refreshed, I'm breathing properly again. At night Reuben encourages or bribes the parrot with a nut to go back in his cage and puts a cover over him so he'll sleep. Sometimes at dawn before anyone else is awake, I go and uncover the parrot with his yellow beady eye.

The cavalry stables contain a sandy paddock where the annual gymkhana takes place with white painted posts and fencing. My memory of it is mediated and supported by a jerky cine-camera film that Dad takes. I'm the skinny boy clinging to a huge horse which any English stables would refuse to let him mount let alone jump. Sergeant Dako, whom I like immensely, is the NCO given the responsibility of taking charge of our group and ensuring we return from our bush rides unscathed and happy. We wear shorts and no riding helmets. Only once am I scared. My horse bolts and I completely lose control. I fall from the saddle sideways and my foot goes through the stirrup. I'm dragged through the bush and scrub for maybe twenty yards and then, I don't know how, my foot slips out of the stirrup and I'm free. Back at the stables, I make light of the bruises and scratches and keep my fear hidden. I know that if Dad and Mum hear what happened, Sergeant Dako will be in trouble and I might not be allowed out riding again. My favourite, rare ride, is when we go out for half a day to the beach, riding without saddles and taking our horses into the surf. Cantering bareback at the water's edge is magical and worth the later aching thighs. I try riding a few times when I return to England. But I find it unexciting, dull and rule bound.

THERE'S AN OPEN-AIR cinema near our bungalow. It only operates Thursday to Saturday evenings. We're usually allowed to go on Fridays. Most of the metal seats are positioned on flat ground in the open air. At the back, there are two raised, concrete huts with corrugated iron rooves and more expensive seats where the children of the most senior Ghanaian officers and the few white ones sit. I prefer being out in the open air in the cheaper seats and not in the stuffy, enclosed boxes. Though there's one advantage of the boxes. In the rainy season, they keep you dry. When the clouds burst, children from the cheaper seats try to clamber into the boxes from the teeming rain. A few succeed. The seats under cover are no great advantage to watching the film as the racket of the rain on the metal seats and the iron roof drowns out the soundtrack. Whatever cowboy or action film is showing becomes a silent movie in the drumming rain.

I can still hear the rain battering the metal chairs and see it streaming down through the light beaming from the projection box. And sometimes, in my bed wherever I am, I hear its soundtrack in the distance with cowboy gunshots as I did from my bedroom in No.23 Burma Villas under the whirring, clicking fan.

I don't remember leaving my primary school or Ghana where I'd been very happy. Perhaps I thought I'd be going back and it wasn't a big deal. I'm already looking forward to my next adventure, on my own, at school in Suffolk, England.

Act 1

The Poor Man's Eton and the Poet

Woolverstone Hall. Richard outside Berners House. Age 11. 1964

WOOLVERSTONE HALL, 'the poor man's Eton', is the result of post-war optimism for a fairer society and opportunity for all. In 1951, London County Council opens a grammar boarding school for London boys in the Suffolk countryside on the South bank of the River Orwell, from which old Etonian, Eric Blair, took his pen name. It's a social experiment with noble intentions. Take a group of disadvantaged but bright London boys, remove them from their home environments and give them an education loosely modelled on British public schools. But if the school is exclusively for boys from modest homes, how would they experience other worlds? A small number of parents pay fees on a sliding scale depending on their income. Some of these are from the armed forces, typically from families who don't have a tradition of sending children away to school.

So here I am, returned from Ghana, waiting with Mum for the coach to school in the rain outside County Hall. In my last year in Accra, I was told that I no longer needed to wear glasses at all. I climb the steps into the belly of the bus. I can see perfectly well without them now and don't have to watch my step. But I can't see whether the drops running down Mum's face are rain or tears. I'm happy and excited to be starting my new life. I'm talking to the boy next to me. I don't notice the coach leaving. When I turn round it's too late to wave goodbye to Mum.

We by-pass Ipswich and the coach trundles deep into the Suffolk countryside. The boy next to me is squinting through the condensation at the smudges of black and white cows. 'Hey mate, do you drink real milk or cow's milk?' I work out that 'real milk' comes in pint bottles with silver or gold foil tops on your doorstep – if you have a doorstep, that is.

The main house, with its central block and curving wings, is a handsome, impressive building with a circular gravel drive and lawn. Later I learn it's a Grade 1 listed eighteenth-century, Palladian structure. I feel privileged to be there in Berners, one of six boys' boarding houses; it's the only residential house part of the original eighty-acre estate. It has the school library with its view of the goddess Diana and grounds sloping down to the Orwell, the school staff room and headmaster's office and apartment in the ground floor wings. Our housemaster, Mr Shakeshaft, and his wife, our matron, live in a flat on the second floor. Other boys are housed in modern glass structures, which look like hastily assembled offices.

In Berners House there's a shared dormitory for twenty boys, the first four years. An adjacent one for fifth formers. Though additional radiators are installed fed by eight-inch diameter, late Victorian pipes, it's always cold in winter. The top third of the roof pitch on both sides is glass. Our dormitory's in the orangery like we're hothouse plants.

Orangeries in country estates were first constructed in the late seventeenth century to grow citrus. By the nineteenth century they were used for home-grown plants to over-winter them and more exotic specimens like orchids. Some had fountains and areas for entertaining, showing off your plants and architectural features.

SOME OF OUR classes take place in Nissen huts. They're heated with stoves which burn solid fuel and we cough until our lungs grow used to the scratchy fumes. In the run up to Guy Fawkes' day, the best master to 'bang' is Jock Cromarty, the Latin teacher.

When his back's turned, and he's chalking a declension on the blackboard we stick bangers in the stove. *Amo.* Bang! *Amas.* Bang! *Amat.* Bang! He's used to it, turns round in his own good time and pronounces: 'Class 1A, fifty lines. I must not buy fireworks under any circumstances.'

'Sir, not even to stop the Germans, sir?'

'I must not buy fireworks under any circumstances including to stop the Germans.'

At the end of our first week we're told about 'Stonehenge Rugby', a brilliant coinage, which consists of the entire first year intake. Nearly thirty first year boys in each team – twice the normal number – one team in ocean blue, the other in snow white. There are three oval balls not one. The aim is to get hold of any ball and touch it down over the try line. There are no scrums or line outs. If someone kicks the ball out, a rugby coach, master or an older boy, all keen to see the new intake, kick it back. You can pass or kick forwards or backwards and grab the ball in any way you like, short of throwing a visible punch or gouging an eye. My outdoor life in Ghana has accustomed me to rough and tumble. This is great fun!

After tackling someone near the touch line a master shouts, 'What's your name, boy?' His voice has a sing-song lilt. Have I done something wrong?

'Walker, sir.'

He coughs a smoker's cough. 'Good boy, Walker, carry on.'

I learn he's 'Taff', a Welshman, the school's First XV rugby coach. Quite slight and not tall, I'm destined to become a scrum-half. The backs are traditionally the glamorous ones, graceful runners, who score eye-catching tries. The stereotype is the forwards have more grunt and less brain power. In the modern game these attributes have cross-fertilised. There are some huge, brutal backs and some highly skilled, ball-handling forwards. I like to think that the scrum-half is a gateway between the dark, hidden thickets of the scrum and the creative, open pastures of the backs. Rugby – and cricket – become important parts of my social life and prestige at the school. I'm never badly injured enough at rugby to miss a single competitive match, except one, for the first XV of my year group in five years of playing. In cricket, I'm an opening batsmen who sticks around, usually I bowl some off spin and occasionally I play wicketkeeper. Once in a competitive match I'm keeping wicket and my friend, Ian – also my fly half – is bowling off spin. Generally, he bowls slowly enough for me to stand up to the wicket, crouching right behind the stumps. We have a system where if he says any number from one to six, I know that number ball is going to be quicker and I stand a yard or two back. We change ends and walking past each other he doesn't whisper anything. His fifth delivery's edged through the slips for four runs. The final sixth delivery comes much faster than I'm expecting. It clips the top of the off stump, the bails tumble, spectators clap and our team cheers. We've won the match!

I'm not celebrating. The ball has clipped the off stump and ricocheted up into my right eye. There's a lot of blood and in minutes a huge lump in the upper eye socket droops over my eye and I can't see out of it. There's a debate in the sick bay whether I should go to hospital. They keep me in for two nights. By the following day the swelling's easing and I'm starting to see. I don't miss the next match though I don't keep wicket. In the fifth form I'm already playing for the whole school First XI. Which means playing alongside boys one or two years older than me.

ONE BENEFIT OF being in the rugby and cricket teams is travelling to other schools. It could be at the least a break from routine with a better match tea than at home. As the teenage years pile up, an increasing attraction are glimpses of girls, or even meeting them. One is the sister of a boy I play cricket against at the end of the summer. An introduction happens with an instant mutual liking. There's a long pause with the summer holidays. A week or two after returning in September, Mr Shakeshaft calls me up to this study.

'Richard, I've had a letter inviting you out for the day. Do you know who it's from?'

'Probably a boy I met at the last cricket match of the season.'

'Well done. There's only one snag . . .'

'But sir!' I've raised my voice.

Mr Shakeshaft, pauses, lowers his head and looks over the top rims of his glasses. 'Steady now. The invite is on a Saturday when you'll be playing rugby.'

'Sir, how do you know I'll be playing rugby. The team hasn't been selected yet.'

'You've never not been selected. I don't see why that will change this term. Assuming you want to go, I'll speak to the coach.'

'Thank you sir.'

A few days later, Mr Shakeshaft tells me he's agreed with the coach I don't have to go on the team bus. He's written to the family to tell them they can collect me from school first thing, then deliver me to the away match ground to play in the match, take me home for tea and return me to school no later than 8pm. I'm ecstatic, more excited and nervous about this than any rugby or cricket match I've ever played.

The muddy, dented Land Rover slurs to a halt on the gravel outside Berners. A large man jumps out who's wearing corduroys. Dad never wears corduroys.

'You must be Richard. I've heard lots about you.' He holds out his hand which is a bit rough and worn like a teddy bear. 'Jump in.'

On the journey he asks about Dad and Mum. He's much younger than Dad. 'Seen any lions out there?'

'Not really.' I don't like to tell him there aren't any lions in West Africa. 'Lots of snakes and a scorpion in my sandal when I was camping. And mosquitoes.'

'Sounds dangerous,' he chuckles and crashes the gears. 'She needs a new box.'

The Land Rover tyres crunch up the gravel drive towards the half-timbered, Elizabethan I guess, house. We park alongside other vehicles including a horsebox. The front porch is like the entrance to a church with benches on either side. In the hallway is a friendly jumble of boots, shoes and coats of all kinds hanging from pegs in a wooden board. The damp, sweaty smell of horses and leather radiates from the garments. Two white and chocolate brown King Charles spaniels rush up to greet and run circles round us. My friends' father leads us towards a large oak door with a black lead latch. He pushes it open, and I see the back of a woman on the far side of the room busy at a counter.

'This is our guest for the day, Richard.'

His wife turns round with a huge smile. 'We've so much been looking forward to meeting you.' She's wearing a blue apron covered in flour and walks round the huge kitchen table to give me a hug. She smells of butter and baking. 'Now why don't you go and find the people you've really come to see not us old fuddy-duddies?' She's a lot younger than Mum.

I spend the rest of the morning with my cricketing friend and his sister, the one I've *really* come to see. She has glossy, ash-blonde hair which on a Saturday she's allowed to wear down to its full length reaching her waist. She glows with health and vital beauty. She's wearing a white blouse and blue jeans which are very tight fitting. I suppose she's about fourteen. She smells faintly of lavender. He's tall, a bit gangly like a giraffe. He probably plays second row or lock.

The three of us spend the rest of the morning with them showing me round the house and grounds. We all talk, joke and laugh together and sit by a small lake for a time where there are two swans sporadically upending themselves to feed off the underwater plants.

'They mate for life. They've been here forever,' she says.

'Like your parents?' I say.

She laughs lightly and wanders off, and my friend from cricket says quietly, 'She says she really likes you. She'd like to have some time with just the two of you.'

'What are you two whispering about?' she asks on return.

'Richard's plotting to kidnap you.'

'Have you had much practice at kidnapping girls?'

And I feel my face burning and glowing like the wood burners in the Nissen huts.

We leave the lake and meander back to the house. Her mother says, 'We promised your school that you'd arrive at the match in your rugby kit. Dear, why don't you show Richard an upstairs bedroom where he can change before lunch.'

I follow her lavender scent to the bottom of the stairs, where she stops and holds out her hand.

'My stuff's still in your dad's Land Rover.'

She smiles, 'I'll still be here when you get back.'

We're touching fingers for the first time, which seem to have a life of their own and entwine themselves round each other as if they're old friends who've met again after a long time. Upstairs she clicks the lead latch on a wonky door and there's a small bedroom with a leaded window at the end. It's quite dark with a single bed. She enters. Our fingers disentangle. I hesitate.

'Come on,' she says.

I enter slowly and put my bag on the bed. She shuts the door with both of us in the room. My heart's pounding. She sits on the pink candlewick bedspread and I follow her. 'You can . . . ,' but I'm already there, my face close to hers and our lips touching. We're slowly locked together like a glue hardening. How long we don't know. A voice is calling, her mother, at the bottom of the stairs.

'Lunchtime. You don't want to miss the rugby,' followed by a tinkling laugh trickling over our near-deaf ears.

We arrive at the ground a few minutes late, and though I'm in my rugby kit the match has already kicked off. The master in charge says they've already started with a reserve player and hands me a flag saying I'll have to spend the match as 'touch judge'. A toxic mix of humiliation, shame and anger swirls round in me as I run up and down the touch line. I've lost my chance of impressing the parents, my gangly friend and his beautiful sister with my skill and bravery. Surprisingly, their parents and the master seem remarkably relaxed about all this. I'm still allowed to go home with them for tea.

It's laid out on the table in the huge kitchen in front of what I now know was an Aga. On entering I'm suffocated by the warm clouds of freshly baked cakes and scones, toast and dripping butter; the zing of egg, tomato and cress sandwiches on brown bread – the mother had asked about my favourite sandwiches. Her brother and older sister appear laughing with their parents about an incident with one of the stable hands, a pony and a gate. The spaniels, now damp and muddy, are shaking themselves and vigorously tracking any crumbs dropped on the flags. The entire tea passes by with a rumbling, occasionally raucous hubbub around us; while we only have eyes for one another and are in some blurred and honeyed dream, barely registering what's around us, both waiting to be alone together again.

We escape to a sitting room with sumptuous but slightly frayed brocade curtains. The curtains are drawn and a log fire's puffing woodsmoke. A standard lamp in one corner stands in weak pool of light. We're supposed to be watching TV – which no-one had in Ghana – and I rarely watch the little allowed at school. The voluminous sofa is comfortable though a little battered. We sink into it and soon begin kissing as if our lives depend on it. Her blouse comes off readily enough, her jeans are more of a struggle, but we manage to slide them down between us while still locked together. For the first time I feel the pubic bone of a young woman's vagina. The mound above it is soft like moss. She holds my penis, exploring this organ with a life of its own and how it responds. I'm worried we'll be discovered. She tells me not to worry, that her parents never enter. Just the cleaner once a week. Its hers and her siblings' room, who will stay away this afternoon. Then suddenly we're called and it's time for me to go.

In the Land Rover with just the father, I remember Dad calling me down from the flame tree in the grounds of the rest house where we stayed by the beach in Winneba. It was just before I went off to school. He wanted to tell me about sex and, if I had it, always to make sure I washed thoroughly afterwards. I wasn't sure if this applied if you and the girl kept your underpants on.

It's a memorable day on two counts. I've had my first sighting and glimpsed a few of the symbols and behaviours, subtle and direct, of the British class system, its signifiers and how it operates. I had, too, my first young adult, intense, sexual experience which went beyond a kiss. It was more than enough for one day. When I return to school, I'm told that though I'd continue playing and training for the rugby team it was my responsibility, not my hosts', to ensure I was on time for kick-off. I should consider myself lucky I'd missed only one match and wasn't suspended.

I think it's a price well worth paying for insights into the world of early adulthood as I'm starting to construct it. The parents were warm and welcoming, their complexions glowed with outdoor good humour. They had a slightly distracted air, a thousand and one things going on in their lives, and whilst they were delighted to have you along, you'd need to fit in as best you could. They were far too busy with dogs, horses, stables, gardens, drains, fields, hedging, baking, the vet to worry about me. I'd never met anyone like them. Nor had I ever met a girl like their daughter. How I wish I could remember her name! I still wish I could recall it. Each time I think I might by concentrating she slips away like a bar of soap in the bath. Peculiar how the possession of a name fools us into thinking we know someone better and betrays us with a nominal sense of intimacy or belonging.

Other sexual intimacies were more rough and ready affairs. As we get older, we're allowed on some Sundays to catch the bus into Ipswich for three or four hours. We chatted to girls in the bus station or the park if the weather's good. Occasionally, this ended in a clinch and/or kissing, but always still fully clothed. Promises are made to meet again, but, in my case, are never met.

From the age of around fourteen, after a rugby or cricket match at home on Saturday, a small group of us wolf down our post-match tea, excuse ourselves and trudge across the fields or the foreshore to the Butt & Oyster in the village of Pin Mill, where barges and yachts are moored or slumped on the mud flats. The landlord allows us to drink two pints as long as we stay in the public bar or outside. The pub is always swept and scrubbed ready for its Saturday night. No doubt the cleaners do their best, but there's a lingering, acid smell of beer and barrels. Through one of those visits in the summer of the fifth form I chatted to a local girl, and we arranged to meet the following weekend on the edge of the village, not at the Butt. I arrive with two large bottles of cider. We make our way into a field of ripe wheat where we can sit hidden from any passers-by. Before the end of the first bottle, we're kissing and lying alongside each other. She has a dress with buttons down the front, which I undo and she encourages me to caress her breasts and nipples slipping her bra down to her waist. We're becoming more passionate and I stroke the insides of her thighs. I can feel her wet through her panties. She pulls them to one side and my fingers play with the outside until I have the courage to push my right index finger inside her. She's enjoying it, she breathes, 'That's lovely.'

We continue like this for until she says, 'But it's so uncomfortable lying here. The earth digging in my back. And it's the first time. Let's meet again and do it properly.' Soon we sit up and finish the first bottle of cider. We agree to save the second one for the next time we met. But we never do, and I still don't know whether she meant it was our first time together or she was, like me, a virgin.

There are always rumours of one or two masters fancying boys and boys who have crushes on others, sometimes mutual. I think there's much more gossip about it than action, but no doubt something happens from time to time. I only experience it once in the last term of the fifth form when I'm fifteen. One evening after nets, I find myself on the same bench chatting to the Head Boy of Berners House after the others have wandered off. He's good at sport and academically, as most head boys of houses are. I like him well enough, but I've never gone out of my way to cultivate him. He says he thinks I'd be a good Head of House; it isn't the easiest of jobs and can make you a little distant from boys in the rest of the house. He's been a bit lonely in his final year after becoming Head of Berners. If I want to chat about it or other things I can come to his room one evening after lights out. We can smoke a cigarette there together. We won't be disturbed, his room's at the top of the house with only one classroom beyond it, which we use for prep in the evenings. Later, no-one ever passes his room until the following morning.

I go a few nights later. He tells me he really likes me, and he's had a crush on me for two years. He's only telling me now because he's leaving soon and wants me to know. He sits at the pillow end of his bed and I sit at the far end, both with our knees drawn up. We smoke cigarettes and chat about nothing consequential and then I leave.

A week later he asks me to come again. Slightly reluctantly, I agree. We start in the same way, knees up, smoking and chatting. Then he says he'd like to touch me.

'What do you mean touch me?' I'm surprised, shocked, afraid of what might happen, anxious about what he might do.

'Anywhere you like. I can hold your hand. Just touch. Nothing more.'

I don't want him to touch me, but I wonder if he'll get aggressive or angry. He asks again. Very reluctantly I uncoil my right leg so it reaches down the bed towards him.

'You can hold my foot. One minute.'

'Two?'

'One. Then I'm going.'

He grasps my foot and quite soon starts to caress it.

'Stop! I agreed hold not stroke. If you do it again, I'm going.'

He restrains himself a while and starts stroking again saying, 'Don't you like . . .'

'No, I don't. It's revolting,' I shout pulling my foot and leg away.

The final weeks of the summer term pick up pace. I see him occasionally in the normal run of things. Twice he tries to persuade me to go back to his bedroom. I feel sorry for him, but I never go or want to go back. It's the sum total of my own boy-on-boy physical intimacy.

I'M FINISHING MY last O-level exams. I've been happy in the First XV for rugby and the First XI for cricket, as well as in the badminton and fencing teams. I've been in school plays and musicals, though I've given up music as too unexciting after Highlife in Ghana. At or near the top in the arts subjects, average or above in sciences, I'm predicted to get nine good O-levels. But I've started to grow my hair as long as I can and listen to John Peel under the scratchy blankets. In the Fifth Form I'm caned – I refuse to cry though I want to – for breaking into the kitchens and eating ice cream. I know it's time to move on, to start to create myself as a young adult.

I tell the school I'm leaving after my O-levels, though I haven't told my parents. Mum's coming home from Ghana to Guildford to put my sister in school. I know she'll be OK about it.

IT'S OUR PENULTIMATE weekend of the summer term coming up! Boy, are we excited! Little do I know how the Duke of Edinburgh Award is going to shape my life. I've already passed my Bronze and Silver and I'm ready for the big one: the Gold Award. The Award God has partnered me with my friend Maurice, or Mo.

We have rucksacks, a tent, sleeping bags, groundsheet, tin cooking utensils and basic foodstuff. We're to be away for two nights, Friday 4th and Saturday 5th July. We set off on our trek through the Suffolk countryside. A couple of miles from school, we catch the bus to Ipswich and buy tickets to Liverpool Street.

We descend through the mouth of a heaving animal, the juddering, clanking escalators into the underground. Waves of warm, foetid air hit us in the face, blowing our hair back and making us screw up our eyes. I half-catch my breath and choke on the rancid fumes. When the approaching rumble rolls through the tunnel, the crowd presses forward like battery chickens at feeding time and we're carried forward with it. As the driver applies the brakes, the hot metal screeches in protest. The tortured whine pierces not just our eardrums but our bodies.

We shoulder our way up the sticky stairs breathing the sour air in shallow gasps. We're coughed up into a walkway of porcelain tiled walls reflecting the brutal fluorescent lighting. And yet how amazing and beautiful even that short but horrible journey has been. It's the full force of urban life in our faces not the nature that surrounds us at school. We've done it ourselves, just the two of us and we're here. On our way. Our adventure has begun. Like we've just circumnavigated the globe.

We stand outside the Elephant & Castle underground at the bus stop inhaling the tainted, metallic air. The mysterious silver box structure overground at the tube station is like something from a sci-fi film. It has a glamour attached to the future and its endless potential. Brave new world!

We catch the bus down the Old Kent Road, passing a pub called The Dun Cow. I've never seen a place less likely to support a cow. Greasy fish and chip papers overflowing from stuffed refuse bins, crushed beer cans on pavements smeared with chewing gum, tramps clutching bottles of cider or barley wine, kids hanging out round betting shops or takeaways; half-empty stretches of ground where the rubble of war bombs has been cleared but nothing yet built. These are playgrounds for adolescents or tips for builders with wrecked baths and doors, ovens and sinks. Over the wasteland hangs a sweet, rotten miasma that crawls down our throats.

We enter the lift with its whiff of disinfectant and urine, and press the button up to his parents' flat – the nineteenth floor of a council-owned block of flats in Bermondsey. Mo knows his parents are away for the weekend. He turns on his mum's gas cooker. We have beans on toast, and Mo deliberately burns the cooking utensils so they look used. We descend in the putrid, graffitied lift to the off-licence where, clearly underage, we buy six large bottles of cider. We go back to the flat and drink one. Dozy with the efforts of our journey and the cider we go to bed early.

WE'RE SURROUNDED BY thousands, tens of thousands, hundreds of thousands, bodies, arms, legs, plain and painted faces, shoulders, knees, eyes, long hair, shorter hair, rare tattoos, elbows, necklaces, smoke, laughter, good-natured shouting, bangles, jeans, kaftans, cheesecloth, denim, bare chests and breasts, sandals, bare feet, baseball boots, plimsolls. But we're safe on our island which is the groundsheet from our tent that we're not camping in. We've brought it in our rucksacks with the five large bottles of cider. We're between and under the shade of two oak trees. When we arrived early it was only a few hundred folk milling around who'd been there all night on a vigil for Brian, wrapped in blankets and shawls. We're about forty yards from the stage. The air is heavy with the pungent sweetness of hash

The first act, Family, comes on. Half the cider's gone, one bottle I'd exchanged for a lump of hash. It's a great deal, which the man with the headband and mirror sunglasses knows. He hands it over saying, 'OK kids, cool.' He cackles as he moves off. 'Don't smoke it all at once or you might miss the main event, man.'

Family's Roger Chapman pierces the roar of the crowd with his rasping, strangled voice crying out like a muezzin. The gig's underway. Mo's crumbling the dark resin along the length of the tobacco and finishes rolling a huge spliff with a cardboard roach torn from a cigarette packet. He cups his hands round the roach of the joint forming a smoke chamber inhaling deeply and holding the smoke in his lungs with his eyes bulging until he's red in the face. I smoke it like a regular cigarette. 'You wanna get wasted?' hisses Mo. 'Do it like this.' He mimes the action he's just made. I try it again imitating him this time.

Then, BHAM! I'm somewhere else. I'm floating with the eerie, bending notes, jazz meets folk meets psychedelic of the Third Ear Band. I'm next conscious of an announcer crying out, 'Give a big welcome to Alexis Korner with New Church!' What's this New Church? Have we come to an evangelical rally? Mo coughs through another lungful of hashish smoke. 'Korner, he's been around forever. He knows everyone, he's played with most of them.' It's deep, deep blues. You can't dive bluer than this.

A huge roar erupts, cheering and whistling rolls a tidal wave through the crowd as Jagger bounds on stage. He's all in white wearing a tunic to mid-thigh with bell-bottom trousers. 'Awlright, OK now, listen. Cool it just for a minute,' followed by catcalls and whistles. 'I'd really dig it if you could be with us. Cool it!'

Jagger reads from Adonais, Shelley's lament on the death of Keats who died from tuberculosis in Rome at twenty-five. Though not before he'd written some of the greatest lyric poems in the English language. Mick doesn't read the elegy well, stumbling through it in his unattractive nasal 'sarf London' twang. He sounds hoarse. Will he be able to sing?

> *Life, like a dome of many-coloured glass,*
> *Stains the white radiance of Eternity.*

Brian had already been asked to leave the Stones. He was too wasted on drugs to contribute any more. Mick Taylor stepped into the studio to play on *Let it Bleed*. This gig has been planned as his first outing with the band. But Brian died two days before, bloated, polluting the bottom of a swimming pool. Mick releases thousands of white scraps of paper that can fly. Some wobble rising only a few feet, some flutter up above the oceanic crowd. 'Butterflies,' says Mo.

Nature's 'white radiance of Eternity.'

The band strikes up 'I'm Yours and I'm Hers', an unfamiliar cover. The wailing chords and Jagger's voice taunt us in the shimmering heat and worm their way into our bodies, charged by the mirage that we can all sing and strut like that. Three of the first four numbers are covers with only 'Jumpin' Jack Flash' from The Stones' own catalogue. Bill Wyman's bass drives through 'Flash', throbbing in my chest. Mick howls, 'I was crowned with a spike right through my head.' And with that phrase I'm out of my body, weightless, the spike is through my head but it's not painful, it's soothing, an anaesthetic it's taken me to a different dimension. How does Mick know I've got a spike of hashish right through my head? I laugh and nudge Mo pointing at my head, 'Spike through my head,' I say. He grins and passes me the remainder of the spliff.

'No Expectations' is the first time we hear why Taylor's been invited to join the Stones. It's a lovely, simple song written by Keef and Mick, but it already sounds like a blues classic. When Mick sings *'Take me to the airport and put me on a plane / I've got no expectations I'll pass through here again,'* Taylor's guitar weeps in counterpoint for all the loneliness and resignation in the song. It speaks to me in my angst that the world is imperfect. *'Our love is like our music / It's here and then it's gone.'* And I'm gone, I'm not sure where I've gone, I'm lost, vulnerable to the beauty of the song sharing my fragility in a cotton wool cloud with half a million people.

Somewhere through the swirling in my head I hear Mick introducing a new song he says they've never played in public before, 'Gimmee Little Drink'. The guitars are bending the notes out of shape, the notes are a woozy liquid and when Mick sings with his customary swagger, *'Gimmee little drink from your loving cup / Just one drink and I'll fall down drunk,'* the clashing, churning wires of the guitars reverberating in my head, the lyrics and how I feel – stoned – are in a perfect trinity.

At the end Mick mutters, 'We were all over the place.' But that's just it! It's raw, a new song, moment to moment in creation. 'All over the place' is how it should be on a baking July afternoon with half a million others at rock 'n' roll's biggest ever free gig.

They go to a classic blues, Robert Johnson's 'Love in Vain'. We concentrate intently on this miniature drama of a man going to the station carrying a suitcase and leaving his lover. Mick discards his white tunic and is down to a lilac vest. Though he stumbles a couple of times on the lyrics his delivery and phrasing are majestic. '*Well, I followed her,*' holding the beat and note on '*her*' before continuing '*to the station.*' Then using the same caesura again, '*With a suitcay, ay ay se / in my hand.*' It's like listening to someone riding a bicycle so slowly, you think they'll fall off. After Mick sings, '*I felt so sad, so lonesome / I could not help but cry,*' Taylor's guitar weeps softly in a desolate place, its notes moaning, articulating the pain of the blues. There's a long pause, then with tens of thousands of others I'm clapping for Taylor's guitar with its eternal emotions of loss and solitude.

'Satisfaction', already anthemic, the three chord rock song to no sex and consumerism, pulls me to my feet. There's no room to move. But I don't care. I'm waving my arms wildly round my head, twisting down and round. Wailing:

I can't get no satisfaction
I can't get no satisfaction
'Cause I try, and I try, and I try, and I try
I can't get no, I can't get no . . .

And yet by getting on my feet wailing these words I feel immense pleasure exploding like a Roman Candle. Crying out something that's clearly not true. I'm overindulging in satisfaction being here on this day and in this moment. I want for nothing. I'm the luckiest teenager alive!

A new song continues the dance party. Wyman's bass and Watts' drums kick off with a solid, secure and comfortably deafening wall of sound churning from my head to my gut. We're in the groove of 'Honky Tonk Women'. Mick quivers and warbles, introducing us to '*a gin-soaked bar room queen in Memphis.*'

This takes us to the summit of the gig, a magnificent first ever outing for what becomes one of their live signature masterpieces, 'Midnight Rambler'. It starts slow but scary with the wailing notes of Mick's harmonica corkscrewing through the sky followed by the funereal, reverberating bass of Wyman, a retreat for Keef's churring rhythm guitar fitting snugly round it. Between these two guitars as they pick up the pace, Taylor's lead guitar slides and screams with a terrible psychodrama. The buzz and hum of metal wires cutting through the summer air, a sinister, sharpened knife. *'I'm talking 'bout the midnight rambler . . .'* Mick's on his knees crawling across the stage, *'Well, hear about the Boston strangler.'* It's visceral. The satanic recess of ourselves. As the final chords sound Mick flops and bows, he and we exhausted by its horror. The steel dagger through the heart of the show.

We're straight into 'Street Fighting Man'. 'This is the first time they're doing it live,' says Mo ecstatic. I'm on my feet. The three guitars chopping and roaring like a dirty old motorbike kicking into life and accelerating us away on the back seat of its engine. Charlie's thundering the drums, an occasional cranny when Taylor's notes punctuate the bellowing, a nightingale in a storm. Mick, provocative, *'the time is right for a palace revolution.'* Then contemptuous, *'sleepy London town . . . no place for a street fighting man.'*

The throb of congas playing a samba lead us to the finale, a soundscape mixing Africa and Brazil. An explosive minute of Yoruba rhythm before the guitars dive in, churring, tropical notes that swoop over the beats. It's Ginger Johnson's drummers laying down the intro to 'Sympathy for the Devil'. An insistent, burning groove that won't let me go, something deeper, an umbilical cord leading to a place I didn't know existed. There's an extended, instrumental passage over the beat of the congas, three guitarists sprinting at full speed down the track, runners abreast egging each other on to squeeze out that final burst of energy. The congas drop the volume and Charlie does some intricate work on the cymbals, ice tinkling in the heat of the song and the afternoon. Mick's words buffeted by the thrash of the guitars and the pulse of the congas slipping in and out, heard in snatches, *'a man of wealth and taste,' 'Jesus Christ his moment of doubt and pain,' 'who killed the Kennedys, you and me,'* like a rare bird song heard intermittently in the forest of sound.

We know time's up when Mick sings, unscripted, *'we gotta go, we gotta go.'*

After it's over and the crowds start to leak away, we adjust our groundsheet and lie staring up at the sky through the oak branches. My head's buzzing, my brain racing. I let the tree bathe me in its steady, green presence.

The acid sweet smell of the hash in the joint Mo had rolled is still in my senses. He passes me another. 'Best to have it now. They won't like us smoking in the Albert.'

We float across the park to the Royal Albert Hall, delirious in clouds of knowing.

WHEN I TELL people what happened next, they explode in disbelief. 'It can't be true! What were you smoking?!' It's a double bill of Chuck Berry and The Who. *Tommy*, the first rock opera, was released two months earlier in May '69. This is a chance to hear some of its numbers live sprinkled with what are already classics like 'Substitute' and 'My Generation'. I love the earlier, raw Who, but I'm not sure about *Tommy*. Yet.

Captain Walker goes missing in action when his wife gives birth to a son. Years later Tommy's Dad returns home to find his wife has a new lover. During an argument, the lover's accidentally killed. Tommy's Mum brainwashes him into believing he saw or heard nothing. His senses shut down leaving him that 'deaf, dumb and blind kid.' The doctors diagnose the loss of his senses is the result of a trauma. Tommy's Mum sees him staring frequently at the mirror. In anger, she smashes the mirror and he's freed from his traumatised state. Nine years after the release of Tommy, something happens with my own Dad, exposing a family secret which recalls something of this story.

We're in good company at the Albert Hall: like us, Keef misses Chuck Berry and, having just played to half a million in Hyde Park, turns up to enjoy The Who a few rows in front of us. We see The Who again weeks later at the second Isle of Wight Festival.

After the Hyde Park gig, it seems modest with 'only' a hundred and fifty thousand fans.

GRANULES OF OUR adventure percolate upwards until they reach the Masters' Common Room. We aren't put forward for our Duke of Edinburgh's Gold Award. We'd already accepted that in planning our expedition. I suggest we deserve a gold medal for vision, initiative and the execution of our goal. We're teenagers committed to experiencing the Zeitgeist. We've no aspirations to be explorers or mountaineers. It's inconceivable now how we made it happen, with mobile phones still a quarter of a century away. It's our last outing from Woolverstone Hall.

Dad's apoplectic when Mum tells him I'm leaving school. Difficult messages are invariably relayed by Mum. She sees her role as a peacemaker and bridge-builder. She does all she can to avoid conflict. It would've been more immediately bloody, though it might have got Dad and me more quickly to the good place in our relationship we finally reach.

Dad claims it will be the end of me. I'm passing up the chance to get to a decent university and a professional career. In the 1920s he'd left school at fifteen and enlisted in the army as a private to escape a poor life in Brownhills, Birmingham. Like Mum, he'd never been to university, but it was his aspiration for me. Woolverstone has given me a platform to achieve what he hadn't and now I'm determined to throw it all away.

I'd discovered a one year A-level course at Guildford Technical College. It was designed for teenagers who'd already completed two years of A-levels. Either they'd partied too hard, been seriously unwell, or there'd been a family disruption.

It isn't until my A-levels that I begin to understand that books and writing will be a lifelong passion. As music and visual art in many genres were, but in a less structured and studied way. I register for A-levels in English, French and German, while Mum's anxious about me taking charge of my own education and Dad's still angry I've left the 'poor man's Eton'. Neither of them understand much about A-levels or university entrance.

I have a Saturday job working for an office cleaning company. It's quite peaceful working in an unoccupied office. I get some satisfaction from using the buffing machine on the flooring to make it shine. If the evening's quiet, on Sunday I sometimes go to a blues/rock club in a Godalming pub, where I see bands like Blodwyn Pig and Caravan, or Chicken Shack who had an unknown singer called Christine McVie. Otherwise by Sunday afternoon or evening I'm focused on my studies for the rest of the week. There's nothing more self-centred than a teenager on a mission, whatever the mission is. I play no sport, don't watch TV, listen only to vinyl rock-alternative-folk-blues-jazz-psychedelic music – Stones, Traffic, Family, Dylan, Cohen, Soft Machine, Velvet Underground, Pink Floyd, Third Ear Band, Roy Harper, The Doors, The Kinks – played on a boxy contraption with a built-in speaker. It isn't automatic. I have to lower the arm and needle to the outer groove of the record by hand, careful not to scratch it. Occasionally, I go and stay in London with Mo. He's become friends with Alexis Korner's son, and we sometimes go and smoke dope in his dad's place in Kensington Church Street.

Dad, having returned from Ghana, takes a job, through contacts, at a solicitor's firm in London. It must have been a huge upheaval to his way of life from the bungalow in Ghana, with the gin and tonic mixed for him and the Highlife parties at the Ambassador Hotel. Now past the age at which he died, I appreciate and admire his dedication and hard work. How oblivious I then was to his sacrifice for the woman and the children he loved.

After supper, I disappear into my bedroom to study and write essays on Keats' *Odes* or *The Winter's Tale* or *Middlemarch* or Maupassant short stories or Goethe's poetry. Sometimes, I join them for coffee or tea, and Dad offers me a cigarette. The offer is a tacit acknowledgement that he's reconciled to my choice of leaving school and that I'm going to shape my own education.

The only time, on leave from Ghana, he'd visited me at school he'd slipped a packet of Rothman's 555 into my hand. He told me *sotto voce* that, if I was caught, he hadn't given me the cigarettes. It was a shared moment signalling that he knew I sometimes broke the rules and that was an acceptable thing to do. But if you got caught, you were on your own.

In the summer of 1970, after my A-level results appear, I'm asked to go and see my English lecturer, Mr Rolf. He's a tall man with a neat beard, upright in a dignified way. I like and respect him, and had made time to take part in *The Hollow Crown*, which he directed. He congratulates me on outstanding results and asks what I'm going to do next. I say as I've done my A-levels in a year, I'm going to take the year off studying, earn some money, travel and then go to university. To step off the education ladder save for exceptional reasons is unknown then, but I've created a 'gap year' for myself.

Mr Rolf smiles, his white teeth glowing through his beard.

'We – I've spoken to colleagues – we'd like to suggest you consider coming back next term and apply for Oxbridge in the autumn. We've never had anyone do this before. We think you're a serious candidate. We'll do all we can to help.'

This is so out of the blue, I've never considered it. I know I want to study English literature – thanks to his teaching – but that's it.

'Thank you,' I pause. There's nothing to lose. 'Thank you. Yes. I'll try.'

Mum's excited, Dad's pleased but refuses to allow his emotions to run ahead. I spend the rest of the summer in Salcombe on the Devon coast. A friend has got a job in a hotel as a waiter. It comes with accommodation: a boat hut in the grounds near a landing dock where a ferry runs passengers to and from Salcombe. I get a job washing dishes in a town centre café and commute by ferry. I meet someone working in the café who's already reading English at Oxford. He's at St Peter's – I'd no idea about any of the colleges. 'Apply there,' he says, peering at me through John Lennon spectacles framed by a beard and shoulder length hair. 'Francis will like you. Here, try this. Afghan Gold,' he breathes out a cloud of sweet smoke.

THE END OF August 1970 brings another Isle of Wight Festival surpassing the highest attendance at any festival worldwide. Conservative estimates approach 600,000. Woodstock was around 400,000. Mo and I have a plan to take LSD for the first time. Probably at the peak of the show on the last night when Hendrix is scheduled. We agree we'll see how we feel and what the atmosphere is like. The first day I hugely enjoy Chicago, who play a long set including 'It Better End Soon', which lasts twenty minutes and references the US war in Vietnam. They're a rock band with horns fusing elements of jazz, rhythm and blues and classical song.

Saturday's Joni Mitchell, who falls victim to angry protests and chronic confusion. There's a hard core of European anarchists who'd experienced the Paris barricades in '68. They're here to disrupt the festival as a capitalist venture. They tear down the fencing round the site, interrupt performances and are aggressive to those of us with £3 tickets. They pitch tents on a hill overlooking the site, with an encampment of hay bales. It's named Desolation Row. Sporadic scuffles break out. One group calls us 'capitalist cunts!' The organisers bow to the pressure and declare the festival free.

Joni's scheduled to play in the evening, but appears in a sun-yellow dress in the afternoon. She has trouble with hecklers during her first songs – including 'Chelsea Morning'. As she starts her hit 'Woodstock', she has to stop when someone needs a doctor. Then she can't raise the crowd to sing the chorus. She continues trying to quieten the crowd, 'You're acting like tourists, man. Give us some respect.' She plays 'A Case of You' and 'California', the crowd turns, and with 'Both Sides Now', she's brought them round.

During her set we hear the choppers of a helicopter landing backstage. It's Miles Davis, who that year had recorded a double album, *Bitches Brew*, taking jazz to places it'd never been. Some jazz purists are alienated but it brings him listeners who 'don't do jazz.' In spirit, *Bitches Brew* feels close to the Highlife my parents danced to, which often has a trumpet coming to the fore early in the song. This then takes a back seat as the vocals kick in and return later giving the vocals a break. Miles dispenses with vocals and his trumpet blossoms as the sole voice. Highlife sometimes uses an electric organ or piano in its soundscape. Miles has both.

It's dusk when the band comes on stage and begins playing without Miles, who appears once they're in their groove. He has a red leather top and red tee-shirt, silver studded denims and stack heeled shoes. His two young keyboard players – Keith Jarrett and Chick Correa – both go on to play hugely influential roles in the development of jazz in the seventies until now. We worm our way to within thirty yards of the stage in anticipation.

Miles is the antithesis of Joni. He says nothing. The first we hear from him is through his trumpet. It's a forty-minute tour de force without a break. Highlife is music in the forest clearing with a pool of sunlight beaming down. This is music which starts in the same place but wanders into the forest where it grows darker, more difficult to find your way. The keyboards bicker and squabble like parakeets. Miles' midnight-blue lacquered trumpet plays notes in a clattering fall of pebbles, one moment the sound is fractured, the next it's united in harmony. One moment serene, another vicious. Somewhere through the matted undergrowth we hear croaking frogs, whirring insects, a monkey scream, the percussionist is at work. Then momentarily an almost silence and the plaintive wail of the alto saxophone, notes of fragile beauty counterpointing the hurricane of unrepentant brass in the trumpet. The wall of sound is threaded through with each musician individually stitching a pattern, a melody, a rhythm which comes together and makes the tapestry whole then rips it apart. The music has an intense focus on nothing but itself. We hear and share it, we try to hold each note or silence in its despair or its beauty while it slips through our fingers like water.

Miles leaves the stage and the band continues playing. It's perfect timing. Miles had arrived on stage at sunset and led us into the dark, but through the music the night is now ablaze. Smoke from the fires make my eyes stream. When asked what he'd played Miles said, 'Call it Anything', an off the cuff remark which is how the set came to be known. Though this was the band which had recorded *Bitches Brew* in the studio, it was only their third and last concert playing together. Within a few years *Bitches Brew* is widely recognised as one of the most important jazz recordings of the twentieth century. Miles' trumpet has spoken. To trumpet: to proclaim, to announce, to shout from the rooftops.

There'd been some doubt as to whether Jim Morrison would be allowed to leave the United States. The band was named after Huxley's book *The Doors of Perception*, featuring his psychedelic experiences. Jim, a voracious reader, considered himself as much a theatrical performer and poet as a singer in a rock band. He's out on $50,000 bail pending charges of drunkenness and lewdness while performing.

The Isle of Wight stage is dark and remains low lit. The Doors are tight and controlled. Jim Morrison's heavily bearded, in a white shirt and dark jacket. His voice is as seductive and moody, as powerful and raunchy as ever. But his movement and behaviour are minimal, stone cold sober, perhaps he is tonight.

'When the Music's Over' and 'Light My Fire' are the twin peaks of their set both lasting fifteen minutes. They finish, of course, with their song 'The End'.

NOW WE'RE GETTING excited, edgy. Jimi will be on stage next. Are we going to drop the LSD? I'm nervous as I've never taken it. Mo's already tried it once in London. He tells me it was fine. I ask him where he took it. In Alexis Corner's flat with his son, he says. There are hundreds of thousands of people here with us after midnight in the early hours of Sunday morning. Will they be kind or aggressive like the anarchists up on the hill? There are dozens of small fires flickering with huddles of people trying to keep warm. Could I get burned in one? Mo reassures me. He tells me he knows how it works. He'll look after me. I'm reluctantly convinced against an instinct that tells me I shouldn't.

'Richard, you'll regret it if you don't. I'm going to,' says Mo. He's holding out his palm with two the tabs of acid squatting there. 'Go on,' he says.

I quickly take one before I change my mind and open the bottle of water to flush it down my throat. 'The first time it took about twenty minutes before it crept up on me,' which is the last thing for a while I hear Mo saying.

We are on a small island off another island. Island. I land. Eye land. My eye is landing and transfixed by a lake of silver somewhere far below me. If I am not careful, I might fall into it fully clothed. I adjust my stance and ensure my feet are firmly planted on the ground. I can feel the earth between my toes even though I'm wearing plimsolls. How has the earth got into my plimsolls burrowing down through my socks and settled itself under the soles of my feet and soiled them? Perhaps if I take off my plimsolls and socks, I can wash my feet in the lake. It looks cold, glinting ice though I think it's still summer or has something happened and we are now here, with winter dark blanketing us. But the ground is soft, it gives under my feet, not hard like winter. It is difficult to know. It is always difficult to know what is. What is not, and what seems. It can stop you doing anything, you can freeze for a long, long time. Yes, I will wash my feet. I have not washed my feet for a long time. I have not washed for a long time. I bend down and begin to unlace my plimsolls. There, one lace is out like a dirty white worm wriggling on the ground. Worms are good for the ground I remember. They let the air in. I take off that plimsoll and can feel the cool, damp earth through my sock. A voice coming from a long way away is saying something. Its words are bending and woozy like they have drunk too much and cannot stand up. Each one slowly unfurls itself at a snail's pace. I have no way to make them move faster or slower or extract more or less meaning. *Yooor... Feeee... Cowhlld...* then in the dark, fleshy lips are close to my face whispering, whispering like there is a secret just between the lips and me and we must not let it out, must not share it because we have it together, it is our secret. The lips are strangely familiar, but I cannot place them. I have never kissed them. They are fleshy, bulbous. I don't want to kiss them, but they are close to my face. There are palm fronds hovering alongside the lips, one frond on each side in a fan of five fronds at the two corners of the huge lips. The fronds are coming to rest on my shoulders where they perch, green crows, and through my rough denim jacket I can feel and hear them skitter on my collar bones. They grip and are starting to push me down firmly and gently, but I am not sure I want to go down. If I go down, I will end in the silver lake. I might drown, I might freeze. I don't know if I can swim. Can I swim? I couldn't once. The sea was barrelling me round. There's a shoal of flying fish springing out of the silver lake below me, they are going to land on my feet. Now I'm sitting beside the lake and it is glittering, perhaps the sun is rising again. One sun is nearby. I notice lots of other suns flaming round me in the darkness. There's an acrid smell which might be burning rubber. Is it the people up the hill beyond the waving iron fencing on Desolated Row? The lake is smaller now, the size of a puddle. There's a splash of dark mud in the puddle. Then a voice finally reaches me though it's still at a distance as though calling down a tunnel.

It's Mo speaking. 'Careful man. That's our stash.'

And he takes up the lake and wraps it round the dope.

There's an explosion of static and electricity which makes me jump and shiver. 'It's been a long time. It's good to be back in England.' 'God Save the Queen' sounds like it's coming from an angry pneumatic drill punching and punishing the air and morphs into 'Sergeant Pepper's Lonely Hearts' Club Band'.

Jimi covers Dylan's 'All Along the Watchtower', where the lyrics, 'and the wind began to howl', are talking about his guitar.

No reason to get excited
The thief, he kindly spoke

We aren't excited, we're ecstatic with the whorls of Dylan's lyrics twisting their way through the barbs of Jimi's guitar. Jimi had joined the US Air Force to avoid a prison sentence. Now here is this ex-paratrooper discharging bullets through his staccato guitar notes in one of the anthemic anti-war songs of the decade, 'Machine Gun'.

It's a frenetic, frenzied tour de force, with Jimi leading his guitar to explore the outer constellations of space where notes might travel and still return. Across the songs the sound goes where no-one else has taken it through an electric guitar howling at the speed of light.

Jimi's performance scales the summits we know he can reach. Three weeks later we hear that he's died choking on his own vomit.

AUTUMN KICKS IN and I have to take Latin O-level in nine weeks – the final year you have to have Latin for any first-degree course at Oxford. I do some extra reading, go to some lectures, take the entrance exams and am invited for interview. It's in Francis Warner's study alongside other dons at St Peter's, my first choice.

We speak about *The Winter's Tale* and how I plan to spend the rest of the year before taking a place at Oxford or elsewhere. I learn an invaluable lesson: the art of non-disclosure. Francis says he can see traces of Ros Coward in my writing. She's a lecturer in English at Guildford Technical College. I know who she is, but I've never been taught by her. I blink when Francis says he sees her influence on my answers, and I don't contradict him.

Then I forget about it. I'm more excited by the adventure I've cooked up with friends in The King's Head. On Boxing Day, we set off for Czechoslovakia in Leon's Ford Anglia saloon, a sixties car with a rear windscreen sloping inwards. Ruth had fallen in love with a Czech man in Paris. She had a girlfriend with her. The Russian occupation of Czechoslovakia in 1968 meant Jan couldn't leave. We're on a mission to get him out. His hometown, Olomouc, is a long way east of Prague. The heating breaks down in the car. I have to stop driving and ask the girls to massage my feet so I can feel the pedals. We think nothing of it, we are on a mission to rescue a Czech from the Russians!

Jan's friends smoke numerous cigarettes, we all drink beer and a gingery spirit, Becherovka. We've brought vinyl presents – The Doors and Pink Floyd are favourites. There are conversations to which I wasn't privy. Months later Jan arrives in England.

We set off to England on New Year's Eve, thinking the roads will be quiet and we'll easily cross the Czech border. I park the car by the guardhouse in front of a barrier which is, strangely, raised. In the freezing night we can see the German side at two hundred metres. We sit in the car waiting for someone to appear. Ten minutes pass. I get out and wander round. I get back in to keep warm and turn the ignition.

I put the car in gear and move forwards slowly, aware of the risk of skidding. We've gone less than fifty metres when two gunshots crack in quick succession. We come to a stop half-way to the German border. There's shouting and screaming behind. In the wing mirror, I see two guards, one still holding his pistol. I try to explain in my basic German that we'd waited at the barrier, but no-one appeared.

'Gehen Sie rein. Alle!' We enter the guard house. We're asked the same questions again and again. Answering them falls to me as the only one with any German.

'*Wo haben Sie sich aufgehlaten?*' Where did you stop?
'Olomouc.'
'*Was haben Sie dort gemacht?*' What did you do there?
'*Freunde getroffen.*' Met friends.
'*Bei wem haben Sie übernachtet?*' Who did you stay with?
'*Bei unseren Freunden.*' Our friends.
'*Woher kennen Sie diese Freunde?*' Where did you meet these friends?
'*Wir haben sie in Paris kennengelernt.*' In Paris.
'*Haben Sie Ihren Freunden Geschenke mitgebracht?*' Did you take any presents?
'*Ein paar Schallplaten.*' Records.
'*Was für Schallplaten?*' What type?
'*Rockmusik.*'
'*Die Beatles?*'
'*Die Pink Floyd.*'
'*Was ist mit Geld? Haben Sie ihnen Geld gegeben?*' Did you give them money? '*Nein.*' A lie. We'd brought three hundred dollars in cash and left it with Jan.

They'd taken our passports when we entered and said it'd take some time to check our story. We can hear martial music somewhere. Midnight comes, the music stops, there are two minutes of spoken Czech then the music strikes up again. An hour later a guard emerges.

'*Sie dürfen jetzt gehen.*' You can go now, he said, edging the passports towards me with his fingertips as if they might be infected.

Outside, the car's been ransacked. We keep quiet scraping the ice from the windscreens and side windows. We get in and the engine coughs twice before firing. Once we've covered the first fifty metres towards the German check point, I accelerate hard.

'*Frohes neues Jahr.*' Happy New Year, says the guard as I wind down the window. We all burst out laughing.

LEON DRIVES ME to Worplesdon near Guildford and drops me

outside my house. Mum has clearly been waiting for us. Before Leon has driven off, she's already on the top step waving a piece of paper. As he accelerates up the short, steep hill out of the cul-de-sac, she calls out, 'There's a telegram. You've got it! You've got your place at Oxford!'

I smile weakly. All I want to do is sleep for twenty-four hours. But with Dad standing behind my mother booming out, 'Congratulations!' that's impossible. And over the teapot I'm soon drawn into the excitement of it all and narrating the adventures of our trip to Czechoslovakia. I don't tell them about the gunshots.

THE PLAN IS to stay in Springfield, Massachusetts for a couple of weeks. I want to get to San Francisco and, now I have my place at Oxford secure, this is as good a way as any to start. The daughter of my parents' friends has married an American. She's in her early twenties, I'm just eighteen when I land at New York's JFK airport. Her husband's studying for a doctorate, but they include me in their life and socialising.

They insist I join them one evening when they have friends round. We're sitting on the floor passing round joints – grass not hashish. The vinyl playing is Crosby, Stills, Nash and Young. There's been plenty of wine with the spaghetti. The next thing I know is something's slowly stroking the back of my hand. It's Linda's fingers and she's leaning towards me, her neck arching in my direction bringing her head close to mine with a dreamy smile on her face. Something breaks the spell, maybe the record finishing. I'm excited and aroused but anxious and confused. I'm younger, she's married, I'm in their apartment as a guest. Perhaps she's homesick! Most worrying of all, although I'd shared beds with three girls in the previous year and we'd been sexually intimate, I was still a virgin. I see the coming days flash by in comic horror as a poor man's version of *The Graduate*. I decide I'd cut short my stay and head north to Canada, where I think it'll be easier hitch-hiking.

ONE OF LINDA'S friends is driving to Toronto. I accept a lift straight north, which gets me over the US-Canadian border. I'm heading west towards Vancouver on the far coast of that vast country. One place I stay is a campsite by a fast-flowing river. The tents are already erected and travellers by car stay in this inexpensive motel under canvas. There's a café for breakfast and other food where I wash dishes. They let me stay in a small tent and give me meals. It's a way of conserving my dollars and a break from standing by the road for hours. Staying by the river gives me a chance to swim in the freezing water. I can have a hot shower and put some clothes in a washing machine.

One night by the communal fire pit, someone with an acoustic guitar plays a song I've never heard. It captures how I feel to be journeying in the flatlands of Canada approaching the Rocky Mountains:

> *As I went walking that ribbon of highway*
> *And I saw above me that endless skyway*
> *I roamed and rambled*
> *And I followed my footsteps*
> *To the sparkling sand of her diamond deserts.*

I ask the singer about the song.

'Oh man, you don't know! That's Woodie Guthrie. He's cool. When he sang those songs, he had a sticker on his guitar. It said: This Machine Kills Fascists.'

By this time Woody Guthrie, activist, poet, songwriter and human rights campaigner, had been dead three years. The Woody Guthrie song I heard by the fire pit was 'This Land is Your Land', written in New York in 1940. Woody had lived in the Oklahoma dustbowl and travelled to California with displaced farmers learning their folk/blues songs leading to his album *Dustbowl*

Ballads. The impact of the dust was felt as far as the Eastern Seaboard, where even the snow turned red. It was the year after Steinbeck published *Grapes of Wrath*, his epic novel featuring the Joad family's disastrous migration from Oklahoma to California. A journey which climaxes on the final page with a young mother who's just lost her baby, offering a starving man her breast.

Woody's is a classic case of a continuous rebellion against everything his father represented.

So many rebellions by young men are a kickback against a dominant father figure. There's an element of this in my own insistence on doing things my way, in making it clear that I wasn't interested in the law, let alone the army – my father's preferred option. Growing my hair long, preferring poetry to contracts, arguing for pacifism not for prosecuting war. These are all in direct opposition to my father and his view of the world. It's why figures like Jim Morrison, Woody Guthrie and other artists of all kinds, genders and periods who live in opposition to a norm expected by a father, exert a fascination for me.

I HAVE A notion, untouched by reality like so many ideas when you're eighteen, that I could take a short cut to San Francisco heading south-west through the state of Montana. I fantasise winding my way through its mountains on horseback.

My dream's shattered by a bored immigration officer. The overweight official bends down to the level of the driver's window and glances at his passport, then asks to see mine. His eyebrows rise when he sees the dark blue document with its Wizard of Oz lion and unicorn supporting the monarch's crown and shield embossed with *Honi Soit Qui Mal Y Pense,* the animals standing on a platform of *Dieu Et Mon Droit.* He turns the passport over without opening it. His puzzlement makes it clear this is his first sight of a British passport emblazoned with fantastical, gold flummery.

He directs his gaze across the driver and addressing me drawls one word at a time, 'What. Have. We. Here.'

He doesn't wait for an answer, but stands up still clutching my passport. Through the car side window I see the fawn shirt of his uniform and the handle of a revolver sitting in a polished holster. As he saunters towards a wooden cabin, he gesticulates to the driver, 'Pull over there, buddy!' indicating a lay-by.

It's the first time I've been anywhere in the world where a British passport isn't recognised. Here on the border between Alberta, Canada and Montana, USA, there's simple ignorance. As a child of the British Empire, I'm challenged that not everyone's world revolves around the British monarchy and unicorns. I'm shaken though say nothing. I hide my feelings with righteous indignation. 'Fool! Doesn't he know what a British passport is!' Now I laugh at the absurdity of my teenage arrogance.

After ten minutes, the official reappears and stops five metres in front of the car with my passport in his right hand. He waves me to get out of the car. I do, as does the driver who'd offered me a lift.

'No sir, you can get back in your car.'

The driver gets back in reluctantly, shrugging in my direction.

'Get your bag, sonny,' says the officer with damp patches under the armpits of his shirt. 'We can't let you in,' he says as I open the rear door to grab my rucksack.

'But I have a visa.'

'We don't care about no visa,' he says. 'This photo don't look nothing like you. We can't be sure it's you.'

The photo taken at fourteen bears little resemblance to my eighteen-year-old self. 'And, anyways, you got long hair. We don't let in no people with long hair.'

As the barrier is lowered on Montana, I turn round and walk back to Canada.

After this failure, I decide to continue hitchhiking to Vancouver, where I get a bus to get me over the border back into the US. I decant myself in Portland, Oregon and continue hitch-hiking south heading for San Francisco.

HIGHLIFE, & MY OTHER LIVES

I TRUDGE THE sidewalk climbing hill after hill with my rucksack. The wide road sometimes flattens out as if gathering its strength for the next ascent. At the crossroads, the surface breaks into a ripple of cobbles. What strikes me are the crows' nests of wires overhead: telephone wires and the electricity supply for the trolleybuses and trams which clatter in the streets clanking in their rails. I pull the scrap of paper from my wallet to check the name and address. 'Just knock on the door, man. It's in the Mission. They'll help you out.'

It's early March, mid-afternoon, and unusually warm. I stumble up the steps of the three-storey house and knock on the scarred front door. I'm level with the front room bay windows. In their reflection my greasy hair reminds me I haven't had a shower in three days. I can hear muffled music from the apartment upstairs. I wait a while, content to rest after my climb, then knock again. The paint's flaking off the clapboard. I'm already wondering what to do if no-one appears. Certain the names I have on my scrap of paper are out, I knock for the third and final time. I sit down on the steps. The stucco's cracked. Five minutes back down the hill, I'd passed a small cluster of Mexican shops. Someone might have a room. I stand and begin to make my way down the steps. There's a rattle and thump, someone on the upper floor has pulled up the sash window. The music is unchained and leaps out into the street barking with excitement and joy. I recognised it instantly: Santana.

'Hey man. What's up?' The speaker has a bandana round his head, I glimpse his ponytail, he's holding a can of Coors beer.

'Sorry to disturb you I . . .'

'That's cool.'

'I'm looking for . . .' I hold up my scrap of paper and say the names.

'They're away, man. Out of town. Hiking. They've taken some stuff with them.'

'I was hoping . . . I mean . . .'

'You're not from round here, are you?'

'No, From England.'

'Hey, come on up and have a beer.' He turns away and through the open window I can hear him calling. 'Some kid from London.' I hear him coming down the stairs. Santana's still bounding down the street. He's wearing a Jefferson Airplane tee-shirt and Levi jeans.

As we climb the stairs and the sounds swell, I say, 'Cool music. Santana.'

He smiles, 'Carlos. Yeah, I was at school with him man.' He hands me a Coors. 'Welcome.' He holds up his can and we clink.

There are a dozen people chatting quietly in twos or threes, drinking, smoking and listening to the music. The room's filled with the sickly-sweet aroma of joss sticks. I glance round the walls with their Fillmore West posters of 'The Grateful Dead', 'Quicksilver Messenger Service', 'Frank Zappa and the Mothers', 'Jefferson Airplane'. One of the LPs I'd left in Guildford was the Airplane's *Bless Its Pointed Little Head.* A live recording of two concerts at the Fillmore East in New York and the Fillmore West in San Francisco. On the back cover the band are lounging or slumped, half-draped over each other on a sofa and chairs with a low coffee table where candles, a pipe, bowls and smoke coolers squat.

The image was a sixteen-year-old, suburban English boy's fantasy of a hip party in San Francisco. Now here I am in the city itself, a similar scene, though there's no draping of limbs and the dope gear was unused on a table.

'Take a seat man.' I sit next to a figure all in denim with a white tee-shirt and cowboy boots. He has a mop of dark hair to his shoulders and the largest walrus moustache I've ever seen. He wears gold rimmed, round glasses and chunky rings encase his fingers including a skull and pyramid.

'Cheers,' I say tentatively holding up my can of Coors.

'So, you're from London.' He holds out a red and white Marlboro packet. I take one.

'Near London. South.'

'Well, I'll be darned. South of London. What're you doing here?'

'Someone gave me an address of a friend. I just arrived today.'

He nods slowly. 'What are your plans for this beautiful city?'

'Umm. I don't really have any. Plans I mean. I want to see it for myself.'

'How long are you thinking of staying?'

'That depends. I could stay six months if I like it and get some work.'

He laughs a little. 'Once they get here, most people stay longer.'

'I have to be back for university in October.'

'Aah. College. So, you're a smart kid, eh? What are you gonna study?'

'I'm going to read, I mean I'm going to study English.'

He explodes with laughter. Then, still trying to control his laughter, he calls out to everyone and to no one in particular, 'This dude speaks better English than any of us but he's still gonna go study it!'

He's taken off his glasses, and is wiping the tears from his eyes. 'It's OK. You're cool. You're really cool.'

I don't feel cool at all. Santana has finished and there's something jazzy I don't recognise playing. Then someone tells me to help myself to another beer and when I return the walrus moustache has disappeared and there's a Joni Mitchell look alike, chiselled, straight, long blonde hair.

'Are you OK?' she asks and without waiting continues, 'Don't worry about him. He's always doing that. We're used to it.'

'Used to what?' I say bathing in her empathy. I don't remember if she tells me her name at that point, but I still remember it today. Jan Swang.

'He does it on his show. KSFN. It's part of who he is.'

I nod as if I understand which I don't until later.

'I don't know the music,' I said. 'But I like it.'

'It's not out yet. He's got an advance copy. It's a band called Weather Report.'

Then a spliff is being passed round and soon a second one. The sequence and scene wobbles and dissolves quietly and dreamily. And it no longer matters, for everything is warm and welcoming and I've arrived in San Francisco.

THE WALRUS MOUSTACHE, Steve, is a highly regarded DJ on the hip KSFN. Before the evening finishes, he's offered me a job.

'You read the commercials. They'll love your accent. We'll sell a shitload of stuff.'

I ask what I'll get paid.

'No cash. Well, not much. You can stay at my place. It's got a basement, its own bedroom. A huge waterbed, man. A shower, a fridge. You can do your own thing.' Steve isn't exaggerating: the house and its basement accommodation are enormous. It's in Oakland over the Bay from San Francisco, surrounded by other spacious plots without fences or other markers of ownership. The lawns are precisely cut, sprinklers came out when it gets warmer. Every house – all different – has at least two large cars and roomy garages. There are mail and newspaper boxes gleaming in the West Coast sun. Capacious sedans drive at a stately pace round the neighbourhood. The streets have large ironwoods and red maples or smaller strawberry trees. It has the first and the only waterbed I've ever regularly slept on. When I know him better, I ask Steve why he lives there. It seems so at odds with being a DJ at a cool radio station in downtown San Francisco. He laughs as he often does.

'I thought you might find it boring.'

'Hey Ricky. Aren't there always chicks ready to come back for a smoke? We make our own entertainment here.'

The working day starts late afternoon when we climb into Steve's convertible. We glide down to the toll and onto the Oakland

Bay Bridge to fly west over San Francisco Bay. As we drive over the bridge, Steve sometimes lights a pre-rolled spliff, takes a couple of hits and passes it to me. I do the same and pass it to an adjacent car. Its occupants wave, smile and make a V peace sign. 'Hey Steve! play that new Country Joe song, "Hold on its Coming"!'

When we reach the station, Steve goes in before me. He has a long session of preparing the show with the producer. I wander round, get something to drink, maybe eat, and turn up half an hour before we're due to air. An assistant hands me a numbered sheet with the commercials. All I have to do is read it through and ask if there's something I don't understand or can't pronounce. Though I'm told not to adopt American English and to keep my English pronunciation: 'toMAHtoh' and not 'toMAYtoh'.

The show runs from eight until ten pm five nights a week. It's the perfect launch pad to move on elsewhere: someone's place, a bar, a gig and often we ended up going home near dawn. Occasionally Steve brings a girl back with us and they go straight to his part of the house; more often, he invites a small crowd back and a girl ends up sharing my waterbed. We're usually too spaced out to do anything but cuddle and fall asleep together until early afternoon. When we have more energy, we dissolve into uncontrollable laughter trying to negotiate the swell of the waterbed underneath us.

One of Steve's favourite bands is Tower of Power. They're an Oakland band with an impressive horn section who play jazz-funk-soul music driving and upbeat reminiscent of the Highlife music I love from Ghana. Whenever they're playing in the Bay area, we go. I ask why he likes them so much.

'They're a change from all that psychedelic acid rock we play. They're grounded.'

I still own the original Tower of Power's *Back to Oakland* album with a photo of the Oakland-San Francisco Bridge we drove every day. Five lanes wide in one direction only! I'm living in an infinitely expanding future. Sometimes I'm there in the convertible, passing a spliff to the car in the next lane. Steve roars with laughter and presses his foot on the accelerator and we pull away gracefully, flying into the evening sun for the show that he curates in the dark studio and which plays out through the night.

INCREDIBLY, IT TAKES just three rides to travel from San Francisco back to Massachusetts. It's three thousand miles, a driving time of three days by bus. We stop for diesel or something to eat but only once to sleep. The trucker says he needs four hours and climbs into a bunk behind our heads. I doze in the front. The beast roars along the arrowing highways of Nevada and Utah scrubland and desert with outcrops of rock poking giant, knobbly thumbs into the clear blue skies; it's early September, still the landscape shimmers and wobbles. We bullet the plains of Kansas and Missouri through thousand-acre fields stubbled as far as the smudged horizon, with the only break on the skyline the rusting windmills like cracked teeth. We thunder eastwards into Indiana and Ohio, occasionally other vehicles drive off the road in terror. The landscape grows rolling and varied, so by the time we reach Pennsylvania we might be in Europe.

I HAVE A week to spend in Massachusetts. I hang out in Amherst with the younger crowd I'd met at the start of my trip. There's an Irish American girl, Maureen, I like. I've no idea whether she wants to see me. She does. I'm excited.

We have a lazy, carefree few days, usually just the two of us. It's still warm in the evenings. We lie in a field and are invisible to anyone passing. Fireflies wink what looks like a blue light. Maureen tells me it is, in fact, green. We're lucky to see them because they're most active in July before the August heat.

'They're normally sexual signals. But they've finished the mating season.'

'They're just doing it for pleasure then?'

Maureen laughs. Our faces are millimetres apart smiling and we're looking into each other's eyes.

'Have you read *Leaves of Grass*?'

I haven't but know it's iconic for American literature and writers including the Beat poets. 'I know I should. Is it a hymn to marijuana?'

Maureen's majoring in biological sciences but still getting credits attending an American poetry course. I lose my virginity to her in the campus room she shares with another girl. She has the foresight to ensure the other girl is out. I wonder if she still remembers the whispering of *Leaves of Grass*. I do remember her freckles – an American with a Celtic complexion. A loving, kind and wise woman far more mature than me.

IN MY FIRST days at St Peter's I find a handwritten note in my pigeon-hole summoning me to see the Dean – the college pastoral and disciplinary officer – in his study at five-thirty pm. Glyn Pursglove is a scholar of seventeenth and twentieth century poetry and protégé of our English tutor, Francis Warner. The room is small with just enough space for a desk and two armchairs. The Dean rises and holds out his hand, affable, a sandy complexion framed by spectacles.

'Mr Walker, a pleasure to meet you. How are you getting on?'

'All's good, thank you, Mr Pursglove.'

'You're one of Francis's first year's, I see.'

He gestures at one of the armchairs. I assume this is a pastoral chat with an added element of common ground as we share the subject of literature. He resumes looking at his notes and is silent. Then looks up.

'Something amusing Mr Walker?'

'Nothing Mr Pursglove. I'm just happy to be here.'

'I'm glad to hear that.' He pauses and puts on what I guess he thinks is a stern face. 'I'm not sure how happy you'll be with this next part of our conversation.'

'Sorry Mr Pursglove. I don't understand.' My heart starts beating faster.

'Do you remember where you were last Thursday afternoon, Mr Walker?'

I stare at a book spine over his shoulder, Herrick's *Lyrics. A Festschrift*. 'I think I was in college, Mr Pursglove.'

'That's right you were, Mr Walker. Do you remember what you were doing then?'

I'm still working out what 'A Festschrift' is. 'I don't think so.'

'Mr Walker, you were seen by one of the porters walking on the grass.'

Surely even Oxford wouldn't rusticate an undergrad for walking on the grass!

'I'm sorry Mr Pursglove,' I say expecting the conversation to move on.

'Have you anything to offer in your defence?'

This isn't a police station, though Mr Pursglove is taking his duties seriously.

'The building work was going on. I just thought it was easier to walk across the quad.'

'In spite of the visible and clear *Keep Off the Grass* notice, Mr Walker?'

'Yes, in spite of the notice. It seemed a sensible thing to do to reach my room.'

The Dean slowly closes the folder over the note on his desk and sighs. 'I am afraid Mr Walker I am going to have to fine you.' He put the tips of his fingers and thumbs together in an arch and gazes at me solemnly. 'Five shillings.'

I'm not sure whether to laugh or to cry. The Dean brightens up, changes his tone, 'This will be the most expensive glass of sherry you have while you're here with us.' He's built the entire exchange around this punchline. Before I can say anything, he's on his feet pouring two glasses from a decanter.

'Welcome to St Peter's and to Oxford,' he says cheerily amused at his own joke. 'Now tell me why you want to read literature,' he solicits, apparently unconscious of the absurdity of the scene we'd just enacted.

For weeks my friends would say, 'Has Mr Walker been on the grass again?' Everyone would burst into laughter, and someone would roll another joint.

A NOTABLE MAJORITY of St Peter's undergrads are from state schools, but I become part of a circle which includes Nick Howard, an old Etonian whose home is Castle Howard in north Yorkshire. It was later used in the 1980s as the location for the TV version of *Brideshead Revisited*. Nick is also reading English, but is more intent on being a version of the Sebastian Flyte of our generation.

Where the unhappy Sebastian numbs himself with alcohol, Nick does similarly with an obsessive fantasy of being a rock star. During the Easter break of our first year, Nick and his nascent band decide to rehearse at Castle Howard. Nick has arranged for the band to stay and rehearse in the Temple of the Four Winds, a folly in the castle grounds. Not a band member and with no desire to be one, I'm invited by Nick to arrive before the band. I stay with him in the east wing of the main house where he and his brother have their private rooms.

It transpires that my role is to have supper with Nick and his parents, George and Cecilia Howard. I have long hair, but I'm not a wannabe rock musician. Nick thinks I might be an acceptable cover for some of our friends in the band. George unexpectedly inherited Castle Howard following the deaths of his brothers in the Second World War. Along with Cecilia they revitalised and restored the house. He's nicknamed 'Gorgeous George' because although he owns a grand stately home and chairs the County Landowner's Association, he wears a caftan when off duty. When I visit, George is a governor of the BBC and a few years later its Chairman.

George is a large, genial figure who makes me feel completely at ease over pre-dinner drinks. It's hard not to smile in the presence of a portly, late middle-aged man who wears a caftan. Thinking of what my Dad, also George, would have asked for, I order a gin and tonic. It's billed as an informal kitchen supper – the cook's night off, though she'd prepared all the food in advance, and it's served in the kitchen by the butler, Henderson. I doubt Henderson ever has a night off, at least not in the sense of dressing down. Though we're in the kitchen – at a table large enough for twelve – he's dressed in the full regalia of dark butler attire, and he waits assiduously on the four of us.

George asks me how they might do Radio 1 differently. I say something like, 'Just give John Peel more airtime.' He knows about John Robert Parker Ravenscroft and his importance to the cultural credibility of the BBC with a younger generation. I tell him how I used to listen to John Peel under our boarding school blankets at midnight when he worked for the pirate radio before the BBC. What made Peel the most distinctive and influential broadcaster of his counter-cultural generation was his championing of the underdog, the offbeat, the bizarre, the comic, the surreal, the beautiful, raucous, melodic, challenging and sometimes in-your-face music.

By the time the kitchen supper is over, the security alarms have been activated to protect the treasures the castle holds. We have to weave and crawl avoiding the laser beams.

'Keep close,' Nick whispers theatrically. 'Do exactly what I do. You're my shadow.'

To my surprise we make it through without setting off an alarm. I may be the only non-Howard family member to worm my way late at night under a copy of the famous portrait of Henry VIII. When I say copy, it's a pretty darn good copy. Holbein painted the original as an early piece of national mythmaking to go on display in the Palace of Whitehall in the second half of the 1530s. The copy in Castle Howard was painted in 1542 directly from the original.

Nick and I duck and dive along the Antique Passage designed by Vanbrugh. No wonder Nick gets bored with reading Restoration theatre. After all, he's spent his childhood, school and college holidays living in Sir John's much greater material legacy, Castle Howard. Once we get back to his rooms, Nick breathes a huge sigh of relief. 'After that, we definitely need a smoke!'

MUCH OF MY time at Oxford is spent on drama. I immediately join the Oxford University Dramatic Society (OUDS), and in my first Michaelmas term have a small part in Jo Orton's 1967 play, *Loot*. The lead male is an ebullient, corpulent second year undergrad with a gruff manner but who is, in fact, extremely kind. He reassures newcomers and gives us some basic stage tips. He's playing Inspector Truscott, who responds to one character's comment, 'The British police used to be run by men of integrity,' with the retort, 'That is a mistake which has been rectified.'

The second-year undergrad, who's reading Experimental Psychology at New College, is Mel Smith, son of a Chiswick greengrocer turned bookmaker.

I'd never heard of Alexander Blok, an early twentieth century Russian symbolist poet and playwright. But I audition for a part with a new, experimental theatre company which aims to stage offbeat, unknown drama. I'm offered the lead role. The play, *A Puppet Show*, uses Commedia dell'Arte characters. I'm the clown with white make-up, a black cap and a baggy white Pierrot costume.

Rehearsals are at the far end of the spectrum from my OUDS experience. It isn't until the third rehearsal that we looked at a text. The first few hours with the cast are all about exercises with the body, posture, relaxation, breathing and trust in those performing with you. There's no fixed rehearsal space, but we gather in a large room above a garage. It has battered, oil-stained, wooden floorboards and you can see through the gaps not covered by our rehearsal mats down into the garage where cars, oil, jacks, tyres, wheels, batteries and all the paraphernalia of a small garage are littered. Fumes of diesel, hot metal and grease percolate the rehearsals.

It happens to be next door to where I'm living in Jericho. In the bric-a-brac shop opposite the synagogue in Richmond Road I buy a copy of an old master, an Italian painting for £5. I like its composition, content and colour palette, predominantly green with some restful russet reds and ochre-beige. I buy it to cover the blank wall space in my study. Fifty years later it hangs in my late Victorian house in East Oxford. Specialists tell me my *Marriage of the Virgin* is a mid-Victorian reproduction. The synagogue is now heavily secured, and somewhat forbidding with security cameras and heavy iron gates. The bric-a-brac shop has become Al Shami, a Middle Eastern restaurant.

In Jericho, we go to The Rickety Press or The Bookbinders and play shove ha'penny with men from the printing works housed behind the neo-classical façade of the University Press. Even after they scrub their hands, the creases of their skin and their fingernails remain stained with printers' indelible ink.

Jericho, though now overpriced, remains an attractive and desirable place to live, with its central location, a mix of bars, restaurants, coffee shops, canal side and Port Meadow nearby. Though there are no print workers in the pubs any longer. And the customers wouldn't know what to do with a shove ha'penny board.

ONE SUNDAY MORNING I find myself in a limousine gliding towards Heathrow. There's a gala fund-raising event at the Oxford Playhouse. I've been asked to go and fetch one of the performers. It's the Anglo-Irish actor, dramatist, painter, founder of the Gate Theatre in Dublin, Micheál Mac Liammóir, who founded the Gate Theatre in 1928 with his lover and lifelong partner, Hilton Edwards. Hilton directed more than three hundred plays at the Gate from Sophocles through Ibsen, to a then unknown Brian Friel. Hilton isn't with Micheál as he exits Arrivals at Heathrow.

Micheál clearly expects attendance of the highest order to his every need at any moment.

'My dear boy. What a dreadful flight. Awful woman nearby, asking the hostess to ask me if I minded not smoking. I said I didn't mind at all and lit another cigarette.'

The chauffeur, in a uniform and a peaked cap, holds open the passenger door for Micheál, which seems to mollify him. I'd planned, as I had on the way to the airport, to sit up front with the chauffeur.

'No, dear boy,' said Micheál tapping the leather bench seat in the back. 'With me.'

'I thought you might like a rest after your journey.'

'A new boy's face and the sap rises once more. You will distract me.'

Fortunately, there's a large armrest, already down, which offers some protection. Every ten minutes Micheál leans over towards me, leering.

'Are you sure you won't join me in a cigarette? Balkan Sobranie.'

At the entrance to the Randolph Hotel, the bellboy takes Micheál's holdall.

'Are you joining me for lunch?'

'I'm sorry Micheál, I've got things to do. I've been asked to come and collect you at four o'clock.'

'Oh! Is John here yet?'

'John?'

'Yes. Gielgud. I only agreed to come because they said he'd be here.'

'I've been told he's coming. I don't know if he's here yet. Perhaps ask at reception.'

Micheál wrinkles his somewhat pasty and pudgy face.

'I'll come and collect you at four. I think there's a read through or a rehearsal.'

'I don't need that at my age,' he snorts.

At ten past four, when Micheál hasn't appeared, I ask reception to ring up. There's no answer. I go and knock on his door, twice loudly. Eventually he opens the door a little, not fully awake. For a moment I can see the confusion in his face. Then the mild terror lifts.

'Dear boy. I was asleep. Beauty sleep. Give me fifteen minutes please.'

As the door's closing, I see that his toupée has slipped slightly, there's a streak of orange on his forehead, the bags under his eyes are darker and his jowls heavier. I'm looking at an old man. A life in theatre.

He takes twenty minutes but appears looking remarkably refreshed and as spritely as any seventy-something year-old who pays little attention to his health but much to his appearance. In the Playhouse there are dozens of people on stage milling round laughing, slapping each other on the back, embracing, false and genuine squeals of surprise; it's British theatre at its campest, most narcissistic. Its pinnacle to which they all aspire, is Sir John – who reminds me of a heron. Tall, erect but slightly hunched in the shoulders, with a high forehead, patrician, and remarkably still given the roaring jollity swirling round him. He's ready to strike in an instant when the right prey is in range. He's holding court as I usher Mac Liammóir up the steps to the stage.

'Richard, what a pleasant surprise to see you here.' It's my tutor, Francis, who is an academic luvvie with photographs in his study of himself with Richard Burton and Elizabeth Taylor and another of Samuel Beckett in full hawk profile. Both photographs are signed to him. He turns back to the circle, 'Sir John, one of my most dramatically-minded students.'

Sir John acknowledges my presence with the slightest cock and dip of his head. I step aside allowing Micheál entrance to the group.

Sir John resumes his anecdote, 'As I was lacing my shoe . . .' Micheál, not to be outdone, booms, 'John, you old rogue. You've never laced your own shoe in your life!'

There's silence and an inaudible gasp. Sir John puts his hand in his pocket, pulls out and waves something imagined while enunciating in his most orotund Shakespearean mode: 'Trifles light as air are to the jealous confirmations strong as proofs of Holy Writ.' Iago's words on Desdemona's stolen handkerchief, recalling Mac Liammóir's Iago to Welles' Othello on celluloid.

Sir John continues in full Shakespearean mode, 'You Irish vagabond. Come here and embrace me!'

Sir John has very deliberately chosen his description of Mac Liammóir as an 'Irish vagabond.' He knows the man famous in the theatrical world in Ireland and beyond was born Alfred Willmore in Kensal Green, London. Alfred had studied at the Slade, but left without graduating to avoid conscription and travelled throughout Europe. He's captivated by Ireland, becomes fluent in Irish, changes his name and never looks back. He himself is his finest piece of dramatic creation, a performance which lasts the rest of his life.

My tutor Francis knows full well that the addictive high of networking, casting, reviews, adulation and gossip which theatre embraces is a glittering lake in which you can easily drown. A year after I leave Oxford, I'm performing at the Edinburgh Festival, where the *Financial Times* critic compares me to 'a youthful Max Wall.' I'm not sure I value the comparison to a music hall dancer and comedian who'd become popular between the wars, but afterwards – on his uppers, divorced and bankrupt – is playing working men's clubs in the north of England. Francis is excited that Wall, rediscovered by Samuel Beckett, among others, has just performed a highly acclaimed version of *Krapp's Last Tape*, Beckett's most autobiographical, solo drama.

'One day Richard, one day, it'll be you!'

I TOY WITH the notion of making my way in theatre, but I have no interest in being a rock musician. Conversely, I'm steadfast in my attraction to rock music and its performers. Walking on Box Hill near Dorking in Surrey, I become friends with a man on a motorbike, Bob Pridden, The Who's sound engineer. He tells me that anywhere The Who are playing he can get me in backstage.

Early in the day I leave a note for him at the New Theatre near St Peter's.

Later I'm confronted by a roadie with few teeth an hour before the gig. 'You better be a friend. What's your name?'

I tell him.

Ten minutes pass and the door opens. 'Good to see you, Richard. I'm busy now. Go down and make yourself at home.'

There's an open door into a low-ceilinged basement room with no natural light. A dozen men and women all stop talking when I enter. Lamps pick out a sideboard full of beer, wine, Jack Daniels, Coca-Cola, rum, Smirnoff, ice-buckets with champagne. A leather sofa runs along the far wall and down one side. On a low table there's a blue bowl half-full of white powder. A woman in a short mini-dress is kneeling with a rolled up bank note to her nostril. Someone says, 'It's OK, it's just some kid.' Then she snorts the powder up one nostril, for a moment she looks startled, her eyes widening and glassy, she giggles to herself, and inserts the bank note in the other nostril.

'You OK?' says a baby-faced man wearing a rust-orange suit. He smells metallic.

'Thanks. I'm a friend of Bob's.'

'Like some stuff?'

I don't reply.

We hear a woman laughing followed by a door banging and a man shouting, 'Oh yes, you doooh!'. The woman bursts into our room with bare feet and a pair of skin-tight denim jeans but no top or bra. She pulls the door back and hides behind it, 'Don't tell him I'm here.'

Moments later a wild-eyed man appears with tousled dark hair and lipstick smeared across his face. His shirt is torn.

He grins theatrically raising his eyebrows and widening his eyes. 'Where is she?'

'Search me,' shrugs the man in rust-orange.

'Jez, I wouldn't search you if you paid me,' says the wild-eyed man.

He walks to the end of the room and sitting on the sofa reaches round behind his back. In an instant he's beating out a rhythm with two drumsticks, lost in its intricacies and absorbed in the soft, sharp thwack of the wood on leather. Everyone's watching, listening to the rhythm of the sticks, rain on a canvas tent.He stops abruptly, jumps up, runs to the door and jerks it open.

'I knew you were there all the time!'

'It's just a game,' she opens her arms.

'Too right it is.'

Everyone turns away busying themselves with conversation or cigarettes.

A voice behind me asks, 'Anything left in that bottle?'

It's the wild-eyed man pointing at the champagne. I pass it to him. He takes three long swigs before handing it back. 'Thanks mate.'

He disappears through the door with the woman, slipping her right hand into the left of The Who's drummer, Keith Moon, drumsticks tucked safely down the back of his yellow trousers.

Bob appears briefly and says there's a seat on the front row at one end for me if I want or I can watch from the wings. 'Make sure you're back here after the first set. Something I need to tell you. Enjoy the show.'

I spend most of the show in the wings near the bass player, John Entwhistle. It's five minutes after the band finish the first half before my body stops quivering, my hearing is still underwater. Townsend and Entwistle are ahead of the curve in amplification. Jimi Hendrix and his manager used to come to them for advice. Bob was part of that conversation.

I make my way back down to the basement. Bob's already there. 'All OK?' he mouths. I hold up my thumb. 'A beer?' I nod. He takes one too and guides me to where we can just about hear each other.

'Richard. You know Oxford. You live here, right?'

'Yeah, I'm a student here.'

'They want to . . .' he pauses. 'To eat Indian,' he looks at his watch. 'By the time we finish and get them out, they'll be closed. Anyway, they'd like it private. The restaurant, just for them.'

Bob sees relief on my face that I wasn't being asked to find more drugs or women.

'It's OK, you can come along too if you like.'

'It's not that, I just hope . . .'

'You'll do it. I know you will.' He puts his arm round my shoulders. 'Thanks man, I knew you would.'

The nearest Indian restaurant is in Walton Street, Jericho, ten minutes' walk. I rehearse my script: looking after famous musicians, giving a concert, we might be late. *Don't* use the words 'rock musicians'. I hurry down Little Clarendon Street passing the vinyl store I go to. On my left is Wellington Square where Patrick lives in a late-Victorian three storey house. He models himself on Keith Richards. Later all these houses are demolished. Now in Wellington Square, I see Patrick suspended in mid-air, cross-legged, scruffy baseball boots, the beads round his wrists jangling against a monstrous bong in a smoke-filled room, painted black.

The Bombay is an institution. They recognise me. I have my script, but no-one at The Bombay has one. But they're word perfect: 'Everything will be alright, it will be a private party.'

No plates are smashed or furniture destroyed. The bill is paid with a handsome tip.

IN 1972, THE grand old man of English poetry, Wystan Hugh Auden, returns from New York to Oxford – to his undergraduate college, Christ Church – with his health failing; and even with his peculiarly high tolerance for domestic chaos, he's finding life difficult to manage on his own. Grand Auden certainly is in terms of his reputation as a writer and intellectual. He's the greatest living English poet and I'm excited that we're going to meet him.

He certainly isn't old, only sixty-five when he returns to take up residence in a 'cottage' – appropriately enough called The Brewhouse – located in a Christ Church canon's garden.

It's a late February afternoon when he shuffles into Francis's study on the third floor of Linton House, the Georgian rectory which is the front entrance of St Peter's College. There's no lift to this floor, so Auden has to climb three steep flights of stairs clutching the wooden banister rail. He must have had to gather himself and catch his breath before entering the room accompanied by Francis. We'd been told to be there at 5pm sharp. Auden enters the room at a quarter past five precisely. One fixed point in the chaos of his personal life is an obsession with punctuality. As if clock-watching were an anchor in the stormy sea of his turbulent emotions. His 1969 poem 'Moon Landing' comments drily that women wouldn't have bothered with such 'a phallic triumph' and men only made it possible

> *because we like huddling in gangs and knowing*
> *the exact time.*

Like the six other undergraduates in the room, I absorb his battered face, a rare skin condition which has coarsened, thickened and furrowed his skin. But it's the shambling, shuffling entry which shocks me more, as if we're suddenly in a hospital or an old folks' home. This is compounded by his footwear: old-fashioned, 'grandad slippers', wool plaid in grey, scuffed, stained and damp. I wonder whether he's dragged himself from Christ Church up St Aldate's, gone left into Queen Street then right along New Inn Hall Street to St Peter's in those slippers.

Once settled in the large leather armchair he pulls out his packet of Players, a Zippo lighter, and fires up his fag. It's like watching the opening moments of a drama. His concentration on the task is absolute and we might not be there. We're the audience whom he's not yet acknowledged and won't do so until this opening scene is set to his liking. It's the slightly weary but consummate professional readying himself for his umpteenth performance, which is what his life seems to him to have become.

Conversing with Auden is like having a conversation with a human-sized lizard turning its head slowly round to meet your gaze. In our discussion about poetry, art, society, science, politics he only allows shades of grey to seep in where he's still gnawing at an issue himself like a dog at an especially enduring bone. Otherwise, he's always decisive and clearly never takes prisoners. We have the discussion under his firm hand of why he changed the line: 'We must love one another *or* die,' to, 'We must love one another *and* die.' And he makes it clear, that his is the last word on it.

Auden's wonderful poem about Edward Lear seems to me as much about Auden himself as Lear. After all, Auden spent nine summers in Ischia before he and Chester, his American lover, bought the only property Auden ever owned, at Kirchstetten near Vienna. Auden writes about Lear's demons – he had epilepsy – whist Auden had demons of his own. The poem climaxes in joy and love: 'And children swarmed to him like settlers.'

At two points Francis provides Auden with a martini. Even his 'Thank yous' sound like they might be cloaking another back story, which is, in part, the shimmering in his eyes, and the over-elaborated and mannered way in which he delivers his 'Thank you, Francis,' with pursed lips.

I see and hear him shuffling back to Christ Church through the throng of ordinary shoppers – fortifying himself by quietly chanting some Lear:

The Owl and the Pussycat went to sea
In a beautiful pea-green boat.
They took some honey and plenty of money
Wrapped up in a five-pound note.

All in preparation for yet another dinner at Christchurch High Table, where Auden gets disgracefully drunk through the courses and asks an unsuspecting, very distinguished guest whether he, like the Great Poet, finds it tricky alone in his room at night, to piss in the sink.

I've experienced the Everest of twentieth-century English poetry, an awesome occasion I treasure still. Though the visible sadness Auden was carrying at the end of his life lingers with me too. He died, like Lear, alone, feeling unloved.

I SIT MY last paper in the Examination Schools in the High Street along with everyone else wearing a black gown, a cross somewhere between an undertaker and a waiter. My head's exploding with fragments of quotations. Is it better to build an answer round the quotations you remember in full or give a different answer with no quotations and paraphrase? This swirls in a heady mix of extreme hay fever when I have to ask permission to leave the examination room because my eyes are streaming and I can't read the paper. I stick my head in a basin of cold water to try and shock myself into clarity.

Out of our gowns in celebration that we've reached The End, we toast not in champagne, but in pints of beer at the Victoria, at the end of Walton Street. I've casually invited Terry Eagleton, the only Marxist critic of literature in Oxford. I've been attending his seminars as a contrast to Francis Warner's. To my surprise he turns up. He asks what I'm doing next.

'I'm going away from all this for a year,' I say. 'Somewhere with music where maybe I can start to write.' I'm thinking of Toronto where an American girlfriend from my first year has a cousin who can help.

IN TORONTO I find a job working in the head office and depot for Sam the Record Man. It's the 1970s Canadian version of then hip Virgin Records. The flagship store is on Yonge Street, one of Toronto's main arteries, the head office and depot are a block away. From there vinyl is loaded onto trucks and distributed to the other 139 Sam the Record Man stores across Canada.

I move to the Little Italy district in downtown Toronto and catch the tram to work along Dundas Street. There are Italian ice cream shops, restaurants, delis and a food market. A quarter of the residents are Italian economic migrants from the impoverished south.

Yonge Street is the centre of Toronto's music scene, a cacophony of music stores, cafes, bars and clubs. The city is one corner of the golden triangle for jazz and jazz-fusion with New York and Chicago. One freezing winter late afternoon, we tumble from the depot and slide to one of the Yonge Street taverns where later there'd be a paid-for gig, but early on it's free.

Some musicians are setting up, checking the sound and its balance. We're joking and drinking beer. Before we know it, the band are assembling on stage. After the first notes on the double bass, Scott says, 'Fuck! It's Dizzy Gillespie!' And there's the hugely extended cheek and throat pulsing with notes which one of the great pioneers of bebop is squeezing out through his trumpet.

The sound's Afro-Cuban, which Dizzy was instrumental in developing with Chano Ponzo, a Cuban percussionist, singer and dancer in the 1940s. Scott's whispering to me, 'It's Manteca, they're playing Manteca.' He tells me Manteca, written by Dizzy and Chano, incorporating Afro-Cuban percussive rhythms into bebop, is a foundation stone of this cross-over genre. I tell him about my childhood experience of Ghanaian Highlife, and how the song seems to have its roots in the energetic and uplifting rhythms of Highlife.

'*Manteca* is Afro-Cuban for heroin,' says Scott, who's the most interesting person I meet at Sam the Record Man.

Sometimes I go round to his parents' house and listen to him play the piano while we smoke a spliff. He's studied music formally and already improvises brilliantly. One day he's agitated as he puts something on his turntable.

'This isn't out yet. I got an advance copy.'

The shimmering opening bars of the solo piano instantly seduce us. So careful, clear and pure. We don't speak for the thirty minutes, the notes are smoothed pebbles skimming the water, skipping and dancing through our senses. It's a slow-motion journey entrancing us through its tinkling cascades of sound and silence. When the music stops and the record arm raises its needle from the surface of the vinyl clicking back softly to its rest, Scott mutters, 'Keith Jarrett, live at Köln.' I can barely hear him as I'm in another, distant place. 'One day . . .' says Scott, the two words hang unfinished in the silent room.

Eighteen months later I hear Scott has died. An overdose of 'manteca'. I still listen to the piece and it transports me to that faraway place I go with Scott.

I leave Sam the Record Man and Toronto for my sister Jane's wedding in Surrey.

FAYNIA, FROM OXFORD theatre days, hears I'm back in England. She's directing a new play for the Edinburgh Festival. Last year she won a Fringe First with a new play by the same writer, Richard Crane. Will I come and audition? *Clownmaker* features the life of the Russian dancer, Nijinsky. I get the part and Romola, Nijinsky's wife, goes to a third-year student, Lauren. She has glorious, ringleted, copper-red hair to her shoulders. I'm struck by her sparkling, opal eyes. She's wearing dungarees with a white cheesecloth blouse. A switchback of curves. Voluptuous. Her elongated, almond-shaped face is a Modigliani. Aquiline. Bold. Her face in my face. I know instantly I want to be with her for a very long time.

Clownmaker wins a Fringe First Award and an excerpt is shown on the BBC. I propose marriage to Romola every night on stage and she accepts. Lauren's already friends with some of the cast and crew. I join them in the Fringe Club after the late-night show, but always in a group. The flat for the cast means sharing a room with three others. She persuades a girl to swap rooms with me so we can sleep in the same room. We push our mattresses together. but there's an unintended chaperone with another girl there. We have to be patient.

We're finally alone on a visit to the Royal Botanic Gardens. In the Palm Houses the star of the show is *Victoria Amazonica,* the giant water lily from South America. We spin a story: one of its white flowers, which open at night, falls in love with the bee that visits for pollination. It refuses to open and release it to pollinate other flowers. We agree to call it 'Captive Love'.

Act 2

Fledglings

Lauren. Seville, Spain. 1977

We take a lease on a top floor flat in the Heaton area near Lister Park. A gallery in nearby Cartwright Hall is dedicated to Bradford's most famous son, David Hockney. Lauren's already a disciple, a flame that burns through her life. I meet her outside the Social Sciences building after her sessions in the Department of Peace Studies. We go and have a curry. She talks about an essay for Paul Rogers, an expert on the relation between socioeconomic marginalisation and security issues. As Student Union Events Officer, she has to look after Edward Heath and Arthur Scargill. Then and later she's always more politically engaged and active than me.

Faynia has a producer for a commercial run of *Clownmaker* in London. I'd be the only member of the Edinburgh cast to transfer with the show. It'd be my breakthrough into professional theatre. I don't think twice. My future is Lauren.

Lauren's mother left her father soon after marriage in 1954. He'd been a perfect gentleman, apparently. Overnight, he became a dominant, dictatorial husband. Doreen had agreed to leave home in Surrey where she was a hospital matron and move to Lincolnshire. She wasn't told the house they were going to live was opposite his parents' home nor that he was leaving the RAF and joining the family architectural practice. Then it was revealed she would no longer be allowed to work. She left him, pregnant with Lauren, and went home to her parents.

After maternity leave, she returned to work and Lauren was, on a daily basis, brought up by her grandparents. Her grandfather was a working-class, self-educated Fabian socialist who'd written a pamphlet about the 1926 General Strike. He fetched Lauren from school while her grandmother prepared tea. She was a Harrod. He introduced Lauren to Bertrand Russell's thinking. Sometimes they went to the opera at Covent Garden. The family had agreed they'd tell Lauren her father was dead. When she's twelve years old they tell her the truth.

She decides, now she's starting her final year at university, that she'll get in touch with her father. She makes the visit to Lincolnshire alone. She not only meets her father but is introduced to a half-sister she doesn't know exists. She's there hoping, on the cusp of adulthood, to start an independent relationship with him. He makes it clear he wants nothing more to do with her.

A month after they meet, we're in bed and the downstairs bell rings. The registered letter is addressed to Lauren. 'Lincolnshire,' she mutters. She reads it slowly then drops it on the duvet. She picks an enclosure from the letter and slides out of bed. 'Bastard!' she says calmly ripping it to pieces which snow in the wastepaper basket.

She comes back to bed shaking and starts to sob. I hold out my arms. The room heaves with her sobbing and laboured breathing. She's worried about missing a lecture. I stroke her hair and tell her it's OK. Later that morning she tells me it was a cheque for £10,000.

We hang out mostly with Lauren's friend Pam and her boyfriend, John, who accompanies himself on the ukelele to his own quirky songs and anecdotes in Bradford pubs. Sometimes Lauren plays guitar, covers and a couple of her own songs. Her guitar playing is competent, her voice is extraordinarily beautiful. John once persuades me to read a poem. Everyone knows who Ted Hughes is. So I'm not going to read him. I chose Edmund Blunden's 'The Pike' instead.

In the final months of her degree Lauren says she wants an adventure. Can I sort?

HIGHLIFE, & MY OTHER LIVES

IN LATE JULY, we fly to Sevilla and catch a bus to the city of Huelva, in the South West corner of Andalusia on the coast. We've had five days' notice. Franco died the previous November. There's turbulence and excitement, a brave new world of democracy unleashed after forty years. Windows, walls and kiosks are smothered with a riot of election posters. Late at night I peel some from round our neighbourhood. If there's only one, I never take it. Lauren's amused by my mania. I'm gathering a collection which I know will become important documents. Later I store them in my parents' attic – thrown out when they downsize from a house to a maisonette! My favourite is a fist in black ink clutching the red rose symbol of the Partido Socialista Obrero Español. Felipe González, its Secretary-General, shifts the PSOE from its Marxist roots to a social democratic party. González, a charismatic, youthful reformer, is seventeen years ahead of Tony Blair. In the first post-Franco elections, the Communists are no longer banned. In Huelva football stadium we attend a rally with La Passionara, Dolores Ibarruri, the legendary Communist leader during the Spanish Civil War and later General Secretary of the Spanish Communist Party. She's famous for her slogan '¡No Pasarán!' during the Battle for Madrid in 1936. We're witnessing the birth of democracy in Spain in 1977!

I have the cushiest job. Lauren and the other teachers give English classes in the mornings to adult women. In the afternoon and evenings, it's children and teenagers. I rarely have to go to the school and then not to teach. I walk into the office of the Director, Patrick, injecting himself. I'm aghast, horrified. He sees the shock on my face. 'Don't worry Richard. It's just insulin.' He coughs the cough of twenty plus a day Ducados cigarettes. I mention it to Lauren. 'Oh, everyone knows except you. You're never in the school. Lucky boy!'

Patrick has just won a contract with the Rio Tinto Zinc company to teach English to its senior executives. Patrick tells me he's no idea if I'm a good teacher, but I get the job because it says Oxford on my CV. 'That'll keep them quiet,' he laughs coughing. The lessons are supposed to be after work from six in the evening in the RTZ offices, where I'll often learn that Jorge or Luis aren't there, they've been called to Madrid. Or Carlos and Pedro appear late saying, '*Hemos tenido un día largo. Necesitamos una cerveza.*' We've had a long day. We need a beer. They insist the lesson is on bar stools talking about politics, football or life in Huelva versus England. I try to insist they use their basic English. But I learn as much Spanish as they do English. The most senior, Xavier, soon dispenses entirely with the office. I go to his apartment where his wife serves him a large whisky and me a beer with homemade *tortilla*.

On Friday nights we meet the other teachers at La Culata, The Dove. Sometimes we go on a late-night hop from one bar to another drawn by the sound of a guitar, clapping and singing. This flamenco is local and communal. The performers and their friends are their own audience. It's *their* pleasure in *their* moment. We're privileged to share it.

The heart of the music is the voice of a man or a woman singer using intervals smaller than a semitone. The greater the brightness of the voice, the higher its wail, as if a soul has died echoing round the bar in a melancholic longing for its loss. The clapping is off-beat, now in support of the voice, then sounding a different rhythm, a counter story. The hard-heeled shoes clatter on the tiles, bass notes beating, the pulse of the earth. Lorca calls them *los sonidos negros*, dark sounds.

The pain expressed by flamenco is the music of a people destined to wander as forever the outsiders. My place not yours! My culture not yours! The mongrel, unique river of flamenco with its many tributaries percolates this lie of watertight divisions.

IN SEVILLA, WE always stay in a small *pensión* on the edge of the *judería* or Jewish quarter. The houses and synagogues are constructed to form narrow streets and alleyways with shaded patios, designed to minimise the extreme heat of Andalusian summers.

We love wandering between the ochre yellow and orange of the houses with their wrought-iron balconies trailing tresses of green down the coloured walls. The pedestrian alleys allow no cars, so we're lulled by the soothing splash of fountains echoing over the cobbles. We peer between the bars of elaborate wrought iron gates into patio courtyards deep inside, dark mouths in a sun-dappled face.

The first monologue I write, *Scar*, broadcast on BBC Radio 3, uses this setting. An unnamed, foreign woman travelling alone visits the *judería*. She gets lost, she talks to a man in a bar, something happens, she panics, then she runs away. It's not clear whether it was a touch on the arm or a more serious assault. I use the multiple and shifting identifies of Seville itself as a location which mirrors the ambiguities of what might have happened to the woman narrator as she wanders through the city's alleyways, cafés and bars.

We stumble on the Murillo Gardens, a dense, hidden forest of green barricaded by the mediaeval buildings of the *judería*. Sitting under the fig trees we're alone listening to the leaves inhale and exhale. The rustle and silence of living things.

In the mid-seventeenth century, Murillo produced a powerful series of paintings portraying the poverty, decay and decimation brought by the plague. Later when visiting the Louvre we admire his 'Young Beggar' in which he uses light and shade like Caravaggio but the contrasts are more muted. The boy sits in a tar-black corner his back against the wall, his legs splayed out in front of him. His closely shorn head is tilted downwards examining and extracting lice from the stained white shirt under his ripped, olive-green tunic. His torn khaki trousers only reach as far as his knees. His lower legs and feet are the most starkly illuminated, the skin of the shins so pale and stretched we see the whiteness of the bone beneath. In the corner is a clay-coloured pitcher next to a fallen basket with two bruised apples on the slate-coloured floor. By his left knee are some half-eaten and discarded shrimps – a staple of the poor. 'It must have been awful,' says Lauren. 'Plague, heat, no family, almost nothing to eat.'

We love visiting the Giralda, its bell tower is a hundred-metre-high landmark and was once the minaret from where the muezzin called the faithful to prayer. This mosque is the foundation of *Catedral de Santa María*, the fourth largest in the Christian world. We are intrigued, fascinated by the layers of its migrant texts in Arabic, Hebrew, Latin and early Castilian.

LAUREN SUGGESTS WE spend the greatest of Andalusian festivals, *Semana Santa*, Holy Week, in the ultimate Moorish stronghold, Granada. Attending the celebration of Christ's crucifixion and resurrection in the city where Islam expired in Iberia, seems poignant.

Blossoming in this enclosed city with palaces, halls and courtyards, we inhale the fragrance of white myrtle, roses and orange trees. The Friday mosque, hammams and complex water system are positioned below the peaks of the Sierra Nevada to catch the run-off from the snow we see in the distance. The site covers thirty-five acres. Twenty football pitches. Ten thousand Arabic words and sentences – many relating to Allah – are used in the stone carvings throughout the halls and meeting rooms which form the interconnecting complex of patios, arcades and fountains of the Alhambra. One of our favourite phrases is: 'Don't talk too much and you'll be at peace.'

Isabella and Ferdinand adapt the Muslim complex into a Royal Christian Court. One of their first acts in the Alhambra is to give royal endorsement to an Atlantic expedition by an unknown Italian, Christopher Columbus. 'In 1492 Columbus sailed the ocean blue,' chants Lauren.

In one of our photo albums from 1977, there are pictures of the *nazarenos* or penitents in the streets of Granada. They're attired in robes with long tunics covering their bodies from neck and shoulders to their bare feet. *Capirote*, hoods with conical tips, some a metre high with a veil attached drop to their chests and hide their faces. We whisper, 'KKK.'

Here are two figures with red grape *capirotes* and veils. Dark eyeholes cut in waterfalls of wine. The tunics below are a deeper burgundy, offset by their cloaks and sashes which shimmer from their shoulders to the ground in throbbing gold. Their white gloves clutch shoulder-high staffs topped with a brass metal cross. The crowds are nine or ten deep on the pavements and spilling from the balconies. The streets are packed with excited children and toddlers. There's an occasional surge forward as a group cranes to see the *paso* or float prepared by their Brotherhood, depicting scenes from Christ's Passion or Sorrows of the Virgin Mary. Many of the floats are accompanied by marching bands. Pipes, drums, flutes, French horns, trombones, tubas, trumpets, bassoons, clarinets – I imagine Lauren marching with hers – and saxophones in the elegiac, slow and mournful cacophony of a funeral march. Which, of course, it is, though it climaxes in a resurrection.

'Nice work if you can get it,' I say.

Lauren mock frowns, her Sunday school teacher surfacing.

MY MUM AND DAD experience a post-resurrection celebration on the fringes of a significant nature reserve in Europe, where the marshes of the Cota Donana breathe over the village of El Rocío. For most of the year, the resident population of fewer than a thousand shuffles along its wide, sandy streets. As if this one-horse town is forever destined to be the dusty backdrop for John Wayne cowboy movies.

At Pentecost, fifty days after the Resurrection, there explodes an orgy of firecrackers, chanting, clapping, drums, flutes, tambourines, guitars and singers following wagons decorated with arches of paper flowers, effigies of the virgin or the white dove, and drawn by oxen patiently churning up the dust. The horses kick it up too with a high-stepping trot, on the verge of breaking into a canter but skilfully held in check by their men and women riders.

Into this mix of wild west meets Andalusian Catholic partying, George and Gwen arrive. I'd never seen them so relaxed and having such fun. Is this a signal we're now adults and they no longer needed to set an example? They take El Rocío entirely in their stride as if they regularly mix with hundreds of oxen, horses, wagons, traps and carts. A sheen of flamenco dresses and their cascading ruffles vibrate primary colours; the men wear tight waistcoats, breeches, leather boots and black, Zorro Cordobes hats.

'It was quite dusty,' says Gwen.

George retorts. 'But there was plenty of *cerveza* and sherry.'

'We liked the music,' Gwen adds. 'It was jolly. I had a little dance.'

'You mean that swarthy chap with long hair and an earring,' George smiles. And they burst out laughing.

We take them by steam train from Huelva trundling up to our favourite mountain village, Aracena, in the Sierra Morena. We pass through forests of oak trees where boar root out acorns producing some of the finest *jamón serrano* in Spain. We stroll out of town down donkey tracks feeling the heat pulse off the stone walls and admiring the trunks of the twisted olive trees. Vines, camouflaged soldiers stalking an invisible enemy, are rooted under the shade of the olives.

We stumble on a farmer puzzled as to what we're doing. He has a straw hat, his jeans hold his bowlegs together. He takes us back to a shed by his shack. In the gloom we make out large wooden barrels. He takes the lid off one and dips a bamboo stick inside the vat. He holds it out to Gwen. ¡*Beber!* Drink! he roars. Gwen tries, but most of it dribbles down her chin.

After two rounds the farmer offers the cane to Lauren. She makes a good job of it, and we copy her. We wander out into the late afternoon sun, tipsy except George who could have finished the vat. It's fermenting grape juice, five percent but it's hot and we're starving.

One evening in Huelva we're out at dinner with them. Lauren laughs when George asks her if he can call her Susan. He can't remember her name and always calls her Laura. He says Susan would be easier to remember. At home Lauren and Gwen both go to bed, but George wants a nightcap. I find a bottle of Brandy de Jerez matured in oak casks used for sherry. I take it with two balloons and some ice onto the balcony. George looks at the tray.

'What's that?' he says pointing at the ice.

'Ice.'

'Shouldn't need it if the brandy's any good.'

'It's hot Dad. It's how they serve it. Just one cube.'

He slowly nods his assent. After I pour the brandy over an ice cube, he lets it sit for ten seconds then plucks it out and throws it over the balcony. He sips. 'Not bad,' he says. 'Not bad.' And swallows the rest of it.

'I'll have another, please.' This time he lets the ice sit longer before discarding it.

Our meandering conversation includes his memory of when we'd visited Madrid on leave from Ghana and he'd taken me to Real Madrid at the Bernabeu where we see two of the first global superstars of football: the Hungarian Ferenc Puskas alongside the Argentinian, Alfredo di Stefano. Many of their goalscoring records still stand.

After I pour him a third brandy and myself a second, he says he has something to tell me that he hasn't told anyone. He's had a dream. He doesn't normally have dreams that make sense. But this one is very clear. He learns he's going to die the following year.

'Don't believe dreams like that, Dad. They're just your worries, not medical facts.'

I'm too callow to react as I would've done later when he was sharing a dream of his death. In fact, I'm afraid. I don't want him to talk about his death. A young adult, I'm only just getting to know him. They've been having a great holiday. It's a glimpse of the man Mum must have fallen in love with. I've never seen them like that. I want it to last. Not to finish abruptly with a conversation about him dying.

He's staring into his brandy then looks at me smiling, clasping his glass. 'Cheers!' We clink glasses.

'Cheers!' I echo.

'It's been a good evening,' he says.

'It was great! I'm really glad you and Mum came.'

As I get up, he says, 'Richard, don't tell your mother what I just told you.'

'Sure.'

'Goodnight,' he says.

As I'm starting to clear up, he puts his hand on my wrist. 'Pour me another please. Just a small one.'

I do. 'Sleep well, Dad.'

He nods. As I turn with the tray and leave him on the balcony, he whispers, 'Thanks.' His voice is breaking. I don't turn round to see the tears on his cheeks.

AS THE END of our year in Andalusia approaches, I raise the idea of marriage offstage with Lauren. 'I'm going to do that postgrad drama course at Bretton Hall, Leeds,' she says. 'Anyway, you haven't got any money. You need to earn some before we get married.' She's half joking and half right. And off she goes to West Yorkshire, the land of the Barnsley chop and last gasp coal mines.

I wake with a cricked neck and look out the plane window. When the door opens, the August dust gusts inside, a hot, sandy fog. Welcome to Kuwait City. I've signed a year's contract to work in the training centre of the Kuwait Oil Company. The minibus taking us from the airport seems to be heading into the desert. Technically, it's Kuwait City, but our apartment block is at the dead end of a solitary tarmac road with few buildings in sight. We see an old Bedouin driving a few goats through the scrub and the only place to eat nearby is a shack servicing indentured labourers from the sub-continent. One night I peer through a porthole into a rusting container. In flickering lamplight, huddles of men squat, chat, smoke, doze on mattresses. It's the nearest they have to a home.

Lauren and I send each other longhand letters on eggshell blue airmail paper. Hers are full of fun: workshops with Hull Truck Theatre company, an Australian TV producer sharing her cottage, someone I'd done theatre with at Oxford, spending a weekend entirely in character, drinking Timothy Taylors, coal deliveries. One letter is signed off: 'am seeing the solicitor and signing the contract tomorrow.'

Letters written earlier, explaining how she thinks we should buy the cottage she's renting, arrive later, out of sequence. As I don't respond, she takes my silence as consent. Her mother loans us the money and I'm to pay her back monthly. It'll buy us our first home. This is a declaration of commitment, but pragmatic signalling how astute she is with money, confident enough to buy a house without my agreement.

The roof of the apartment block is flat, you can see flares on the horizon, tiny candles on a child's birthday cake. We hang washing out to dry, but only when the air's a kiln and there's no desert dust. The flares are gas burning off from the oil fields which employ us. Our block houses twenty employees. Two couples are married with children, three have wives. The other fifteen men are single, at twenty-three I'm the youngest. A few are in their fifties, keen to make some cash before it's too late. Unaccompanied men share three-bed flats with two bathrooms. In our flat one bath's usually full of beer brewing. I share with Mike – a fifty-plus Australian, a keen photographer with a slight limp – and John, a bluff Yorkshireman, who's left a wife and children in Leeds.

A minibus takes us to the Kuwait Oil Company training centre at seven in the morning. If you aren't waiting, you miss it and have to call an expensive taxi. The bus brings us back in the afternoon. Some of us stay on to play football and Ron who's been an England rugby triallist persuades me to join rugby training. I haven't played for seven years.

I still have the front page of the *Kuwait Times,* 8th October 1977. The rugby match report is sandwiched between stories on renewed violence between Israeli gunners supported by 'right-wing Palestinians' bombarding left-wing Palestinians in Lebanon; and OPEC agreeing $50 million dollars interest-free loans to developing countries hit by global oil prices. 'In a game not noted for its sound defence there was a magnificent tackle by Richard Walker on Van Dalen going full steam.'

Ron and I buy an old-school Mini together as a run-around for the year. It costs £90 including insurance. Fine for me at barely five foot nine inches. Ron, a second row forward at six foot four, has to drive with his knees poking up on either side of the steering wheel. For most of the year, the only time we meet Kuwaitis is in the classrooms at the training centre supposedly teaching them English for Special Purposes: drilling, extraction and pipelines. They have three topics: football, girls and whisky.

An exception is Maher. He invites three of us to go 'camping in the desert with my family.' This is a flat landscape with rock-hard sand and a gravel surface. They've erected two Bedouin tents, a large one for Maher and family divided into two sections and a smaller one for us at some distance. They'd thrown rugs and cushions on the floors. We aren't allowed to see let alone talk to the women swathed in black who cook for Maher, his brothers and us. They plug TVs into their car batteries and play Egyptian films with the music up loud. We provide the whisky. Gas flares on the near horizon burn all night.

I RETURN TO England at Christmas to see the two-up, one-down, terraced, stone cottage in Holmfirth that Lauren's chosen and I'm buying. It costs £3,000 and has magnificent views across one of the valleys and a coal shed with an outdoor privy. At Christmas, I ask Doreen if I can marry Lauren. She claps her hands and hugs me. 'I'm so happy for you both!' We tell Gwen and George that we plan to get married in August after Kuwait. Then I fly back to the desert.

Lauren visits me at Easter and we travel to Persia, now Iran. The Shah's still on the throne. We base ourselves in Isfahan, the most beautiful of its southern cities. It's kept much of its mix of Persian-Islamic architecture with beautifully tiled mosques echoing some of the buildings we've admired in Seville and Granada. There's a Persian proverb: *Esfahan nesf-e-jahan ast*, Isfahan is half the world.

The Naqsh-e Jahan Square, a World Heritage Site, is one of the largest on the planet. Iranians claim this is where polo was perfected. Under the arcades men throw ropes of sweet paste embedded with nuts and dried fruit making nougat. We eat duck with chocolate, sit on plumped up, glittering cushions smoking water-cooled tobacco in a shared hookah. A decade later, I use this setting with the call of the muezzin to prayer in my novel, *A Curious Child*.

After Easter, Lauren returns to Yorkshire and the days fall into an arduous trudge. One afternoon I have a message that Julian Velarde wants to see me. There's a car waiting to take me from the training centre to his apartment. Julian's a long-term resident in Kuwait and the fixer. He's the man who oiled the wheels to ensure the contract goes to a London company. There've been three or four occasions I've met him but we aren't friends – he is in his fifties – and I'm not senior enough to warrant a business or social call.

'Come in Richard,' says Julian under his pencil moustache. He's nearly bald and slightly overweight in a comfortable way. 'Welcome, make yourself at home.'

Over his shoulder, I see an attractive, dark-haired woman at least a decade younger. He half-turns. 'Please meet my wife.'

'We're sitting over here,' she says gesturing to the far end of a spacious living room. She speaks English fluently with a French accent. Lebanese, I imagine.

'What're you having to drink?' asks Julian. 'I'm on whisky.' It's about five o'clock. He's fiddling with the cuff links on his shirt.

'I'll have a small beer if you have one, please.'

'Of course.' His wife disappears to fetch one. 'How are things?' It seems an odd question. I'm not sure how to answer. 'Work I mean. Or life generally?'

It's awkward. He's searching for what to say and how to say it. Julian's wife returns with the beer. 'Some pistachios too,' she smiles then leaves us.

Julian clears his throat, sips his whisky then speaks.

'Richard. I'm . . . I'm sorry. I don't really know . . . I have some very bad news for you.'

He pauses, unsure how I might react. I half hold up my hand indicating for him to give me a moment. I swallow a sip of my beer. I take one of the pistachios, concentrate on prising it open from its shell and pop it in my mouth. Then another sip of beer. And that evening in Huelva returns with another older man sitting drinking together, swamps my consciousness.

'It's my father, isn't it?'

He nods.

'Has he died?'

'Yes. Yes, I'm sorry, he has.' He's swirling the ice round the bottom of his whisky glass. I remember the ice in Dad's Spanish brandy. I choose another pistachio nut.

'These were his favourite.'

My chest heaves, I can barely catch my breath, my heart hurts and then it explodes and I'm flooded with tears. Everything's blurred.

'I'm sorry,' I say, 'I'm so sorry.'

Julian has the wisdom to know that I'm not talking to him. He stands and comes over to put his hand on my shoulder for quite a long time saying nothing.

'If you like, I'll leave you for a little while.'

I whisper, 'Thank you.'

The evening disintegrates, buffeted by storms and waves of tears and breathless grief. Endless apologies to Julian and his wife for imposing my sorrow on them. They are very kind. I stay for supper. Twice I try phoning my mother. No answer. She's probably at Jane's but I can't remember the number. More than once Julian's wife hugs me. I remember getting drunk on Julian's whisky and falling asleep on the sofa.

When I wake it's dawn. I'm stretched out on the sofa with a pillow under my head, covered in a blanket and no shoes. Julian's wife appears with a cup of tea. 'Hangover?'

I nod.

'I put some honey in the tea, that might help. When you're ready, I'll call you a taxi. Julian says to tell you, you're booked on a flight tonight.'

'Do you mind if I try calling my mother again?'

'Of course not.'

But there's still no answer.

The intercom phone buzzes. 'Your taxi's here.'

'Thank you so much. Please thank Julian too.'

She steps forward and hugs me.

I stare out the taxi window at the flares wobbling in the haze on the horizon. How could Mum not tell me sooner?

I REMEMBER NOTHING of the journey back to England and my arrival at the maisonette. My mother hadn't wanted to give up her plants. 'It'll be so much easier to manage without all that garden,' George had said.

Lauren arrives from Yorkshire. She comes with me to see him laid out in the funeral parlour but doesn't want to go in. I enter alone. He looks supernaturally calm and already an exhibit in the museum of my memory, with a glossy sheen on his skin and his full silver head of hair immaculately brushed back from his forehead. He would've liked that. He would have been less happy that while giving him a final shave someone has nicked his upper lip and there's a tiny pool of dull, coagulated blood, purple on wax white.

Mum, Jane and husband Brian, Lauren and I sit in the front row. I don't turn round. The vicar says a few words we've supplied him. The coffin rumbles forward on the body's final journey and the starched curtains stiffly close to hide the mouth of the incinerator. We file out, a slow march under the rose arbour trying to read the names and words on the wreaths. At the end of the arbour, we swivel round to see the guests behind.

As I turn, I step into another dimension. I see my Dad, standing across the lawn on the far side of the pergola. My heart's racing, my breath's in shallow gulps. No one else is paying attention. It's him and me alone looking at each other across the grass. My mouth opens to call out, but nothing arrives. He's younger, and how I remember him as a child. Brimming with vitality, upright and healthy in a dark suit with a head of brushed back, wavy, luxuriant, silver hair. Is this what happens when someone you love passes away? You see them at a moment of their perfection. Like picking the best photo to put at the front of the album. I'm mesmerised and in shock. Something terrible has happened and I can never go back to how it was.

The next scene I remember is back in the maisonette where the guests have been invited for sandwiches and tea, or sherry or beer. George is there too, he's more present, less strange this time. He's talking to other guests; I have to go and speak to him. I wind my way in his direction, stopping to take condolences and memories from friends and relatives, familiar and unknown. Then, there he is, my dead Dad, George, standing in front of me, only a little taller than I remember, but a powerful-looking man with his trademark silver hair, a beer and sandwich at his own funeral wake.

He has a Birmingham accent, as do my father's brothers except the one who emigrated to Australia. An accent which my father had long since lost. As he speaks, I remember being on leave from Ghana and going to Brownhills to see my father's diminutive mother and the family. His six brothers work on the car assembly plants in Longbridge producing the original Mini and Rover. Their team is Wolves and I'm taken to Molyneux. They drink pints of beer before we push through the turnstiles hoping to see Derek Dougan score in his gold strip. We stand on the terraces and I can't see a thing. They take it in turns to have me on their shoulders.

This man looks like he would have done that. He tells me his name is Brian. He's my father's son from my father's first marriage. A marriage I never knew about. A half-brother I never knew existed. Or exists.

I'm stunned. In a panic, the ground beneath me falls away. No sense other than the world around me has shattered and nothing makes sense any more. I can't see or hear a thing. Or speak. Like Tommy in The Who's rock opera. I have no memory of what happens next. Only when I next come back to a changed consciousness my half-brother, Brian, isn't there. I look everywhere, but he's gone.

I RETURN TO Kuwait in June, the first of four months when it never rains and regularly reaches the mid-40s centigrade. I'm back in England two months later, wearing an all-white suit. I don't recall who suggests it, perhaps someone who remembers Mick Jagger wearing all white in Hyde Park. I'm standing in sunshine by St Peter's Church, Laleham on the banks of the River Thames with my best man, Mike, who needs more looking after than I do. I've had to give him the money to buy a new pair of shoes. Inside we wait for Lauren to be led up the aisle by her Uncle Stuart. Lauren's all in white too with her curly hair even more tightly ringleted. When we kneel one of my shoes shows a price tag of £24.99. £159 in today's money.

The Reverend Ron Carter who christened Lauren has come out of retirement to officiate. Doreen's all in pink, and Gwen's all in blue and now on her own like Doreen. They'd agreed the colour scheme between them. Maher from Kuwait turns up wearing a full-length *dishdasha* in white cotton buttoned in the centre to his ankles and a headdress consisting of a *keffiyeh*, skull cap, with a *ghitraa*, a white cloth and *agal*, the black cord that holds it in place.

After the service, the wedding breakfast is in the church hall where, until sixteen, Lauren was a Sunday school teacher. Our friends walk with us by the river to spend the evening sitting outside on our hotel terrace where it's warm late.

The letter confirming our honeymoon reservation of 'one double room (with double bed) overlooking the river for the night of Saturday 19th August, 1978, only at £16.00 (including service charge and VAT) covering apartment and breakfast to be served in the bedroom at a time indicated by you . . .' is signed by the manager, a Mr A. Porter – he'd had little choice but to enter the hotel trade, I think.

The next morning, we drive off in our newly sprayed, mushroom-coloured, former post office van with no side windows, cans and Mike's old shoes tied to the rear bumper.

WE'RE HEADING NORTH to a new life in Holmfirth, West Yorkshire. Lauren conceives in two months – relatives to whom these things matter, count on their fingers to see if we'd *had* to get married. 4 Gully Terrace is so tiny, a bedroom and bathroom up, one room down, we know we need to move. We call her Rowan because we like the tree and its crimson-orange berries. Her second name, Frances, is Doreen's second name. She's born in Huddersfield Royal Infirmary in July 1979.

Lauren breastfeeds Rowan our first winter with ice whirling patterns on the inside of the window panes. We've just bought another cottage for £10,000 but it needs a complete renovation. It's in a valley outside Holmfirth overlooking a mill in a lane that runs to a small holding at its end. 'But the views over Arrunden Lane across the valley are fantastic,' is our response to Doreen and Gwen anxious that Rowan might freeze to death, or we're all poisoned by spring water.

We install solid fuel central heating by the following autumn. In the back of the house is a well room which is the only water supply. The previous owners used buckets. We get a pump installed so we can have taps with running water. Rowan's hand-washed, cotton nappies sometimes appear in shots of the TV sitcom, *Last of the Summer Wine*.

Lauren gets a full-time job in Huddersfield as an Education Social Worker, which means tracking down children who don't regularly come to school and finding out from their families why. She gets shouted at, told to 'fuck off' by some parents. Or no-one answers the door for weeks. She has to ensure that the family of Ruth Lawrence and Ruth herself are happy with being home-schooled. Ruth, a maths genius, wins a scholarship to go to Oxford aged 10, but has to wait until she's 12 before taking up her place. I spend more time looking after Rowan than Lauren, and teach English literature A-levels part time at Huddersfield College and sometimes at Manchester University to foreign postgrads. It gives me time to write.

We're happy with a set of quirky, alternative and artistic friends: Jane and Gareth both with French degrees, he's a postman, they have three kids, keep animals and serve an excellent curried goat. Later, they move to the Dordogne and we spend time with them there while Rowan goes to French school with their kids. Andy an architect – who designs the renovations in our cottage – is in business with John, a furniture maker who's married to Cathy a conservator. We spend post-Christmases with them in Southwold in a large house by the lighthouse with John's extended Norfolk family. We stand on the beach at night pretending to fish and drinking whisky to keep warm. Later Cathy works at the Castle Museum in Norwich. Alan's a lugubrious cartoonist for national and international publications. Andrew's a sculptor, mainly in wood. He and his partner later move to the Forest of Dean where his work extends into environmental and landscape issues. John and Audrey are both social workers with three girls. Rowan's friends with Joy who, on my watch, falls off a wall in our garden into the road. There's blood everywhere. Teeth are lost. I'm mortified. John later becomes a lay preacher. Audrey sticks to social work. Another John owns the smallholding at the end of our lane and is a builder who does the work on our cottage. His wife runs kennels. Their daughters Melanie and Emily are in love with Rowan and wheel her endlessly up and down the lane in a buggy. Mike who taught Lauren on her Master's in theatre at Bretton Hall, and Jackie, are an older couple across the valley who are ecstatic when Jackie becomes pregnant and has a baby. Brian makes electronic music and his partner Leaf, who works with Lauren, is openly bi-sexual. They don't want children. Once or so a week we go to the local pub, the Nook, run by David, a maths teacher in the local comprehensive. We play darts and drink Timothy Taylor's. All these and others are a great mix of friends, and we learn how to manage with a child arriving so joyously out of the blue while still having fun walking the moors, getting the cows moved from the field where our spring is and keeping the solid fuel burner alight all night.

AFTER ANOTHER SEVERE, snow-drift Yorkshire winter, I answer an enigmatic ad in *The Times* and attend an interview at a smart hotel in London where I meet a tall, tanned, good-looking, public school-educated man in a crumpled, linen suit. Martin's looking for someone to partner him in the language school he owns. He isn't looking for capital. Just some brain and commitment. Work there for a year on a decent salary then decide whether it suits me.

'Us,' I correct him. 'All three of us,' I add.

'Don't worry about the little one. She'll do anything, she's with you,' he chuckles.

'And the big one?'

He roars with laughter.

Martin phones the next day to tell me I've got the job and the potential partnership. I tell him Lauren and I are still discussing it and I'd like to see the contract. 'There isn't one. Will you agree in principle by tomorrow and I'll get someone onto it.'

'No contract. No final commitment.'

We let the cottage and drive to Tenerife with Rowan in a clapped-out Ford Estate. We spend a week driving from Santander through to Cadiz. I want to visit Salamanca, the oldest university in the Hispanic world.

We're getting ready for the evening *paseo* with Rowan, thirteen months, lying on her back on our double bed. A thump and cracking sound from the floor. Rowan's rolled off the high bed onto the tiles. Never has the dark, ornate furniture of a Spanish hotel felt more sombre. Then, blessed relief, she starts crying. She's fine, but we need that glass of wine more than ever. We trail from tapas bar to tapas bar with Rowan in the buggy the centre of attention. '*¡Rubia! ¡Que guapa! ¡Rubia!*' Blonde! Beautiful! Blonde!

We arrive in Cadiz to catch the ferry to Tenerife, exhausted but exhilarated. We haven't completed half our journey in Spain. We've driven a thousand kilometres from Santander to Cadiz in an arc curving west of Madrid: Burgos, Valladolid, Salamanca and Mérida, brushing the Portuguese border, then Sevilla. From Cadiz to the port near Santa Cruz, Tenerife's capital, is one thousand three hundred kilometres.

Millions of tourists visit Tenerife from northern Europe for winter and summer sun. We arrive in August in a way few do. The ferry takes two nights leaving Cadiz in the afternoon and arriving in the morning two days later. Our approach towards the island at seven in the morning is sublime. It's a clear dawn, the sun's rising, the summit of Mount Teide, volcanic and the highest peak in Spain, pokes through a pillow of pink candyfloss. A head disembodied from the trunk of the island below.

We stay in a hotel north of the capital Santa Cruz, its beach created with sand from the Sahara. On our first afternoon we hear broad Yorkshire accents. They come from Brockholes, a village adjacent to Holmfirth, and flew in from Manchester that morning. Lauren and I look at each other and burst out laughing. It's taken us ten days to drive. We have memories that aren't passport queues, plane wings or baggage carousels.

Martin's married to the tempest who's Annette from Corsica. Wild hair and flashing eyes. He's the sort of person who might have left school and joined the French Foreign Legion. They have five children each named after English counties. I'm certain about Devon and Somerset then it gets hazy. Cornwall? Durham? *Not* Middlesex. Three girls and two boys, all stunningly good-looking, sun and wind bleached hair, skin burnished hazelnut. They recall the song from *Cymbeline*,

> *Golden lads and girls all must,*
> *As chimney-sweepers, come to dust . . .'*

After two Yorkshire winters, we have a wonderful time in what forever seems a glorious English summer. We rent a small apartment in a fantastical construction built into a rock cliff overlooking the sea with its own stony beach. It's in Tabaiba, a quiet settlement fifteen minutes' drive south of Santa Cruz. Rowan learns to swim by the time she's sixteen months, her blonde hair turning lime green from a mix of sun, sea and chlorine.

We become friends with Tony, a Spanish doctor from Barcelona. Rowan opens the fridge door where we've left a can with a jagged lid. The more she tries to pull her finger out, the deeper the lid cuts into it. Tony's there in a moment and does something which saves her finger. Later I always remember Tony whenever Rowan goes to Mrs Morton, the Reverend Morton's wife, Anthea, for her piano lessons.

Pepita and Carlos are a couple as young as ourselves from the green cool of Galicia in North West Spain. Together we try the ascent to the peak of Teide. Three hundred metres from the summit, the air's getting thinner and we have to pause to catch our breath. We're being buffeted by the wind. I'm carrying Rowan in a backpack so I can't see her, only feel her warm body and legs on my back, her hands on my head and neck. Lauren's screaming through the wind.

'Back! Back! We have to go back!' She's gesturing back down the way we've just climbed. I'm disappointed but do as I'm told. Once we're out of the wind, I'm told why. Carlos has spotted that Rowan's lips are turning blue. She isn't getting enough oxygen. Thank you, Carlos.

At Easter, I tell Martin we aren't going into business with him. He's disappointed, tries to persuade me to stay another year but in his good heart of hearts knows we won't. We're having a great year but don't see a long term future in Tenerife.

WE RETURN TO Holmfirth in early summer and I'm offered some weeks teaching foreign postgraduates at Manchester University. One lunch time I pick up someone's *Guardian* and browse the education jobs section. At home that evening after we've put Rowan to sleep I say to Lauren, 'What do you think about Thailand?'

She looks at me as if I'm having a minor seizure. 'I've never thought about it. Should I?'

'The British Council are advertising a job there. It's aid money. Looks like a really good package. Could be interesting and fun.'

'Apply,' she says, 'It'll give us time to think.'

In less than a month I've been invited to an interview in Spring Gardens by Admiralty Arch and, to my surprise, offered the job working in a Thai ministry. 'What about that Masters in Social Work you were thinking about?' I say to Lauren when I tell her I've been offered the job.

She pauses. 'As long as it's safe for Rowan.' Then smiles. 'It sounds much more fun than social work.'

Act 3

Merry Go Round

Lauren and Richard with Rowan (age 5)
in the garden at Soi Sukhumvit 39, Bangkok. 1984

W E'RE EXHAUSTED, AND it isn't just the twelve-hour nonstop flying time. It's been the effort of packing up the cottage in Holmfirth, which we've finally made warm and comfortable, only to let and leave for what we think will be two years.

Rowan picks up the menu and reads slowly, 'Spy. See. Frog. Will I like that?' We're in the restaurant of the White House, a traditional two-storey hotel built entirely of wood with decorative carvings threaded through its verandas and balconies. The glossy green leaves of mango trees below tremble in the wind.

The heavy clouds mass overhead and open their taps. Shortly, the ground floor of the hotel is underwater. It's August 1983, and we've arrived in central Bangkok, which is regularly flooded. Too many of its canals carrying the tidal and monsoon waters have been concreted over. We're moved nearby to the Dusit Thani, a skyscraper five-star hotel.

'I'm sorry,' Valerie apologises, 'I thought you'd find the White Hotel charming.'

I say we did until we saw snakes swimming in the muddy water below our rooms.

I'm employed to run a project in the Thai government Department of Technical and Economic Co-operation. All my immediate colleagues are Thai women. I report on the project to a senior Thai civil servant and to the British Council.

We're given ten days to find somewhere to live and sort other domestic issues, like registering Rowan at the Bangkok Patana international primary school. We trail in the wake of the property agent, unable to find somewhere we like which ticks the boxes of access to the school, my work and the British Council office where Lauren might work. Bangkok traffic jams are monstrous. I readily agree to prioritise Rowan's school and work for Lauren over my travel, since I learn that as a 'foreign expert', I'm entitled to a chauffeur-driven car to work and back.

With time running out, we're shown a beautiful apartment with teak floors and a wide balcony along its entire frontage. It's a stylish development in tropical gardens with a shared swimming pool sculpted as a shell. Just two apartments on each floor. The top ones are the most favoured, they only have neighbours below. One of them is free. The agent says the owner, Khun Tak, is happy for us to take it as he knows the British Council and its work. He's an educated aesthete, charming, gay, with a light American accent.

The world of British civil servants isn't so sympathetic. Valerie has the job of going back to the British Council in London to consult ODA and the Foreign Office. The rent is seventy pounds a month more than the accommodation allowance.

There's an easy answer to that. 'I'll pay the difference,' I tell Valerie.

She smiles weakly. She'll have to get sign-off from the Director, Audrey, who's up-country bird spotting. There'll be a delay. We're in danger of being gazumped. Then the Deputy Director, Tim, says he's willing to sign it off. Finally, here is *reason* in the machinery, with Tim ready to sidestep the rules. We become friends.

THE NOVELIST WILLIAM Golding is awarded the Nobel Prize soon after we arrive in Thailand. A few months later, I learn that he's been invited to present the South East Asian Writers' awards in Bangkok. I send a handwritten letter to him care of his publisher, Faber & Faber. I write that I admire his writing, especially the novel he'd written after a twelve-year silence, *Darkness Visible*, which I'd used in a book I'd written about teaching literature. That I'd recently arrived with my family to live and work in Bangkok. If he'd like to see life away from formal dinners and ceremonies, I'd be happy to help in any way.

I receive a handwritten reply saying he'd be pleased to meet me and that he's given my name to Faber to pass on to the Thai organisers of his visit. I'm invited to a welcome Saturday lunch for Golding and his wife, Ann, hosted by the Thai Minister of Culture. The invitation doesn't include Lauren. It's in a private dining room of the penthouse of the Mandarin Oriental, one of Asia's top hotels on the banks of the river Chao Praya. I recognise the British Ambassador, who knows who I am. If he's surprised to see someone so junior there, he doesn't show it and is perfectly courteous.

Bill, Ann's name for him, shakes my hand firmly, the laughter lines round his eyes crinkling. He's seventy-two years old and has grown into the age he's looked for the last couple of decades. I'm thirty-one.

'You must be Richard. This is Ann. We're looking forward to spending an evening with you and your wife.'

The only tricky moment during lunch is when a Thai guest asks him a question about one of his novels. He pauses and frowns, looking mildly puzzled. 'Not sure I know the answer to that one.' He looks down the table towards me with the slightest of winks. 'But Richard can answer; he's read my books.'

My first thought is how to avoid the person asking the question 'losing face'. Something to be avoided in Thai culture. Ann comes to the rescue.

'Don't be silly, Bill. You know that it came out of your being a schoolmaster.'

A couple of days after the lunch, I have a message saying the British Council Director would like to see me. Audrey Lambert is then one of the few women Directors in the Council's global network. She's the generation when a senior woman has to pursue a global career alone. So, she is single, and when she isn't working, she explores Thai birdlife with her binoculars. She asks how Lauren and Rowan were getting on. Then, 'So how was William Golding?'

She sees that I'm at a loss for words.

'The Ambassador mentioned you were at the lunch hosted by the Minister.'

I explain how the invitation came about. Audrey nods and smiles. 'I'm sorry, I should have mentioned it.'

'Don't worry,' she says. 'It meant I didn't have to consider cancelling my field trip as I didn't know anything about it.' There's a twinkle in her eye.

It's an early lesson in how careful one needs to be in judging when something's purely personal or might have wider resonance for the British Council. I tell her about the informal supper I've arranged for the Goldings in our apartment the next evening. Would she like to come? She thanks me but she's already busy.

'Are you claiming expenses?' she asks.

'I didn't think about it.'

'I think you can and should.'

I drive myself to the Mandarin Oriental. I'm casually dressed in a short-sleeved cotton shirt, chinos and deck shoes. The last a jokey nod to myself about WG's time in the Royal Navy. The Goldings are staying in the Noël Coward suite. The contrast of Golding's dark horror with Coward's camp Englishness squeaks in irony on the marble floor.

The Nobel Prize Winner for Literature stands at the top of the marble steps outside the carved, teak doors which lead into the suite. His long, unruly hair and beard to his chest glow silver, a dishevelled saint. He's rigged in full evening dress, black bow tie, dinner jacket and trousers highlighting the shimmer of his hair and beard. He's screwing up his eyes, looking for the young man he'd met earlier in the week, scanning the horizon for a friendly vessel. His gaze focuses on me with a look of astonishment which holds for three seconds. Then laughter erupts through his cavernous mouth while, simultaneously, his right hand reaches up to his bow tie and rips it out from under its collar.

'Thank God!' he roars. 'Come on up!'

I hear him shouting. 'It's alright, Ann! It's a proper party!' He grins. 'Ann's getting ready. She'll be a little while.' He holds up a half-full bottle. 'I'm on the Campari. Would you like one?'

I nod. 'Thank you.'

He clunks blocks of ice into tall glasses, three-quarters fills them with Campari and splashes in a little soda. He whirrs a swizzle stick, hands me a glass and we chink. 'Hell, this is really, fucking bitter!' I think.

'What is it exactly that you're doing here?'

I give a summary: a project to improve the levels of English of Thai postgraduate students studying abroad on government scholarships.

'You write?'

I nod. 'Yes.'

'I thought so. What?'

'I've just had a half-hour monologue broadcast on Radio 3. Told by an unnamed English woman visiting Seville. Something physical, maybe sexual, happens. We're not sure what.'

He's silent and takes a long draught of his Campari.

'Good', he says. 'Good and good luck.'

His response sets a template for the many writers, famous or not, I meet in the following decades. If they are solely writers, not also academics, teachers or run creative writing work courses, they are essentially saying, 'You're on your own in this, get on with it. I hope you get published.'

Golding goes to the drinks trolley to fix himself another. He looks in my direction.

'Thanks. I'm driving.' I hold up my drink, still three-quarters full. I don't tell him that I'm well into my first novel, writing in the evenings with a portable typewriter on the balcony of the apartment they're about to visit.

When Ann appears, William is mixing another Campari. She says she doesn't want a drink, and Bill downs his in three quick draughts.

On the drive home, I stop outside a supermarket, saying Lauren's asked me to get something. I leave them in the car with the air-con running so they'll be cool. I open the boot and place the Campari in its brown paper bag alongside some orchids.

Lauren gives her genuine, effervescent welcome and settles them in immediately. She manages an aside once they're talking to others, 'You were a long time.'

I hold up the bag. 'I had to get him this. Campari. He's drinking it like water.'

The rest of the evening goes perfectly. The Goldings are charming. Ann occasionally reminds her husband he's human. 'Stop being so pompous, Bill.'

The guests are interested but not too intense. Rowan appears in her pyjamas and finds her way onto his lap so she can touch his beard. 'You're like Father Christmas.'

A month later, I have a charming note from the man himself with a memorable phrase – I know he means my writing: 'Keep up the good work.' It's all the encouragement I need. We've discussed neither the content nor craft of writing, but I learn something from him. I drink Campari at parties because it's so bitter I can't drink it quickly and don't get drunk.

One of the guests I'd invited to the supper is Mike, an older Brit on a similar contract but in Thailand for a decade. We share a love of books and tennis. We often play at the Embassy in its extensive gardens in central Bangkok, land now sold off.

An element of our enjoyment is the magnificent late nineteenth-century estate with palm trees, bougainvillea and gravel drives. Today the plot is hemmed in by high rise offices, shopping malls, hotels, luxury apartments and highways. An apt reflection of Britain's change in status, it's just one of many inconspicuous properties.

Mike's completely bald with the polished head of a Buddha.

He's canny on court, and though generally my age and energy prevail our matches are closely fought. We enjoy our green bottles of Kloster beer afterwards chatting about books. He suggests I join him in the poor North East of the country, Khon Kaen, on one of his teacher-training projects. At the end of the day, he says we are going for a couple of beers, somewhere I might find interesting.

In the bar a Doors song, 'Riders of the Storm', is playing its churning organ.

'Howdy friends. How can I help you folks?'

As our eyes accustom to the gloom, clusters of men with long, thinning hair emerge. Several have caps with baseball or American football logos. They're in tee-shirts with names of rock bands – New Riders of the Purple Sage, Joe Walsh – some wear lumberjack shirts, every man's in denim jeans and cowboy boots. We might be in a bar in Texas.

Mike goes over to the pool table and puts some coins on its cushion as a marker to get ourselves a game. When the next round's up, someone calls, 'Table's free. Doubles?'

Mike stands up. 'Sure. Thanks.'

The object is clearly the game, there's no chatter, an occasional 'Shit man!' They beat us easily. They don't look at us except right at the end when we shake hands. 'You guys from London?' the first and only interaction.

'I'm Alabama,' says one.

'Arkansas,' says the other.

Over a somtam and red curry Mike and I reflect on what an odd place it was. From other visits Mike knows they all served in the Vietnam war. A few are deserters, though he doubts anyone's looking for them. Some had been reported as Missing In Action and disappeared. Some have told their parents, friends or even wives they can't face living in America. What a strange half-life it is, napalm in their dreams, the sound track to Coppola's *Apocalypse Now,* a cacophony of helicopter blades in their heads, the horrors of brutalising war. A few have taken Thai partners as a way out of their nightmares. Others continue with the solace of booze or dope.

IAN'S A PIG farmer exiled from South Africa through his loathing of apartheid. He's taken a job with Thailand's largest conglomerate of pig farmers because he can wear shorts to the office. Gill, his English Home Counties wife, does his accounts and enjoys a hearty G & T.

We take many trips in rural Thailand with them. In dense humidity the five of us walk three miles along a forest path, including a long section with a tunnel through rock. Lanterns are strung from the cave's roof. The generator's fired up every hour, so walkers can splash through a stream along the cave floor. Leaving the dark, the ground rises steeply, we have to scramble up to reach a simple Thai *wat,* or temple, perched on a rocky outcrop. A monk and two novices with shaven heads and burgundy robes greet us.

The *phra*, or monk, speaks for ten minutes explaining that Buddhism is not a religion but a way of life. Buddha is not a god but an enlightened human being; that Buddhists are not interested in who created the world or why; and how they are focused on the here and now to live respecting others. We're all moved by the purity and simplicity of the monk's words.

On our return trek halfway through the caves, the generator fails and the lights go out. Our group is shouting or crying. Rowan at six is the only child. Fortunately, I'm close by. It's darker than a pint of Guinness. I call to the others I have Rowan, and they should make their own way forward as best they can. Or wait for someone to come with a torch.

Rowan and I hear and feel the water inching our way downstream over slippery stones. After fifteen minutes of edging forward we see a light flash in the distance. The mouth of the cave prints itself slowly out of the dark. As we reach the entrance, the generator kicks in and all the lights come back on. Rowan's unperturbed, calmer than most adults. We're the first to exit the cave. Lauren runs out and hugs Rowan. We hug each other. Ian asks Rowan if she'd been afraid.

'A bit,' she says. 'But I knew the Buddha would help.'

Koh Samet is a favourite place three hours from Bangkok where a fishing boat loaded with ice takes us to the small island with no vehicles and thousands of butterflies. The restaurants have generators to serve cold drinks and food but there's no other electricity. At night the sky is a canopy of fireflies, and the fireflies glittering in the undergrowth are fallen stars. By day, walking along the pale primrose sand is gliding through sieved flour and coral rings the island in undisturbed, vibrant colours beneath the waves.

We'd brought Lauren's mother, Doreen, to Koh Samet and are waiting on the beach, our bags packed, for the fishing boat to return us to the mainland. Suddenly Rowan starts screaming, holding her head on one side and squeezing it with her hands. Doreen calms Rowan who's crying, 'My ear! My ear!' There's blood trickling down her jawbone. Doreen runs up the beach café returning with a small bottle and pours oil into Rowan's ear. 'There it is!' cries Doreen rummaging in her bag. A pair of tweezers grasps the body of a huge red ant longer than a fingernail. Rowan is still sobbing quietly but the worst is over. Even paradise has its pitfalls, I think.

AT SIX IN the morning on weekdays, Tong arrives to work on our immaculate, communal gardens before it gets too hot. She always wears a battered straw hat that looks like an upside down flowerpot. This is complemented by a worn tee-shirt usually with a faded logo. 'Love is All You Need.' I doubt she understands it. And a sarong with flip flops. Her first task is to take a long stick as tall as she is, five feet and a bit. She stalks the garden methodically metre by metre. In one flashing movement she twirls the stick rapidly on the ground then raises it in the air to flick a snake, which sails over the hedge into next door's garden. I once see one fly into our garden. Tong flicks it over the wall into the small *klong*, the canal beside our apartment, not back into the neighbours' garden. If she sees me in the morning, she's always cheerful, waving and smiling.

I give our maid, Noi, some money for Tong to buy some new headgear. She soon appears with a smart new hat, its weave crisp and clean, though it still looks like a flowerpot. She's ecstatic with the pleasure of it. I write a monologue imagining her life, which is broadcast on BBC Radio 3 as *Tong's New Hat*. It's the happiest story I ever wrote.

We go on a *klong* trip through quiet backwaters and ten metres away a cobra, its neck and hood extended, swims alongside. I make Lauren swap places so I'm nearest the cobra with Rowan between us. In the monsoon season the *klongs* swell into the nearby lanes. The floor of the office car is flooded inches deep. Outside I see snakes coiling in the filthy murk. I wonder if one could swim up the exhaust into the car.

ALAN, MY BRITISH Council manager, has a salt-and-pepper beard, glasses with heavy frames and thought work was meant to be fun. He holds meetings in Nong's cocktail bar next door to the British Council in Siam Square. He loves scheming and plotting *sotto voce* over beers and cigarettes. He's working on a proposal to open a British Council office in Chiang Mai, northern Thailand. When my role at the Ministry finishes would I like to be its first Director?

He's frustrated to learn that I've applied for the British Council's quaintly named Overseas Career Service, a scheme designed to recruit and develop the next generation of British Council senior managers. There's a small intake of a dozen a year. It's modelled on those hoping to join the Foreign Office – though it requires individuals with at least five years' work experience not those straight out of university. 'Never mind,' I say to Alan. 'I probably won't get in.'

I am summoned to London by telex. Three days of written exercises and analysis. A made up wooden inbox. Group interactions.

Role plays and a formal interview panel. A month later Alan asks me to come and see him in Nong's.

'Chiang Mai. I've got the approval. Opening in six months. Perfect timing for you.'

'That's great. You got the approval I mean.'

'So, you're interested?'

'I'm still waiting to hear about the Overseas Career Service.'

'Chiang Mai'd be more fun.'

'For now maybe.'

'Christ, Richard, I'm pretty much offering you the job. A small interview here. We can fix it.' Kloster beer in hand he spends twenty minutes trying to persuade me to take the Chiang Mai role. I'm adamant I won't do anything until I hear the result of the OCS process. Alan sighs and orders more beer.

'Anyway, who is this William Wood?'

It takes me a while to process Alan's question before I remember. 'He's in personnel. He was on my interview panel.'

'He rang me. He's in charge of your recruitment. He wants to know if you'll take the OCS option if they offer it, before they do all the paperwork.' Then, the first time that afternoon, he smiles and chuckles. 'Congratulations,' he says raising his glass. 'I'll tell him you'll accept.'

THE ONE SHADOW of our time in Bangkok was Doreen's health. She'd had a double mastectomy in April of our first year in Thailand. We went back for summer leave and the cancer was in remission, she'd gone back to work.

It's October when we learn it's returned more aggressively. Lauren takes Rowan out of school early in December. I join them for Christmas. We fly back together in the New Year in time for Rowan's school term. We've been back in Bangkok four days when we hear Doreen's died. She was fifty-seven.

Lauren insists I shouldn't come to the funeral. I'd seen Doreen shortly before she died. She'd fly in with Rowan for three or four days and return. They set off and two hours into the flight have to turn back, there's a rumour there's a bomb on board. Lauren doesn't want to dwell on the bomb or her mother's death. 'Too morbid.' Her approach to death, even her own mother's, is pragmatic. It's the future, Rowan and me, she's focused on.

RETURNING FROM BANGKOK we sell the cottage in Holmfirth for a considerable profit. The impact of the popular TV sitcom, *Last of the Summer Wine*, is huge. Many in Sheffield, Leeds and Manchester have discovered the mill town on their doorstep.

The British Council office is by Admiralty Arch off Trafalgar Square. Lauren's adamant that she wants a home with a garden in a countryside environment low on crime, a network for baby-sitting and a tennis club. We settle on Haslemere in the corner of southwest Surrey adjacent to West Sussex and Hampshire. I write a play, broadcast on Radio 3: *Two Miracles on the Last Train to Haslemere*.

We find a small, detached house in walking distance of the station. It's worlds away from the literary, academic and intellectual circles I'm working with. Its dinner party circuit is dominated by 'the markets', meaning house prices, or the best prep schools. But gradually we make friends through the tennis club, Lauren's involvement in the Liberal Party, a book club and conversations at the school gates.

Now I have a job which looks like it'll go some distance, it's time to think about another child. It takes two years. William George Arthur is born in the Royal Surrey, Guildford in September 1987. His second name my father's, his third, Lauren's grandfather.

A few months after I start work at the British Council, I'm invited to go and see the agency where I'd sent my first novel. I've chosen Anthony Sheil because I'm a fan of John Fowles, regarded as one of the major writers of the post-war British novel. Anthony is Fowles' agent. The jury has somewhat retreated from the judgment of Fowles as a big hitter, but I think *The Collector*, *The Magus* and *The French Lieutenant's Woman* alone are enough to win him a place in the pantheon.

Anthony explains how unusual it is for a novel to reach him off the 'slush pile'. It had to go through external readers and two of his colleagues before it landed on his desk for the final judgment. He puts me at ease by saying he really likes it and thinks it has great promise, that the agency will be taking me on, but there's work to do.

DURING MY INDUCTION to the British Council's Overseas Careers Service the words which followed me through my career come from Lloyd Mullen, a northern Irishman: 'Richard, when it gets tough and you think things are falling apart, don't worry,' he pauses then peers over his glasses. 'Just be amazed the whole fucking thing works at all!'

I'm assigned to a role as the Deputy Director of the British Council's Literature Department. Its Director is the wonderful Dr Harriet Harvey Wood, who has had a long association with the British Council. Her father helped create the Edinburgh Festival in 1948. She's managed an orchestra, and when I arrive just finished supporting Frances Donaldson in writing the History of the British Council. Her hair is long but always pulled back from her face and tied back in an elaborate bun. Some find her fierce. I love her clarity. She's a superb guide and mentor to the British Council. The annual Cambridge Contemporary Literature Seminar features British writers, established and new, who read from and discuss their work over a ten-day period. Academics, translators, writers, journalists and publishers are invited from across the globe to attend a smorgasbord of British writing.

The printed programme sent to the global guestlist has a slot which reads: 'Surprise Guest'. On the day of the Surprise Guest I accompany the close protection officers to trace the route of his arrival and to answer questions. Where would he stay until he was called? Where were the nearest exits and entrances? How long would the session be? Who was chairing? (Harriet.)

The final session of the day in Downing College draws closer and the sky darkens. It begins to rain. As it grows heavier, we have to close the French windows opening onto the lawn. It's humid and fifty people are a tight fit in a conference room with no air conditioning. We haven't factored in the torrential rain on the windows making it impossible to hear. The gusts continue to batter the windows with no sign of stopping. We're tense. I'm sure the Guest is too. He'd hardly have anticipated his reading would start in a violent storm.

'We'll give him a couple more minutes,' says Harriet. 'Then I'm going to have to ask him to come in.'

The rain continues to whiplash the French windows; in a short while she leaves.

She returns chatting to him through the cacophony of rain on the glass. As soon as they enter, the participants are on their feet applauding, cheering his name, whistling. A drum roll rises to a crescendo then a deafening explosion of thunder followed by sheets of lightning flooding the darkness. Seconds later there's a rumble of thunder echoing over the water meadows beyond the city; the sky and the atmosphere lightens, the rain dies to a light patter. Then stops altogether.

The participants are still on their feet applauding and shouting. Harriet smiles and raises her hand in recognition but asks them to stop now. She gestures the Guest sit in a chair near hers to begin the session. The participants quieten and sit. The first thing Harriet says is: 'That was some entrance Salman. Shall we do it again?'

Everyone, including Salman, shakes with laughter, and the session is underway.

Towards the end of the drinks reception, I'm in conversation with the security team ensuring everything is in order for Salman's exit before the participants go to dinner. I hear one of the close protection officers saying, 'I didn't get much of what he said, but I warmed to that Mr Rushdie when he chose a pint of Guinness.'

IT TAKES US nearly a year to get *A Curious Child* ready for submission. I continue in the British Council's Literature Department because I'm having a great time working with new and established writers at international conferences and tours. There's a tap on my shoulder. It's time to move on. I'm asked to consider Milan, Lagos or Bogotá. We rule out Milan because it'd mean living in a small flat with two kids. Bogotá with its cocaine mountains seems a step too far for a young family. Which leaves Lagos. We find tenants for the house, have dinner with friends in Haslemere who'd been at the High Commission in Nigeria, and set off.

I'VE JUST BOARDED an internal flight from Kano in northern Nigeria, where I'd been meeting colleagues at the British Council. The building alone had been worth the journey with its triple-arched walkway decorated with vibrant tribal art designs in gold, ochre and green.

Femi isn't thirty I judge. He's a journalist for the Federal Radio Corporation of Nigeria. We chat, the usual stuff, General Babangida's military dictatorship, the corruption everywhere, oil pollution in the Niger Delta, Fela Kuti's music, his politics, and his Shrine.

I plan to get a taxi from the airport to the compound we shared with colleagues on Ikoyi, created as an island in the early twentieth century by the British colonists for themselves. Post-independence in 1960, it became an exclusive district for privileged Nigerians and foreigners alike. Real estate in Ikoyi is now the most valuable per square metre in the entire African continent.

I liked to walk the half mile to the office through the dusty lanes until security urge me to go by car. They have a point. In our first month, I come out one morning to find a dead body in a ditch outside our house. Cyclists and other pedestrians are ignoring it. I stay long enough to see the angry halo of flies buzzing around the dead man's head, a vibrating crown of barbed wire. There was an acid reek of urine, sweat and blood.

As we touch down in Lagos, I offer Femi a lift in the taxi to Ikoyi. It'd be a minor detour to drop him at the FRCN headquarters. Neither of us has hold luggage, we pass quickly through the terminal and head to the taxi rank. I have a wheelie that stutters over the cracked, pot-holed tarmac. Femi has a substantial black shoulder bag, which he's kept close during the flight. It's already night. The taxi rank is on the other side of a single-lane each way road encircling the airport. Femi is a step or two ahead.

From out of the dark with no lights, the front bumper and grille of the vehicle make a sickening impact. I feel and hear the muffled, heavy thud of the speeding metal slamming into his body. The car doesn't stop but is momentarily slowed by the impact. Femi is collapsed between its front wheels and somehow snagged to its undercarriage. To my horror, the car drags Femi thirty metres up the road until the driver stops. A passenger jumps out and pulls Femi from under the car but leaves him in the road before jumping back in and the car shoots off. Dragging my wheelie, I run as fast as I can towards Femi's body while the traffic in that lane builds up. The first driver arriving after Femi's been dumped in the road, mercifully refuses to drive over him. I think he's dead. The cars on the other side of the road slow to a trickle, their occupants craning out the windows to gaze at the body.

I leave my wheelie by Femi's body as a marker. I run back to the taxi rank. I ask four taxis, but they refuse to take Femi to a hospital whatever I offer to pay. I return to Femi. I can't be sure but think his chest's moving. The driver of the car by Femi and his passengers have disembarked. They refuse to become engaged. I stare into the dark recesses of the approaching vehicles now slowed to a halt. I try to explain to drivers leaning out the windows. No one wants to listen. I spot an ambulance stuck in the jam. I run up to it and explain what's happened. The driver puts on his siren, pulls out of the jam into the lane free of traffic and drives to where Femi lies motionless. They look closely but don't touch him.

After a short while, one of them says, 'He no good. Maybe he go die.'

I'm not sure whether he means Femi's already dead or he's going to die. 'Please take him to hospital. Maybe you save him.' They remain silent. 'I'll pay you. How much?'

They walk off out of earshot and have a brief conversation. One returns. 'We go take him. You come.'

'I don't know him. He's not my friend. I met him on the plane.'

'You no come. He no go.'

'How much?' I ask. 'You take him. I give you one hundred *naira*.' A comparatively large sum around US $15.

He shakes his head. 'No *naira*. Only you come.'

I hesitate. 'OK, I come.'

They drag Femi onto a torn, filthy stretcher and carry him into the back of the ambulance. He groans quietly. So, he's alive! They secure him to the stretcher with strapping and gesture at me to get in. I climb in with my wheelie. The inside is dirty and stained. Only when they're closing the back doors I suddenly remember.

'Femi's bag. His bag!' I shout.

One of them picks it up from the road and gives it to me. The ambulance doors bang shut.

I can't see. If there are any lights in the back, they aren't working. I don't mind. I don't have to look at Femi or the state of the ambulance. Femi groans gently. As we drive on, the siren blaring, the jolt of a pothole throws us in the air and his groans grow louder. By the time we reach the hospital, and the ambulance doors are opened, Femi's screaming in pain. I speak to the doctor asking why they aren't giving him any pain relief.

'You go buy dis outside,' he scribbles something on a pad and hands it to me.

'But I don't know him. I only met him on the plane.'

He smiles wearily. 'You dey come with the man. We have no drug. You want him dey have drug. You buy drug. One chemist outside,' he points round the corner.

When I return, they've taken Femi inside, into what passes for an Accident & Emergency reception room. He's still screaming. The room is disgusting. The sheets are stained and ripped. There are smears of dried blood on the wall. The disinfectant can't hide the stench of faeces. I hand the doctor the drugs. There'd been no receipt available.

'The machine, he broke,' the man in the private dispensary had said. Soon after the doctor injects Femi, his screams stop and he's quiet. Though once he coughs, blood dribbles down his chin. No one wipes it clean.

I'm determined that I've done more than enough and to leave before I become further implicated. I ask the doctor where I can find a taxi. He ignores my question. 'You say you no know this man?'

'All I know is he works at Federal Radio on Ikoyi.'

'You live Ikoyi?'

I can see where this is leading and try to head it off. 'You should call them and tell them he's here. His name is Femi.'

The doctor shakes his head. 'Better from you. You see what happen.' He pauses. 'We have no phone.'

It was my turn to be weary. 'OK. Please write your name and the address of this hospital for me,' I say reaching under the table for Femi's bag. He writes on his pad and hands me the details. 'I'll give this and Femi's bag to the radio station on Ikoyi. Where can I get a taxi?'

'Outside and left,' he gestures.

'How much should I pay to Ikoyi?'

He shrugs. As I'm walking out, he calls softly behind me. 'Twenty maybe.'

The radio station is deserted with a feeble light cast from the gatehouse. I get out with mine and Femi's bag asking the driver to wait. The guard appears from the shadows. 'What you want boss?'

I tell him the story and that I want to hand over Femi's bag to someone. He returns to the gatehouse. I hear the static of a walkie-talkie radio but not the conversation. Then it's quiet. Bats jerk through the flame trees. After a while, I hear a burst of louder static like a round of machine-gun fire. Then the guard comes out. 'They see you,' he says.

I pay the driver. It costs thirty naira. Fifty percent more for a white man.

The duty manager holds out his hand welcoming me. He's dressed in the long white garb of a northern Nigerian. I explain that I've just flown down from Kano. He smiles, 'Home,' he says. Inside his office, I tell him the story and hand over the paper with the doctor's scrawl. He just listens. It's not clear if he knows Femi.

I point at Femi's bag. 'I haven't opened it yet. Perhaps something will give us a home address.'

We're standing with the bag on a table between us. He moves towards the bag and slowly unzips it. There's a dark shirt on top. 'You look,' he says. I remove the shirt. When I see what I see, I want to zip up the bag, walk out and make the evening disappear. The duty manager sees the fear on my face and bends over the bag. He draws back instantly as if there's a snake inside.

The bag's stuffed with thick wads of crisp US dollar bills. We stand in silence glancing at each other and the bag. We're both hoping for a way out wishing the bag would catch fire. We're stunned. The air conditioning unit wheezes exaggerating our silence. Eventually, I say, 'Shall we count it?' The duty manager nods.

We take turns removing one wad of bills at a time and counting the one hundred US dollar notes. Each wad is secured with a paper wrapping as if straight from a bank. We try to keep the wrappings inact but some tear. The notes have never been used, the cleanest cash I've ever handled. Each wad has a hundred notes, so totals ten thousand dollars. Except for the last wad which has seven thousand dollars. We count it three times but it always comes to seven thousand. There are nine wads plus this one. A total of ninety-seven thousand virgin US dollars. Someone has already taken their three per cent commission. There's nothing else in the bag. We lapse back into our separate silences. The manager then places the wads of cash back in the bag, returns Femi's shirt, and zips it up.

'I go put in the office safe. Please come.'

He picks up the bag and we walk down the corridor to a small room with a safe in the wall. The fluorescent light flickers like some demented stroboscope. The duty manager produces a notepad and writes, 'The US$97,000 (ninety-seven thousand).' He signs and dates it.

'Please you sign.'

I do as he asks.

He unzips the bag and puts this paper with our signatures on top of the shirt. He dials the safe number, the door opens and the bag goes in. He scrambles the dial, and we leave. As we walk through the dingy corridor, I tell him I work at the British Council.

FLIGHTS IN NIGERIA are often delayed so Lauren's used to me arriving late. Rowan and Will are already in bed.

'Good trip? How was Kano?'

'Kano was fine. It's a beautiful office.' I pause. I can hold it back no longer. 'It's what happened just now that's the problem.'

Then I tell her the story: Femi hit by the car, the ambulance, the gruesome hospital. Taking Femi's bag to the radio station. The cash.

'You should have come straight home. Not offered some random man a lift.'

I'm shocked by her callousness. Later I understand it. When we go to bed, I'm still in shock, my charity unappreciated, regarded as irresponsible.

The next day, mid-morning my secretary says someone on the

phone wants to speak to me about the accident. I assume it's the duty manager at the radio station and agree to take the call. But it isn't the radio station or the hospital.

'Where is the money? We want our money back. You steal our money.'

'I don't have your money,' I say and put the phone down. I tell my secretary I wouldn't take any more unsolicited calls.

Lauren calls. 'They just rang the house. They wanted to speak to you. They said they knew where we lived,' she's half-sobbing. 'You fool! Do something!'

'I'll be home soon as I can. Don't answer the phone.'

I go upstairs and speak to my boss. We agree extra guards will be visibly stationed at the compound gates. We discuss security for Rowan's school journeys.

At home, Lauren's fear of what might happen is marginally tempered by a growing anger at me. I've been home only half an hour when the phone rings. I answer it. As soon as the voice starts, I cut the call. Lauren looks at me with a mix of fear and outrage. I've put our family at risk through my careless arrogance.

'Perhaps they'll just give up, when they realise I haven't got the money.'

'Don't be stupid. These people will stop at nothing to get their money. Nothing!'

In ten minutes the phone rings again. 'I don't have your money. Your money is at the radio station on Ikoyi. If you call again, I will tell the police.' The voice at the other end laughs.

I double-check the cast-iron security gate at the bottom of the stairs is locked. In the morning, I walk round to my boss's house and tell him what's happened. That I, not Lauren, will take Rowan to school. Some mothers with toddlers Will's age are coming round. They'll be a distraction. The safest place to stay is home.

We agree it's time to get the High Commission intelligence team involved. There are several calls to my office that morning, which my secretary doesn't put through. After I collect Rowan from school, I show the most senior British intelligence officer and one of his Nigerian colleagues into our sitting room. The furniture and designs were chosen by others. We perch on sofas and armchairs with flowered Laura Ashley fabrics. Emmanuel brings in tea and biscuits. Lauren's in and out checking if Josephine, the nanny, needs a hand with the children.

How had I met Femi? Was he particularly curious about aspects of my or the British High Commission's work? How was his behaviour as we walked to the taxi rank? Why hadn't he seen the car coming? Did the duty manager at FRCN know Femi? Did the stash of US dollars look real? The intelligence officer arranges for armed guards at our compound. 'Just for a few days. Until things quieten down.'

I don't know exactly what they did or how they did it. Intelligence and security work is often a dirty business. It means dealing with criminals or those with criminal intent, sometimes directly, sometimes indirectly. Whatever it was, they did it quickly.

There are no more calls to the office. Lauren doesn't want to put the phone back in its cradle until I come home. Within an hour the phone rings. My heart's hammering. The voice speaks fluent though accented English.

'Is Lauren there?'

'Who's calling?'

'It's the Dutch school. We've been trying to get hold of her all day. Is she available?'

I smile, the first time in two days and gesture to Lauren to come and take the call. 'It's the Dutch school,' I whisper. She takes it and I disappear.

When I return, the receiver's back in its cradle. There are tears streaming down her face, but she smiles. We sit hugging each other on the sofa not saying anything until she stops crying. Then she wipes her face. 'They want me to do another half-day.'

'Did you say yes?'

She nods and bursts into tears again.

For several days we're on edge especially when the phone rings.

But the calls have stopped as abruptly as they'd begun. Though she doesn't say anything I know she's still cross with me, but her justified fury has subsided. Gradually our outward lives return to their routine and the incident fades as a topic of conversation.

Every day I feel the impact of the car on Femi's body and see him dragged up the road. I wonder how long it took for him to die. I wonder what'd happened to the US$97,000. The accusing voice. 'You steal our money.' I'm afraid it'll come back. The stench of death follows me like a mangey, stray dog.

Two months later I'm in the office and my secretary says, 'There's a man at security. He says he wants to thank you. Says you know him. His name is Femi.'

The fear churns in my stomach and into my chest with my heart pounding. I can hardly breathe. I gather myself.

'I'm glad. Tell him I'm glad he's OK. Tell him I don't want to see him. Now. Or ever.'

I FIRST MEET the Nigerian writer, sometime politician, businessman, screenwriter and activist, Ken Saro-Wiwa, at the British Council Contemporary Writers Seminar in Cambridge two years before Lagos. Ken has a huge grin, eternal energy and a curved, meerschaum pipe, the kind Sherlock Holmes smoked.

Ken's something of a detective in his own country. He's from the Ogoni ethnic group in Rivers State where the global oil industry and extraction are centred. When we meet in 1986 his wonderful novel *Sozaboy: A novel in rotten English* has just been published. In the late 1960s, working as a civilian administrator, Ken saw the gruesome civil war with Biafra trying to secede from the Republic of Nigeria. The story is narrated by a young soldier – Sozaboy – in a chaotic, vibrant rhythm mixing Nigerian pidgin, broken English and a young man's creation of a language through which he's trying to make sense of the world. It's Joyce's *A Portrait of the Artist* set in the tropics during a horrific war. Ken writes in a note to the novel: 'To its speakers it has the advantage of having no rules and syntax. It thrives on lawlessness and is part of the dislocated and discordant society in which Sozaboy must live, move and not have his being.'

I work on a couple of literature projects with Ken and the Nigerian Writers' Association, forging a partnership and we sponsor a prize for fiction. I see him at the Nigerian Writers' Association AGM with Wole Soyinka as the keynote speaker. After the event's over, we return to our concrete bungalow where we're staying as 'guests of honour'. We stand outside in the dark drinking Star Beer while Ken smokes his pipe furiously. I ask if he'd smoke it by my bedroom window. The mosquito netting on my room's ripped. I'm bound to get bitten.

Seven years later in India, I'm shocked, outraged to hear of his death at the age of forty-four. He's been leading a non-violent campaign against the devastating impact of Shell's oil extraction on the Ogoni. The Nigerian military government is complicit with Shell in its operations. He was imprisoned and tried by a military tribunal on a spurious charge. Along with eight others, he's hanged in 1995. Ken's the first to climb the scaffold. So incompetent is the hangman that it takes five attempts before Ken dies.

Much of Soyinka's speech was focused on road-deaths in Nigeria. The country then had the worst ratio in the world of road deaths to vehicle ownership. Soyinka is President of the Nigerian Road Safety Association. I love that he and Ken used their influence to try and make a difference. Wole sits across the aisle from me on the flight back to Lagos and thanks me for the British Council's support.

It's heartening to know that the Council's prize for Nigerian fiction doesn't come across as 'interfering'. Working in former colonies where there's a history of British slavery, abuse and exploitation, any suggestion of 'meddling' in others' business is always a factor in developing a partnership or project.

WE NEED A High Commission Land Rover with discreet security for our trip. It's eight in the evening and driving to north

Lagos will take an hour. The area outside the venue is crammed with taxis, station wagons, four-by-fours, dozens of battered and dented vehicles, with smashed windows and cracked windscreens. A brand new, tar-black Mercedes snarls like a shark. The crowds milling about shout in Yoruba or Pidgin. Women with toddlers strapped to their backs, carry food trays on their heads. Men huddling pass round bottles of Star, children sell yo-yos, fake watches and cigarettes.

We push through the crowds towards the entrance, I catch a whiff of sweetness as we arrive at the box office. A woman with bloodshot eyes collects cash which she stuffs in a money pouch round her waist. I pull out a wad of naira. 'Five of us, please.'

The woman collecting the money says, 'I see.'

It takes a moment to understand she wants to see who's in our group. 'Four,' she says.

'No. Five of us.'

'Woman no pay.'

'Aah! We should have brought more women,' I try to make a joke.

She stares at me stonily, then says, 'Forty naira. And you buy me one beer.'

I count out fifty naira and hand it over waiting for some change. None comes back. I nod, 'Thanks. Enjoy the beer.'

As we move off through the entrance gates, she says, 'Plenty women inside.'

Outside under the chaos of the traffic, the hawkers, the high-spirited shouting we'd heard an insistent throbbing from the venue. But we aren't ready for the explosive blast of bass, drum and brass which hit us when we step into The Shrine.

Fela Kuti was a cousin of Wole Soyinka with whom he shared a house in Shepherd's Bush in the late fifties; he'd abandoned medicine and studied music at Trinity College. By the time we're entering The Shrine in the late eighties he's a global musical force and influential in the culture and politics of Nigeria and beyond. He'd been arrested over two hundred times with a twenty-month prison stint starting in 1984. He opened the first incarnation of this club, popularly known as The Shrine, in the early seventies. It was constantly raided with Fela, his family, musicians and his entourage harassed and beaten. In the late seventies a thousand police were sent to burn down The Shrine and Fela's mother – a women's rights activist – was thrown out of a window, dying from her injuries.

The pulsing bass lines explode in our ears with two bass guitars and the drummer Tony Allen, Fela's key musical collaborator, laying down a rhythmic weave and groove. There are about twenty people on stage. Guitarists, trumpeters, saxophonists, keyboard players – all men in orange shirts open to the waist and matching orange trousers, women singers in white dresses with dark triangles, and women dancers in multi-coloured bikini-like tops, and skirts cut in strips allowing them more freedom to gyrate and grind their hips. The band's in full swing but no vocals yet. Just a single dancer on the floor in front of the musicians. I can't see Fela. Then I spot him, the only performer with white face paint, a Yoruba design. He's at the keyboards lost in the crowd of musicians until ten minutes later he steps forward onto the dance area.

He's naked to the waist with an elaborate necklace of animal hide with tight white trousers and smart white shoes. He's incredibly lithe, not an ounce of fat but not pumped up either. As a musician, not a trained dancer, he's the best male mover to his own creation, Afrobeat, I've ever seen. He breaks into vocals. Pidgin English isn't easy to grasp when spoken. In front of a waterfall of sound it's near impossible. Towards the end of the number, which lasts about thirty minutes, I figure out a refrain of 'Teacher Don't Teach Me No Nonsense'.

I go off in search of beers. The fog of marijuana is so dense that we don't need to buy any. There are open booths and rooms off what is a quadrangle. This is where the clouds of marijuana billow from as if the entire building is about to mushroom into a smothering blanket of reefer smoke.

In the booths are groups of women sitting sharing one beer. 'Mistah! Mistah! One beer for me,' comes the occasional call. I smile and ignore them.

One of our security detail is talking to my colleague and friend. They'd heard the place was likely to be raided that night. Whether it's true or not, we'll be in trouble if it happens and we ignore the warning. Leaving aside the risk of getting beaten up by the police, it wouldn't look good in the press to have 'High Commission staff arrested in raid on The Shrine.' The High Commissioner wouldn't thank us for having to explain to the Foreign Ministry what his colleagues were doing at a notorious anti-government venue where illegal activities take place.

We stay another half hour then slip out. I'm mindful of Lauren. I've already used up most of my credit on the Femi incident. I'm content. I've made the connection through Fela back to Highlife and my parents dancing the night away at the Ambassador Hotel in Accra.

WEST – NOT EAST or South – Africa was known in the nineteenth century as 'the White Man's Grave.' Our first inkling of this is the tumbu fly which has laid its eggs in Rowan's shoulders. We have to cover the holes with Vaseline to suffocate the larvae and squeeze them out.

Will, about eighteen months, is playing one morning with other children in the compound on his tricycle. Lauren comes home to find he's fallen off and grazed his knee. Our competent – five children of her own – and cheerful nanny Josephine has washed the cut and doused it with Dettol. Lauren removes the plaster and dressing to check it's clean. She submits him to the Dettol treatment again and puts on a fresh dressing.

I come home from work and don't need to go out again. We have a regular family evening ahead. Tea with the children, showers and stories.

We sponge Will down in the bath so the dressing on his knee doesn't get wet. He's a little hot but not complaining and goes to sleep quickly. An hour later he wakes saying he's hot and thirsty. Lauren gives him sterilised water and settles him down. Soon he's crying again. I sit him up in bed and don't need to ask what the matter is. His upper body is pocked with a dozen small boils that haven't yet burst. I call Lauren. She picks him up, 'He's absolutely boiling.'

I can't get hold of the British High Commission doctor and try the French Embassy. I tell their doctor what's happened. He asks me a few questions and says he'll be with us in twenty minutes. 'Try and keep him awake.'

Will gets much worse. The first eruptions have enlarged, some have burst and more are appearing. The ceiling fan is turned up to maximum. However hard we try with a cold flannel on his head or body, he keeps nodding off.

I hear the doctor's car come through the security gates and go out to meet him. He jumps out of the car with his bag leaving the driver to park. He looks about my age. He holds out his hand. 'Michel,' he says.

'Richard.'

'Where is 'e?'

I tell him. He runs to the house and up the stairs.

'Left at the top and straight on,' I call.

By the time I'm up there he's pulling out the thermometer from under Will's arm. 'Your son is very hill. Forty-one degrees. *C'est tres serieux.*'

'Hospital?' says Lauren.

He shakes his head. 'There is nothing there for 'im. We 'ave to act now.'

He rummages in his bag and pulls out a dark bottle. 'Bathroom please.'

We hear the taps running and him washing. We stare at each other. Both of us rigid, speechless with fear. As he returns, he says. 'I suppose 'e's 'ad no penicillin before?'

'No penicillin,' Lauren whispers.

He's ripping the sterile packaging from the needle and draws the liquid from a small bottle through the needle into the chamber. 'What is 'is name?'

We're both momentarily stunned.

''Is name? Your son.' He holds up the needle and presses with a light touch. A tiny spray arcs through the air blown away by the breeze from the fan.

'William,' says Lauren.

'Will, if you like,' I say.

'Will is heighteen month, yes?'

We nod.

'I 'ave to tell you something. I ham going to give 'im a very large dose. More than double usual. It is the only way I think. Probably 'ee will be allergic to penicillin in the future. You agree to this?' He pauses.

'Whatever you think's best,' I say.

'I cannot promise it will work.'

'What is it? What's he got?' asks Lauren.

There's a missed beat before Michel speaks. 'Will 'as severe septicaemia. Soon it will haffect 'is brain and then,' he shrugs.

Lauren bows her head.

'We 'ave a fifty-fifty chance,' says Michel then bends to inject Will.

We all stay in the bedroom a few minutes discussing what next. There should always be someone with Will. The next two hours are crucial. The penicillin, if it works, should act very quickly in such a tiny body. If, in two hours, his temperature hasn't gone down, we should call him. In any case, we should call him in three hours to report what's happening. We should keep sponging Will. Offer him sips of water if he's awake. We should listen carefully to his breathing. If he goes limp, we should call Michel immediately.

He holds out his hand to Lauren and smiles gently. *'C'est tout pour maintenant.'*

Lauren nods, chokes, unable to speak.

'I'll see Michel out.'

We stand at the bottom of the stairs by the cast iron security gate. I open the front door for him. He turns and holds out his hand. 'There is some science. Some luck. And who knows what?' he says.

'*Merci*, Michel. *Merci*.' I let go of his hand. He smiles and turns towards his car giving a half-wave as he opens its rear door. The engine starts up and the compound security gates begin to grate back. I go to Rowan's bedroom and tell her everything's going to be alright, she should sleep now. She isn't convinced. 'How do you know Daddy? How can you be sure?'

'The doctor says it should be OK.'

'He has a funny accent.'

'He's French. He's a good doctor.'

'Do they have the same medicine in France?'

'*Oui*,' half-perjuring myself again.

'Can you come and tell me when he's alright?'

'Yes. I will. Good night. I love you.' I kiss her on the forehead.

'I love William. And you. And Mummy. Good night.' She turns over. As I'm leaving, she says, 'Don't close the door, Daddy.'

Lauren is sitting on Will's bed. The fan's still kicking up the air. He's unchanged, the boils covering his body. 'Gin and tonic?'

She shakes her head.

'Tea?'

'Just tonic,' her voice cracks. I give her a hug and go to fetch her tonic.

Once she leaves Will's bedroom to go to the loo. At some point, I pull a mattress into the room and sit down on it. 'Whatever happens, I'll sleep here tonight.'

'Whatever happens?' she quizzes me.

I don't answer.

An hour or so later we debate whether we should take his temperature. He's asleep and seems to be breathing normally. Is it better to let him sleep or take his temperature? And maybe try giving him some water? What if it's gone up? We can't see any new boils appearing. We decide to wait another thirty or forty minutes. The fan spins its journey to nowhere. A mechanical Dervish. Still sitting on the mattress, I lean against the wall.

I jerk awake.

'You were asleep.'

I look at my watch. 'Only ten minutes.'

We shake him gently but for an age. He opens his eyes. Lost. 'We need to take your temperature,' whispers Lauren. I pass her the thermometer which she inserts in the scoop of his armpit. Exhausted but conscious he doesn't protest. He lies there staring up at the dizzy fan. She slides out the thermometer and holds it to the beside light to take the reading but her hand's shaking. Gently, I take it from her. I have to be certain. I read it and close my eyes. I pray it's right. Let it be right. Let it be right.

'What is it?' says Lauren, quiet but urgent.

Just to make sure I read it again. Yes it's right! 'Thirty-nine. It's thirty-nine.' Never has a number seemed so important. Lauren's shoulders are shaking, tears are running down her cheeks.

"ater, 'ater,' croaks Will. Lauren holds the hard plastic Tippy-Toppy cup with its spout to his lips.

An hour later I call Michel and tell him that Will's temperature had fallen to around thirty-eight. He's drinking water and has just asked for a piece of cheddar cheese, which has become his night-time comfort food.

'Je m'excuse. C'etait Cheddar pas de Camembert.'

'That is the real medicine,' he laughs and says he'll call by in the morning.

I go in to see Rowan. She's fast asleep. By the time I go into our bedroom Lauren's already under the sheet curled in her sleeping position. 'I'm going to sleep in Will's room.'

She grunts, 'Mmmm . . . ,' and squeezes my hand.

I take a pillow, sheets and make up the mattress. When I turn in the dark, I hear the fan whirling the angels of the night air in a dance above our heads.

Neither of us have ever felt more vulnerable, powerless. Or fortunate.

WHILE I'M IN Nigeria, *A Curious Child* is published by The Bodley Head, Graham Greene's and Muriel Spark's publisher. The novel garners some good reviews, the best in *The Times* and *The Irish Times*, and sells its 3,000 copies in hardback, more than covering the advance. Neither a spectacular success nor a flop, it does fine for a first novel by an unknown writer. It's quickly sold to Sceptre, the literary paperback imprint of Hodder.

I've finished the main draft of another novel and know I have more work to do. It'll be difficult to sustain the demands of the bigger job I have in Nigeria with the demands of becoming a successful literary novelist. I'm ambitious to be one.

A consultant I'm working with offers me a job as a senior lecturer at the College of St Mark & St John in Plymouth, Devon. I feel it's the last chance I have while the good reviews of my first novel are still fresh in the memory. I can't manage the Council career and writing novels. I negotiate a three-year period of unpaid leave. If I'm not being published and making reasonable money, it'll give us a way back.

We leave colleagues and friends in Lagos with mixed feelings, but not unhappy to leave behind the challenges of the security and the health issues. By the time we arrive in Devon, my second novel is in the in-tray of my editor, Derek Johns, at The Bodley Head. The contract's waiting for his signature.

FROM A DISTANCE, the house looks like a Georgian wedding cake. It gazes down the long garden beyond the ha-ha to the Brunel viaduct that connects the railway from Paddington via Exeter to Plymouth. Inside, the stone fireplace is tall enough to stand up in with an oven and seats on either side of the hearth. Its oak beams sport hooks where the game was hung. We install a Rayburn for hot water and central heating. There are three floors, rare in a domestic dwelling constructed more than five hundred years ago.

The house is so cavernous that two central heating systems are needed. The middle floor has a room with its Georgian panelling in prime condition. But the heart of the house is mediaeval with a Georgian facelift. It's Grade II listed. In Pevsner, the 46-volume architectural guide to the *Buildings of England,* Stowford Barton is featured for its gargoyles and steeple chimney, one of two left in England.

In the valley below Harford church a one-way bridge crosses a rushing, boulder strewn river, the Erme, running down off the summit of the moor. The lane leads up to Clive and Gilly's farm where Rowan and Will can run off to the barns and fields with their boys. Sometimes I camp with Rowan near there overnight. She learns to sail in Newton Ferrers, the South Hams. Will breaks his collarbone for the first (but not last time) at Ermington school.

Shortly after we move in, early autumn, there's a knock at the door.

'Aah. You must be the new owner. I'm Amanda.' The speaker's a woman in a Barbour jacket and green wellingtons.

'Yes, I am. With my wife,' I add.

'Could I have a word?'

'Of course.'

'Inside?'

While the coffee's brewing, I take her through to the sitting room with its oak beams and fireplace. We return to the kitchen and as I pour out the coffee, I say, 'It's in Pevsner.'

She looks at me blankly.

'The house. It's in Pevsner's architectural guide.'

'Oh,' she says, lost but doesn't ask what I'm talking about.

'Anyway,' she says brightening up. 'I should tell you why I'm here.'

'Go ahead.'

'Before the house was empty we always used to have the stirrup cup here.'

Ha! I think. A house with its own social calendar.

She explains. Boxing Day. Twenty horses and riders. Which

means about fifty people with the dog handlers and support. They're the South Dartmoor Hunt. It isn't a real fox, she says quickly. Just something dragged for the dogs to scent. This would be where they assembled. Protesters wouldn't come up my drive because it was private land. Oh shit! Damned if you do, damned if you don't.

Our neighbours are chaotic, lovely, both vets and with three boys. Charlie becomes good friends with Will and they play on zip-wires. Rowan enters a winter sailing competition, the Frostbite Series. She distinguishes herself by the highest number of capsizes in any race. We're proud that each time she capsizes she rights the boat herself.

Avonwick Lawn Tennis Club has the most perfectly manicured grass tennis courts we've ever played on. I'm still playing tennis thirty-five years later, but nothing surpasses the cushioned perfection of those courts. The people are charming and there are some good players. The wooden clubhouse has no electricity but the summer supper party is illuminated by candelabra. It's where Rowan and Will have their first lessons.

Amanda phones. The Master of Foxhounds is grateful but has decided the entrance and exit to Stowford Barton is too narrow, making them an easy target for any demonstrators, so they're going to look elsewhere. I'm relieved. The ban on live fox hunting isn't passed by the Blair government until 2004, but there are still protests against hunts, which have switched to drag hunting before the new law.

THERE'S A SCRIBBLED message on the desk in my college office. Please call Jane at Anthony Sheil. I phone her, excited that Derek Johns has signed the contract and my second novel's properly in the pipeline. It's a blow. Derek Johns has been told to clear his desk. The Bodley Head, one of the oldest imprints in the business, is having its fiction list closed, a result of its purchase along with Cape and Chatto & Windus by the American conglomerate Random House.

Jane's upbeat and softening the blow. They've decided to submit the novel to Faber & Faber. Anthony Sheil himself has agreed. Then, as they still are, *the* literary publisher where most writers would be over the moon to be published. In little more than a month, there's a page and a half of typed A4 from Robert McCrum, Faber's fiction editor, saying how much he'd enjoyed the book. He's tempted to make an offer. Instead, he asks for some further work and resubmission. I discuss it with Jane, saying I could live with the two main suggestions. The work takes six months. It goes back to Faber. Two months later a shorter letter arrives saying it's a great improvement, but would Richard address another issue. I tell Jane I want to meet McCrum.

It's a cordial affair. He recognises me from the work I'd done with the British Council agreeing a memorandum with publishers, agents and authors. I don't fully get what he wants. He tries to explain. I say I'll give it a go. Four more months. Back it goes. When McCrum asks for another revision, I agree with Jane I won't unless he offers a contract. He doesn't. I never learn what happened to his initial positivity that for a first submission 'this is a very near miss.'

My second novel is dead in the water. The third, which I'm half-way through, no longer seems worth the huge effort. I know I'll be much happier, and better paid, at the British Council than the Senior Lecturer's job when my heart isn't in it.

WHILE I'VE BEEN away the British Council has moved half its London operations to Manchester. Would I go and lead a team in a new department there? It was a rhetorical question, but I get it in writing and it's for eighteen months. The tall house built of red-orange bricks is an Edwardian rectory, and over three floors has five bedrooms, three bathrooms, box seats in the windows, a chandeliered dining room with an oval walnut table, a gracious sitting room, with comfy sofas and chairs looking down the lawns. It's perfectly shabby-chic. And the British Council pays the rent!

With extensive gardens its location is superb. I walk to the Altrincham tram and am at the office in fifteen minutes. At the end of a cul-de-sac, a hundred metres up the road is a pet shop where we get our first – and last – rabbit. A lop-eared one. I come home early to find a huge puddle on the kitchen floor, the fridge defrosting itself. Then I see the lead from the socket to the back of the fridge is cut in two, in fact, bitten in two. The lop-eared vandal has done it without electrocuting itself.

Anthony and Jennie introduce us to Bowdon Lawn Tennis Club, which becomes a hub for friendships. It's a sizeable and wealthy club, but tiny Avonwick's grass courts are not outdone. Jennie has been a designer at Liberty's and is becoming a painter. Anthony's a highly successful criminal barrister on the northern circuit with more professional distinction to come.

We agonise about Rowan's schooling. She's been very happy with her short periods in Haslemere C. of E. primary and the state Devonport High for girls in Plymouth. She'll be moving into her GCSE period during our time in Manchester. There'll be another interruption in the middle of her GCSEs. With some reluctance we float the notion of boarding school for three years – two of which we'll be in Britian. To our mild surprise, she's open to the idea. Lauren's view is that if she's going away at all, it should be somewhere with a name. So it's Cheltenham Ladies College. We haven't set out with this plan for our children. Life is full of surprises and compromises.

Rowan's happy there. We see her at half-term, holidays and some weekends. Now well into her teenage years, she likes visiting Manchester and its nightlife with a friend from CLC. She and Jenny badger me to take them to a karaoke bar round the corner from the rectory. They're underage but I relent. I take them, reluctantly warning them I've never done karaoke. I prepare myself for a challenge that I'm bringing in underage girls.

'Sorry guv,' the doorman's arm came up in front of me.

'Is there a problem?'

'Are those girls underage?' He gives a cheesy grin.

I step back shrugging at Rowan and Jenny.

'It's alright, girls, you can go in.'

I step forward.

'Not you sir. Thank you.'

At the end of Will's first week in his new primary school he's tearful. He's the only person in the class who doesn't have 'a team.' That means City or United. It's the start of the 1993/94 season. The previous year was the inaugural Premier League, which United won – their first title in the English top division for a quarter century. So Will happily becomes a Man U fan. What a first season it is! They're only the fourth team in the twentieth century to win the premiership and the FA Cup in one season. Cantona, who's come on a transfer from Leeds, is the leading scorer. The irascible Irishman, Roy Keane, dominates the midfield justifying a record fee of £3.75 million. The Beckham, Scholes, Neville generation soon to join the party on field.

Anthony's a season ticket holder and takes us to our first game. Will becomes a life-long fan. Later in his teens and into his thirties, wherever I'm working, I ensure we go at least once a season.

In London, I show Prince Charles round an exhibition to launch the project I've been leading, *Look Ahead;* post the Berlin Wall collapse and Russia's meltdown, a multi-media package for learners of English behind what was the Iron Curtain.

AGAINST FIERCE COMPETITION I get the senior role in India that I want. Lauren's over the moon. She wants to tell Aunty Pat immediately. Pat had been an officer in the Queen Alexandra's Royal Army Nursing Core, the services' nursing regiment. She was a hospital matron in New Delhi after independence. There's a photo of Pat in an emerald-green sari. She has a good sense of humour but is a stickler on the social etiquette of her generation. She's remained a spinster all her life.

It's our *Passage to India*. My father's father built railways there in the early decades of the twentieth century. I discover that the title of Forster's novel was taken from Walt Whitman's last major poem, 'Passage to India!', celebrating the opening of the Suez Canal in 1869.

We pack up the house in Hale, excited to be going to India having had an unexpectedly fun year in Manchester. Stowford Barton in Devon is already let. We roll the contract over but need to get some things out of storage to ship to India, not least Lauren's childhood piano. It's cross strung with a handsome walnut casing. It's the piano Lauren then Rowan learned on and played.

Its greatest player, and yet to come at its advanced age, is the wonderful Julian Joseph, British jazz pianist, arranger, composer and broadcaster. Whenever I hear Julian on Radio 3, I remember his visit to Delhi and elsewhere on a tour we organised. We have a reception at our house in Vasant Vihar. He's a big man and when, unasked, he spontaneously sits down to play Lauren's piano I'm astounded at the size of his hands and the reach of his fingers. They're gentle and deft like his mellifluous voice with its strong bass line. In concert, before playing one of his compositions, *The Language of Truth*, he explains that part of the song is in 7/4 time, and part in 4/4 time. The Beatles 'All You Need is Love' is in 7/4 time. Julian wasn't making a mistake. 'I couldn't make a mistake; I'm the composer.'

The British Council in New Delhi occupies a magnificent building designed by the Indian architect, Charles Correa, who studied under Buckminster Fuller. He invited the British painter, Howard Hodgkin to collaborate on the design of the new office. Like his other buildings, it has 'rooms open to the sky', an auditorium, library, art gallery, seminar rooms and offices. The front mural, designed by Hodgkin, based on a banyan tree, startles visitors with its Makrana marble, used for the Taj Mahal, and black Kadapa limestone from Andhra Pradesh. Howard comes to New Delhi in 1997, one of many visitors, to celebrate the 50th anniversary year of India's independence. He's a lovable rogue flirting with every young man in sight.

THE JEWEL IN the crown of the state visit by HM Queen Elizabeth features the largest international exhibition the British Museum and the British Council have ever mounted. *The Enduring Image* is drawn from across the range of the British Museum's collection.

Some Trustees raise serious objections to the exhibition going ahead. They are fearful on two counts. The sheer scale and logistics of mounting such a huge exhibition in 'a less advanced country' with all the security, environmental and technical challenges it involves. There's more than a hint of condescension in this attitude. The second is whether all the pieces will return once the exhibition is over. Eleven pieces originate in the Indian sub-continent.

I am one of four High Commission and British Council colleagues nominated by the High Commissioner for a private audience with Her Majesty before she leaves India. This is ten minutes in his gracious Lutyens drawing room. I'd met her at the opening of *The Enduring Image* with the Indian President, at her visit to the British Council building and at a reception on board the Royal Yacht Britannia, which sailed out in support and is docked in Bombay, now Mumbai. So she recognises my face. I tell her the last time I'd been on board the Britannia was her state visit to Ghana in 1962.

'I don't recall that we were introduced then.'

'Perhaps my father, Ma'am.'

WE HAVE THREE *chowkidars*, Hindi for 'watchman' or 'gatekeeper'. Each *chowkidar* does an eight-hour shift. This fails to take into account that most *chowkidars* have at least two, and sometimes a third job. So, of course, they fell asleep. There is a wooden sentry box outside our front gate, which they use to shelter from the freezing New Delhi winter nights or the forty degree plus summer days. In winter they build dung-fuelled fires in the dust. The biggest risk to us isn't a robbery but the house catching fire. I give them money to buy a crude brazier so the fire's contained for their and our safety.

During the day in summer, Usha, the housekeeper, is instructed to ensure they have a regular supply of cold water from the fridge. They're always cheerful and enjoy running errands to the local 'C'-block market. It gives them a break from the routine of the sentry box, our gate and garden. They aren't supposed to come inside the house, but I tell our cook, Mr Singh, they can go round the back and use the bathroom that he and his family use. This doesn't happen often so they no doubt piss or crap somewhere up the road out of sight of the house. There are no pavements just rubble or dust. The *chowkidars* are part of the ecosystem of those earning money without begging but who live on the streets, homeless.

Some taxi drivers fall into that category. They congregate under the mango trees outside 'C-block' market where there are usually half a dozen dozing on rickety, beaten-up *charpoys* – rope beds – pulled round in a cluster like a circle of Wild West wagons. It's a temporary home where they drink chai and chew betel nut with or without tobacco to speed up their metabolism and keep them awake.

It isn't uncommon for there to be snake charmers with their baskets and flutes on the street outside our house. Occasionally, elephants lumber by in twos dressed to the nines and decorated on their way to a wedding party. They're a symbol of good luck bringing loyalty, wisdom and long-life. They're often draped with cloths in bold colours and dramatic designs embedded with small mirrors or tassels. Their foreheads or trunks are painted in glowing, swirling designs.

The elephants are often accompanied by the *hijra*, a group of people who are intersex or transwomen, and since 2014 legally recognised in Indian law as a 'third gender'. Like many Indian women they dress in saris with nose rings, earrings, bracelets and bangles on arms, wrists and ankles. They perform at wedding ceremonies, singing and dancing to bring good luck and fertility. When passing E24 Vasant Marg, they wave, giggle and call out. They are full of energy and joy, but for many the only job they can do is sex work.

There's one cleaner to wash outside: the windows, balconies and terraces. He isn't allowed inside. We have another to wash inside the windows who's also allowed to clean the toilets. Usha presides over these and the man who comes to wash and iron our clothes. There's invariably tension between Usha and Mr Singh, the cook. Usha is clearly the more competent, brighter and harder worker. It's easy to know when she's about because you hear her ankle bells tinkling as she mops or makes up the beds.

The only person we employ ourselves and not through the office is our driver, Mukhia. He's an invaluable help for daily life around Delhi; especially in running Rowan – who joins us after her GCSEs at Cheltenham – William and Lauren to the international school where Lauren has a full-time teaching job on the International Baccalaureate programme.

It takes considerable adjustment to this caste-led system of employment and strict division of labour. We've been briefed by the office not to try and upset it. It provides an entire network of interdependencies and attempting to unravel a nationwide system which everyone accepts as their fate would end in turmoil. Our briefing is good advice. But disaster lurks.

Because he's male, Mr Singh considers himself in every way superior to Usha. We take on Usha but inherit him, his wife and four children from a predecessor. They are in the privileged position of having the two rooms and a bathroom, an annexe to the main house. They cook their own food outside on charcoal in the yard. The squabbles between him and Usha are tiresome but we live with them.

Nearly midnight and the front doorbell is ringing. I hurry down the concrete stairs pulling on a sweatshirt. It's the night-time *chowkidar* grasping a cudgel.

'Sir, come,' he gestures at me to follow him.

Outside it's cold, damp with swirling fog. The *chowkidar*, bundled in an army surplus great coat several sizes too big, leads me under the bougainvillea and neem trees to the gate for Mr Singh's quarters.

As the *chowkidar* is unlocking it, I hear high-pitched crying; my first reaction is, 'cats fighting.' The *chowkidar* switches on his torch. I see his hand is shaking and the beam trembles winking on the glossy leaves of the hedge. The cries grow louder, piercing, human. Mr Singh is screaming, the children crying.

With a nod I signal to the *chowkidar* to knock on Mr Singh's door. He bangs three times with his stick. Mr Singh's raging stops, there's a black quiet, then he starts again. The *chowkidar* beats the door several times. It's wrenched open. Mr Singh appears dark-faced and drunk. I see an empty bottle of whisky on the floor. His wife and children are cowering in the back of the room.

'Mr Singh. You have to stop now. Do you hear me Mr Singh? Stop now.'

He screws up his eyes and peers at me trying to focus. His head slumps onto his chest and he stares at the floor swaying.

'Or I'll call the police. The PO-LICE. You understand?'

His wife steps forward, bowing her head with the pointed palms of a *namaste* – the traditional Hindu greeting of respect – and then puts her hand on his shoulder.

'Good man. Please. No Po-Lice.'

In the morning, I ask one of my Hindu colleagues to speak to Mr Singh. If it happens again, I'll get the police involved. Given their reputation we're all between a rock and a hard place. If he's taken into custody, he'll be beaten up and have to pay a bribe. If I do nothing, Mr Singh will continue beating his wife and children.

Which, weeks later, he does. So he's taken away and beaten in his turn. His wife, of course, doesn't press charges and he's released the next day. He appears in our kitchen, bruised and contrite. I speak to the office. 'This is your last chance.'

Six months later I dismiss him. He has a month to find a new job. I supply a reference about his cooking only. He finds one but without accommodation. His family have to leave New Delhi return to their village.

Mr Singh, his family and mine have all lost out. Neither my colleagues nor I could find a solution.

SIR NICHOLAS FENN is a remarkable man. Impeccable, incisive and empathetic when appropriate. This is his final posting. A richly deserved reward for a life in service not just to his country but to making the world a slightly safer, more civilised place. He carries the same quiet confidence and calm into chairing the weekly High Commission meetings as he does into playing the part of Theseus, Duke of Athens, in *Midsummer Night's Dream.* Sue, Lady Fenn, plays Hippolyta, Theseus' wife.

We choose April, before the May heat, to perform in the gardens of the Residence. It's an ice-white Lutyens' wedding cake with tiered terraces where the invited audience sits. The shows are at dusk and into the evening played with a sub-tropical backdrop including the horseradish tree shimmering in its white-grey bark and ghostly flowers, the leaves of the white fig glow orange in the dark.

Lauren plays Titania, Queen of the fairies who gives as good as she gets from Oberon, King of the fairies, played by John, Head of the Department for International Development in Delhi. Falling in love with Bottom, the mechanical who's woken with his head transformed into a donkey, isn't Titania's finest moment, though it's Puck's spell that's to blame. Peter, an accompanying husband, who has a Cambridge PhD in philosophy, is Bottom. Julia, a DfID official, is Puck. I'm Peter Quince, the carpenter who writes and directs the awful *The Most Lamentable Comedy and Most Cruel Death of Pyramus and Thisbe.*

New Delhi is a very literary place. I review fiction for Indian magazines and papers. Through that I'm introduced to Indian writers and journalists, including Pankaj Mishra who has recently published his hilarious first book, *Butter Chicken in Ludhiana: Travels in Small Town India*. He's working as an editor at Harper Collins India. In 1996, recognising the uniqueness of a manuscript called *The God of Small Things*, he sends it to three British publishers. The book receives an unprecedented £500,000 advance and rights are sold in 21 countries. It sells six million copies across forty languages.

Arundhati Roy gives the first public reading of *The God of Small Things* at the British Council in New Delhi to an invited audience, including much of the world's TV, radio and print media. I broker the evening, chair it and handle the questions.

EVERY FOREIGN RESIDENT of New Delhi wants to see a tiger. We make five tiger spotting expeditions and only fail once. The most spontaneous is on the back of a working trip to Lucknow. I've decided that this city, whose sometimes at war relationship with the British Raj is one of the key steps in India's long march to independence, is where we should take Shared Experience's adaptation of *The Mill on the Floss*. I'd seen the production at the Tricycle Theatre – now the Kiln – in North London. It's a wonderful piece of ensemble playing which has acute relevance in late twentieth-century, provincial India.

Walking through the remains of the British Residency in the morning mist is an evocative experience. Some of the buildings on the thirty-three-acre site have been left pockmarked by cannon shot, windowless and roofless as they stood by the end of the hundred and thirty-day siege in 1857. The brickwork is blackened first by fire, more recently by humidity.

In the photo album, Lauren stands somewhere on the outer edges of the estate where trees have seeded themselves and the grass is long between ruined walls and bombed out buildings though a tower has survived. She's dressed in a white blouse and calf-length pink gingham dress with straps, her arms are down in front of her holding a guidebook with both hands. She looks uncharacteristically subdued. She's contemplating the terrible violence and history of this place.

Our visit to the Bara Imambara on the banks of the Gomti, tributary to the Ganges, is more uplifting. In a photograph, Lauren and I are relaxed and smiling, shoeless and sitting on a flat roof in the sunshine with a view through ornately carved Mughal columns of an extensive complex of buildings including the Badshahi mosque.

We're visiting one of the most spectacular sites of late Mughal architecture, a mongrel mix of Ottoman, Persian, Central Asian and Indian architecture. The most stunning building is a vaulted room fifty metres long and over fifteen metres high with no structure supporting the ceiling. Constructed in the 1780s, it was then the largest unsupported ceiling in India and possibly the world. It was built from the ash of burnt rice husks, which are still used today to strengthen concrete.

We endure a seven-hour ride in a black and yellow Ambassador taxi, two hundred and fifty kilometres from Lucknow to the lodge in Dudhwa National Park, a mix of grassland, marshes, swamps and forests. It covers five hundred square kilometres. On its northern edge the Mohani River marks the border with Nepal. The last part of the journey is a mud track bumping forty kilometres on dust potholes. We arrive wrung out. Lauren says she's going to have a lie down. I ask the driver to take Will and me on a drive in the forest to orient ourselves before the next morning's tiger spotting from the back of an elephant.

In second gear we drive up a gentle incline through the forest of *sal* trees, a major source of hardwood in northern India. *Sal* forests have been around for at least 50 million years. Traces of amber in the lignite from mines come from the resin they produce, which is burned as incense in Hindu ceremonies. Some *sal* are over a hundred feet tall and their slender, mottled trunks produce a flickering limelight as the taxi chugs uphill.

'Stop. Look!' I whisper fiercely to the driver pointing up the slope.

Idling up the incline away from us, its hips swaying, its black and lightly toasted tail curling, pads a tiger. It pauses and looks briefly over its shoulder before sauntering off the track and sliding into the forest of *sal*, where its stripes merge into the speckled sunlight stippling the tree trunks. An instant camouflage.

The driver has already cut the engine. I indicate to let the taxi roll in reverse down the slope and use its momentum to swing it round and head down to a bamboo cluster by a waterhole. The black and yellow taxi is disguised halfway into the clumps of bamboo. We can see the muddy waterhole through khaki shafts and olive-green leaves of bamboo.

In less than ten minutes a tiger – I assume the one we've just seen – appears on the far side, noiseless on its pneumatic pads. It ghosts to a halt and stands motionless. Will scrambles across the bench seat to see it padding forward slowly to the water's edge. Its front legs bend as it lowers its head but keeps its neck muscles taut while scanning the horizon and dipping its shocking pink tongue into the water. Though drinking, it is a study in perfect concentration of the moment, aware of every presence. When finished drinking, it steps forward so that its back legs are in the water but still in the shallows with the pond's ripples wetting the underside of its belly. It stays like this for some time, on a restful alert. Suddenly, it turns its head swivelling its body to stare into another clump of bamboo on the far side of the waterhole. It has sensed or heard something. And then there *she* is. We instinctively know that the tiger in the water is male. It's about three metres long and a metre tall. The second tiger is adult but smaller in stature and weight.

She pauses at the water's edge. The male waits, then launches himself onto her and they roll in the dust by the waterhole. He springs up, half turns away, feints as if he's going to run off, then returns. She raises a paw and places it on his neck, caressing not aggressive. They both half-stand on their haunches, shadow boxing with their front paws lightly smacking the other's shoulders and flanks. They're rolling in the dust again when she escapes and plunges into the water. He follows and with their paws they splash each other, children at the seaside. They duck and dive with beads of water sprayed and arcing in the fading light, its intensity shot and glowing, as the prelude to dusk.

They exit the water and lay beside each other on the dust to rest, half-panting with exertion and pleasure. They seem to be enjoying a moment of peaceful intimacy free from their default state of alertness. But no. The male suddenly stands to attention looking in the direction of where we're sitting, watching through the open windows of the Ambassador behind our bamboo screen. He pads half a dozen steps towards us and stops staring at our clump of bamboo. I motion to the taxi driver to wind up his window and I do the same with mine praying it won't squeak. Now we're in a state of high alert. If he comes closer, I suppose he'll spot the taxi. But if he does, will he run at us? Will he try and break the glass and attack? I try not to show my fear to Will. I whisper, 'Don't move. Stay still. Keep quiet.'

He takes three or four more paces forward. I'm paralysed. He stares at us for an age. He turns his head slightly and I can see the white spots, flashes on the back of his ear. Then his shoulder dips and he pads back along the water's edge to his girlfriend. 'Wait,' I whisper to the taxi driver. In a short while they melt through the bamboo into the *sal* forest on the start of a night-time hunt for dinner.

I read that tigers, the largest of thirty-six cats, have hearing five times sharper than humans. Their night-time vision is six times more acute.

I FLY FROM Delhi to Hyderabad, then the capital of Andhra Pradesh. Today it's the capital of Telangana, known for pharmaceuticals. Until the nineteenth century it was the location of the world's best quality and largest diamonds – Golconda diamonds.

I haven't come in search of diamonds or drugs. I'm after a more pervasive product: the English language. Hyderabad is the main campus of the Central Institute for English and Foreign

Languages, the only university in India solely focused on the learning and teaching of English and other foreign languages.

I'm here to meet its Director, Professor Verma. This is a critical relationship in the British Council's English language work and its teaching English. I want the British Council to be doing things very differently by the time I leave India in five years. Given the history between Britain and India, the position of English, the tongue of the coloniser, was, and still is, highly contested.

Professor Verma is the government's *de facto* adviser on English language policy in the country. This means I intend our first meeting will be conducted by my keeping mum. It gives me plenty of time to contemplate the distinguished Professor's slight frame and stature, sliver-tinged hair, and his fierce, intelligent eyes.

It's an unremarkable meeting: how I want it. I make it clear I have much to learn from him. I'd welcome his advice on anything the British Council might do in this space. I hope he'll come and see me when next in Delhi or, if the opportunity arises, I'll invite him to one of our conferences or events. Perhaps he'll be kind enough to say a few words. He smiles and bobbles his head enthusiastically from side to side.

By the time I get to the hotel I'm ready to show the stamped document from the airport proving I'm 'a registered alcoholic' so I can purchase a beer at the bar. This is a joyously Indian way to proclaim that alcohol is prohibited in Hyderabad, and they have expunged drunken and disorderly behaviour. Only foreigners addicted to alcohol would be given this exemption through a stamp issued on medical grounds. This state-wide ban merely increases black market prices for booze.

Over three years I build a relationship with Professor Verma based on mutual respect and trust. With his endorsement we hugely expand the British Council's UK examination business, particularly of Cambridge University English language exams.

But there's a higher peak to scale. We want to establish British Council English teaching centres in India. My predecessors had tried and failed. The Government of India regards the British

Council as a political operation and only allows us to operate under the umbrella of the High Commission. Issues of culture and language are for many Indians Political with a capital P.

The British Council isn't a government department. It's an independent charity with its own Board. It works closely with the UK government and other public institutions, companies and individuals, but isn't part of the political machinery of government. India, China and Russia are the significant states who don't accept the distinction.

If I get it wrong, it'll be decades before my successors can revisit the matter.

In my third year, I judge we're in a strong position to make the case. It's time to remind the High Commissioner and his colleagues how I've been positioning the British Council to teach English in India. What a quagmire I've stumbled into! I spend months working with our London legal adviser alongside the Foreign and Commonwealth Office to resolve the situation. The key issue is the status of the High Commission which, as a diplomatic mission, isn't permitted under the Vienna Convention governing diplomatic operations to charge for services other than visas. The British Council's English teaching and examinations services are, in agreement with the Treasury and the Foreign Office, not subsidised with a single penny of government (taxpayer)grant and they have to operate by charging for all direct and indirect costs plus make a 'surplus' – 'profit' isn't used in the charity sector. This means that Indians wanting to study English with us will have to pay for the service. Any surpluses made are re-invested in the English teaching business or other Council work, especially in the Arts.

As part of this process, I spend weeks working with Mr Shankar Dass, the High Commission's and British Council's legal adviser. When we first meet he says, 'I understand you are in a pickle. That is alright. We know all about pickles in India.'

I explain I've already had an informal meeting with Salman Haidar, the Cambridge-educated Foreign Secretary, and he's been supportive. But I want to move quickly now while he's still in post. Shankar Dass smiles. 'Very astute,' he says.

Permission from the Government of India for us to teach English arrives in the last month of Salman Haidar's tenure. We finesse the British High Commission, which applies for our teachers to have technical, not diplomatic, visas allowing them to work.

I'VE COMPLETED THE two main tasks I was asked to deliver: a successful, high-profile array of cultural events to celebrate India's 50th Anniversary of Independence alongside the State visit; and positioning and establishing a successful English language examinations business alongside winning permission to establish British Council teaching centres, and launching that enterprise was all done with the unstinting support of my ebullient boss, Colin Perchard.

On a visit to the sub-continent, our corporate Director HR asks how I'd feel about a posting to Oman. Lauren reads up and thinks it sounds gloriously stress free after New Delhi and India. Sir John Hanson, our Director General, follows her and talks to Colin. A week later Colin says, 'We think Oman is too small for you. We're thinking about something else. Can't tell you more at the moment.'

Act 4

Eleftheria i Thanatos

(Freedom or Death)

Will, Richard, Rowan, Lauren at Toshali Sands, Puri, Odisha State. 1996

To fly from New Delhi means an overnight stop in Switzerland. By the time I arrive at Sao Paulo Guarulhos international airport I'm exhausted. I'm met and driven to a downtown hotel by a man built like a heavyweight boxer. His name is Domingo.

In spite of Lauren's reservations about living in this megalopolis of a city, we'd worked through the pros and cons, spoken to a number of people, and agreed that I'd accept the posting, although that isn't the end of the process. The British Council from its side are appointing me to be the British Council Director, which also wraps in the role of Superintendent General or Chief Executive of the Cultura Inglesa. The Sao Paulo branch of the Cultura is the most successful and wealthy of the English language businesses in Brazil and more widely in South America. It has influence in London too.

As CEO of the Sao Paulo Cultura Inglesa, I'd sit on its board reporting to its Chairman and the Board. From their perspective, the British Council has nominated me, but the Board has the right to turn down the nomination. Nowhere else in the one hundred-plus countries where the British Council operates does the host country have the right of veto over the appointment of the British Council Director. Rarely, governments refuse to accredit the nomination of an Ambassador but not the British Council. It's a bizarre anomaly and indicative of the Cultura's influence.

There's a session with the full Board, which is billed as a discussion of the Cultura's work, and I'm invited to respond and suggest where my experience might be useful. Board members have a copy of my CV and are invited to comment or ask questions. It's an interview, though not branded that.

Then there's the 'knife, fork and cocktail interview.' These are social occasions ranging from a formal dinner at a top restaurant with the Consul General and the Head of Lloyds Bank in South America to a BBQ beside the pool of a mansion in Morumbi, a wealthy area of the city adjacent to a *favela* or slum. The Board Chairman or other senior members are invariably present. I'm being scrutinised.

I'd entered a time-warp. Many of the Anglo-Brazilian Board members' attitudes and assumptions seem to be of a Britain that still had an Empire, or were stuck at the high water mark of 80s Thatcherism. With one exception they weren't culturally sophisticated. One says without irony, 'Spice Girls, fantastic! Best thing we did the British Council!' I can see it's going to be hard work. Just how hard I don't know.

The most fun meeting I have is with Casey McCann, the Head of St Paul's school, affiliated to the Headmaster's Conference of Public Schools in Britain. Casey was previously Deputy Head at Sevenoaks. St Paul's is the leading international school in Brazil and the rest of South America. We expect will to go there if we come to Sao Paulo. The British Council Director sits on the school's board. Casey's heard Lauren's teaching in Delhi and asks for her CV. We mainly speak about books. I know we'll get on.

By the time I arrive back in New Delhi a message reaches me that the Chairman of the Cultura has agreed to my appointment as the Superintendent General.

LAUREN LIKES THE house. Sliding glass doors and windows run along the inside of an 'L' which overlooks the swimming pool. At the far end is a BBQ area with a hammock. Sunday mornings we have tea and papers in bed with the shutters open onto the balcony, a profusion of honeysuckle and hibiscus. It's usual to see a solitary *beija-flor*, a swallow-tail hummingbird, hovering by the open window manoeuvring itself like a miniature helicopter – the only bird which can fly backwards – to reach its long, hollow tongue down, a straw for the nectar. The dark shimmering sapphire head and neck, the iridescent emerald of its lower body and wings beating a hundred times a second. Loosely translated *beija-flor* means 'flower kisser'. We never saw them, but two eggs are laid in a cobweb nest the dimensions of a thimble.

The house is in a green part of the city, Alto do Pinheiros. We have electronic gates and twenty-four-hour guards, but they aren't armed. We employ Margarida, who lives alone with a comfortable bedroom and bathroom in a separate dwelling at the back of the main house. We're happy for her to prepare her own modest food in our kitchen. She's very slight, hard-working and gentle, patient with our rudimentary Brazilian Portuguese. She comes from Parana, the poorer, adjacent state south of Sao Paulo. She has no family in the city and few friends. No partner or children. Every few months she asks to take some days off to visit her parents. I think she's lonely but as time winds on I understand she's content. She's excited when we bring back a small black mongrel with curly hair. It's an impulse buy to free him from the cage where he's being bullied by larger, snarling dogs. We call him Max, and he becomes Margarida's dog as much as ours, sleeping in her bedroom. Max follows her round the house, his nails clicking on the tiled floors and wooden balconies.

On the way to the supermarket, we stroll along the street lined with fig and palm trees admiring the waxy, traffic-light red leaves of the flamingo flowers. We buy local lemons, avocados, papaya, passion fruit and guavas. I walk to some clay tennis courts for a session with the coach before work, which is twenty-five minutes on foot.

Casey McCann, the headmaster of St Paul's, unsurprisingly impressed with Lauren's CV, offers her a job. I tell him if he wants to employ Lauren, I'll resign as a Board member.

'Richard, this is absolutely not necessary. This is Brazil! I need an ally on that Board.'

But resign I do. We become good friends, perhaps more so because I'm not on his Board. Our friendship includes Lauren too. Sometimes the three of us meet for a quietly raucous dinner where we can be ourselves.

Casey is that generation of gay men who's found it a challenge to come out. He likes our company because he knows we know, and we make no judgments. With the Anglo-Brazilian community, he's always watching his step.

It's a remarkably easy existence for life in a megalopolis. Occasionally, we're reminded of 'the other side' of the city. Driving home along the ring road we stop at traffic lights and our Land Cruiser is surrounded by a swarm of prostitutes, women and transgender. Once I park the car and give a boy a few *reais*, a dollar, to look after it. When I return he's gone, the front passenger window's smashed and the radio's been ripped out of the dashboard. But we're never subjected directly to any violence. This happens to others we know. We're lucky.

I don't blame the boy for the loss of our car radio. It's all about surviving poverty.

THE BRITISH COUNCIL invested considerably in earlier decades in helping the Cultura develop its professionalism and product. By the time I arrive, the Cultura doesn't need a British Council Director as its CEO – indeed, the Cultura does its best to keep me at arm's length except when something ceremonial is needed. Or when the British Council's global brand might confer some status, or privileged access.

The Cultura was devaluing the British Council brand and its values. Some British Council staff were paid for by the Cultura, and they regarded themselves as Cultura employees. So there was no performance management system. This had been a long process with each British Council Director taking up post and remaining silent about this and other deviations, particularly financial, from standard British Council practice. Did I too keep silent in exchange for the comfortable life that came with the role? As the weeks passed, I knew I had to act. It'd be a game of chess. I'd need the backing of our main board in London.

I started with the small things: the personal car and driver, Domingo. He was using the car for his private business. I reminded him that he was only allowed to use the car to get home and fetch me in the morning. A wide grin across his huge, stubbly, Desperate Dan jaw. 'Of course, Mr Richard. I do this.'

It continued despite a written warning. Three months later I wrote a letter dismissing him. I handed Domingo the letter thanking him for looking after me in my first months in Sao Paulo. I wished him well. He smiled. *'O Brasil e diferente,'* he said, then quietly, *'Voce descrobrira.'* You'll find out.

IF THERE ARE no work commitments, our default is to drive out of Sao Paulo for a long weekend. We head east dropping down off the Sao Paulo state plateau and through the Mata Atlantica – the dense rainforest which curtains the coastal beaches of Sao Paulo state. We either stay at the consulate hut, lush in the forest a hundred metres inland, or at the adjacent Juquei Hotel fronting the pale lemon beach.

Sometimes families with boys from Will's class come. The boys spend ages waxing their surf boards, though we all find it a challenge to stand on them. They're sun-blessed, carefree days, worlds away from the roar of Sao Paulo. Who wouldn't relax after a day on the beach and in the waves when drinking the spirit of Brazil? Mexico has tequila. Colombia has aguardiente. Cuba has rum. The spirit of Brazil is *cachaça*, fermented and distilled sugarcane juice. The Portuguese introduced the cane in the early 1500s alongside importing African slaves who worked the mills.

After a few months experimenting, we agree you should drink classic caipirinha made with quality *cachaça*, unmolested by anything other than limes, lime juice, a little sugar and mountains of ice. The only exception allowed is *caipirinha de maracuja*, or a caipirinha made with passion fruit. Cut open the pithy skin and it's a riot of colour, smell and taste, with each of its olive-green seeds embedded in an orange jelly exhaling a tangy, sweet perfume. When mixed with *cachaça*, ice, a touch of sugar and limes it's transformed into a caipirinha that comes with a warning. It's perilously drinkable, with the *maracuja* camouflaging the potency of the *cachaça*.

BY THE TIME we've moved into a spectacular new building, the Centro Brasileiro Britanico, we're divorced from the Cultura Inglesa, though still co-habiting. It's been a painful process to get us there. Meetings with the Ambassador in Brasilia, the Consul General Sao Paulo, the Chair of the Cultura Inglesa, Board members, others Great and Good. I feel the pressure of a network of powerful people unhappy with the proposed separation. In London: the British Council Deputy Director General, Regional Director for the Americas, FCO officials in King Charles Street. All have to be listened to, their misconceptions gently dissolved. I write the paper for the British Council main board on why we should radically change the relationship. The Chair, Baroness Kennedy, ensures the paper is approved.

The Cultura has dipped its hands into its bottomless coffers and the architects and designers have done a magnificent job on a generous plot in Pinheiros in central Sao Paulo. Unlike so much city architecture the building breathes with space around it, walkways and waterways planted with grasses and gravel, a scattering of trees including a flowering cherry surround the building of 13,000 square metres. St Paul's Cathedral is about 8,000.

The glass atrium forming the entrance rises the entire height of the building and we find a British artist who fills the space with transparent waves, curtains of glass beads. Our revised contract with the Cultura means we are commercial tenants in this new build, which allows us to design our own office space. It is, by common consent, the best designed of all the tenants' offices including the Consulate and the Cultura itself. Everyone loves the open-plan space designed around the notion of the Amazon River. And its curving glass walled conference room. My favourite place is a garden deck with a mahogany floor sweeping to the edge of the water surrounding the building. It's scattered with boulders and planted with Mata Atlantica ferns, climbers, creepers, bamboo, mosses, epiphytes – or air flowers, which grow on other plants like some orchids and bromeliads bristling rosettes of stiff, spiny leaves.

The British sociologist Anthony Giddens, Director of the LSE, is in Brazil in 1999 giving lectures and seminars, which I attend, and he's going to see his friend from Cambridge days, the Brazilian President, Fernando Henrique Cardoso. I have some private time with Giddens and float the idea of Blair coming to Brazil to launch the new building. Cardoso like Blair is a fan of Giddens' *The Third Way*. We hear nothing, though Blair's name is still in the frame until shortly before the opening in 2000. At the last moment – the way with senior politicians – we hear that he's asked John Prescott, the Deputy Prime Minister, to come instead.

I'm in the reception party which greets 'Two Jags' at the entrance of the Centro Brasileiro-Britanico. It's mid-morning. He's much as I'd imagined: stocky – he'd been an amateur boxer – affable, and easy to talk to. The plan is to walk him slowly through the building to the rooftop, stopping to meet heads and selected employees of all the organisations in the building. When our lead group enters the glass atrium a waiter steps forward with a tray of drinks.

As soon as the word *'caipirinha'*, Brazil's national drink, is mentioned, he says, 'I've heard about those. I'll try one. Don't want to upset my hosts.'

'Mmm that's cracking!'

He downed it.

'I'll have another.'

The visit continues with John clutching his second caipirinha. The tour round the building and conversations pass without incident. I can hear the Brazilian steel band warming up. When we arrive, the roof party is in full swing with an irresistible rhythm and beat.

More waiters are stationed with trays. John needs no encouragement, and heading straight over grabs a third caipirinha. His special adviser, Joan, is standing right next to me and I hear her mutter in exasperation. John's enjoying himself hugely, jigging and swaying. The tempo increases and reaches crescendo after crescendo. The adviser has discreetly manoeuvred him to the edge of the crowd to stand and watch the drummers. A waiter passes in front of us. Prescott's arm is craning for another caipirinha. Another arm shoots out and locks on to Prescott's wrist.

'John, that's enough!' comes the fierce whisper.

'Aah. That's what special advisers do,' I think

BY THIS TIME my relationship with the Cultura Board is at a low point and I'm feeling professionally isolated. The best support I get is from Casey McCann, Headmaster of St Paul's, because he understands the context and its complexities. Our favourite time with Casey is when we're all free of commitments on a Friday and have dinner together.

On such an evening in our second year (2000), Casey tells us that he's retiring the following year. It's been agreed with his Board but not yet announced. The conversation ranges over the customary mix of books, local and global politics and the current challenges we face in running St Paul's and the British Council. Everything's on the table, big stuff and trivia, like the parent who's pressing Casey to have a helicopter pad installed at St Paul's ostensibly to mitigate the risk of kidnap from a gridlocked car. Lauren's a great foil, allowing us to get some of this stuff off our chests before moving us on to more interesting topics. A large G & T or caipirinha each to start, plus at least two bottles of wine also help.

That evening Casey waxes lyrical about the apartment he's already bought in Barcelona ready for his retirement. There's a wonderful café nearby where he'll have his morning coffee and *The Times*. Numerous bars and restaurants where in the evenings he'll enjoy the anonymity of being no-one of note and during the day he'll write his 'memoirs'. Which, he says, will of course contain lots of stories about his time at St Paul's, including some of the dodgy dealings that have happened around him as its Headmaster.

Lauren and I go to bed on Sunday hoping for a night's good rest to charge our batteries for the week ahead. The landline by my side of the bed is clamouring me awake. The clock's showing an illuminated, throbbing green 0550 something.

'Richard, it's Iain.' The Consul General.

'Yeah, what's . . .'

'Some terrible news. Casey's dead. Foul play probably. I'm going straight to his apartment. No need for you to come. Let's meet later for coffee.'

'OK. Ten o'clock. Your office.' Lauren's stirring under the bedclothes.

'What is it?'

'It's Casey.'

'Casey what?'

'Casey's dead.'

An electric charge shoots through her body stiffening next to mine. She sits upright, staring nowhere then turns her face to mine, her mouth shapes to speak but she can't. She continues staring. It reminds me of the nights she used to wake but not wake. Sometimes mumbling words fell out that made no sense; she'd slide out of bed, go and bang on the windowpane with both fists.

'Out! Out!' she'd be sobbing. I'd put my arm round her shoulders and guide her back to bed. But she hasn't done that for years. Her head slumps and she holds out her arms for me to enclose her.

Later I hear the story. The cleaner had found Casey in his bedroom naked and tied up with hands behind his back and ankles bound. It seems to have been a sexual game gone wrong. He had a plastic bag over his head and died from asphyxiation.

The twenty-four CCTV security cameras at the ground floor entrance have been wiped, as have many key documents on his office computer.

He's cremated quickly without a thorough police investigation. I'm told that the Chair and St Paul's school board 'in consultation' had decided it was better that way, both in honour of Casey's memory and the school's reputation.

I don't believe it was death by sexual misadventure. This is Brazil. Casey knew things. But accident or murder the case remains unsolved.

Three days after Casey's death Lauren and I receive a postcard sent through the regular Brazilian postal service. On the front is an erotic photograph of a muscular black man shot from behind with his hands clasped over his right shoulder. It's by Robert Mapplethorpe, from the late '60s while he still had the rock-poet Patti Smith as a girlfriend, and was photographing the BDSM gay subculture in New York.

On the back of the postcard is a scribbled note saying, 'Thanks for a lovely evening. Let's do it again soon. Casey.'

For the rest of our time in Sao Paulo I'm a little on edge wondering if, after the divorce I'd engineered from the Cultura, my life might end with me too having a terrible 'accident'. Domingo's *'Voce descrobira'*, You will discover, rings in my ears. But then I'm nowhere near retirement and have no intention of writing 'my memoirs.'

Fortunately, I'm unexpectedly offered a big promotion to a new role as Regional Director for our work in East Asia to be based in London. It's a timely release.

IN MAY 2005 we set off from Haslemere to drive through Europe, stopping with friends in Burgundy. The next night we stay in a small medieval town in France, just short of the Italian border. I know it's the French side because I take a photo of Lauren over an apéritif outdoors. In the background alongside the wall of the half-timbered building is a wooden sign: *Epicerie*, not *Fruttivendolo*.

The photo is a half-length portrait of her sitting at the café table in a characteristic pose – leaning slightly to her left, her chin in her left hand with her elbow on the marble tabletop. The engagement ring I'd had made, with diamonds set in parallel in overlapping bars of gold, is visible. She has a simple white blouse with a frill by her left elbow. The copper ringlets on either side of her face corkscrew down below her jawline. She's smiling softly and gazing at the camera through half-closed eyes, infinitely relaxed. This might have something to do with the glass she's holding in her right hand on the tabletop. Inside is a generous serving of some local apéritif which, at a glance, you might think was brandy-based, but she didn't like brandy so I guess it's a sparkling wine with *cassis*.

Before the end of the year, she's using this photograph professionally – just the upper half, not the aperitif. It'd become one of her favourites. She says I always take the best pictures of her. It isn't a comment on my limited skills as a snapper. I'm the only one she can fully give herself up to in front of the lens expressing something beyond the image.

We drive through the Gotthard tunnel, the intestines of the Alps, heading across northern Italy for the overnight ferry from Ancona to Patras in the northern Peloponnese. Lauren's worried. She's had several text messages from her cousin, the nursing home and Aunty Pat herself. She's always been close to Aunty Pat, who treated her when a child as older than her years. After her post-war career in India, Malaya and Ceylon, she comes to live with her sister Doreen, Lauren's mother, and their parents, Lauren's grandparents. When Doreen dies, Aunty Pat becomes *in loco parentis* to Lauren. It's the only time she ever asks Lauren to stop what she's doing to come and see her.

We drive east from Patras towards Athens, two hundred kilometres away; the first part of the journey is where the road hugs the Gulf of Corinth on its left. We soon pass the Charilaos Trikoupis bridge named after the nineteenth-century Greek Prime Minister who built the Corinth Canal. It was opened for the Athens Olympics in 2004 and is widely acknowledged as a twenty-first century design and engineering masterpiece. The challenges were huge: a depth of sixty-five metres onto a shifting seabed, prime earthquake territory, winds in excess of seventy miles an hour. The bridge appears like a spider's web of four diaphanous pyramids, fairy skirts which float over the Gulf of Corinth.

The messages coming out of Sussex mean Lauren cancels her Cyprus flight and finds one back to London. She leaves by taxi to the airport, not knowing when she'll see me in Cyprus. I drive to the Piraeus docks and see the car loaded on the freight ferry to Larnaca.

CLOSE TO THE anonymous office block housing the British Council office stands a portion of the fortified, circular Venetian Citadel framed by its original walls enclosing a complex web of streets cut in half by a waterproof and smudge resistant grease pencil. This green line was drawn by Major General Young in 1963 after repeated outbreaks of violence between the Greek Orthodox and Turkish Moslem communities.

You can walk from the office and within a minute be inside the ancient Citadel. Some of its streets are only wide enough for one vehicle and it was easy to get half-lost. It isn't uncommon to find yourself abruptly confronted by a street blocked off with concrete-filled oil drums. They're often painted green and white with layers of stained, fraying sandbags slapped on top with rusting coils of barbed wire scattered along the upper tier, gigantic julienne strips of burnt orange peel.

The barricades stand as they'd been erected in the rush and chaos of the Turkish invasion in 1974. Some are elaborate affairs with viewing platforms, some just red brick with a peep hole. A lot are graffitied, some have UN or EU signs proclaiming authority over the dead space – the buffer zone – which has been created. A few have been adopted by local residents with benches and flowerpots alongside.

The zone created by the Green Line is a ghostly presence which runs through the dusty heart of Lefkosia forming a morbid space of refuse-filled streets, collapsing schools, rotting churches and rusting cars. In conversations with older Cypriots you can hear the echo of the fear still pumping its way through their veins. The Turkish Cypriots are between a rock and a hard place. The fear or indifference of the Greek Cypriots on one side, the Turkish military invaders now stationed there permanently, on the other. Since the 1974 Turkish invasion it had been policy to populate northern Cyprus with Turkish citizens, illegal under numerous UN resolutions. But once Erdogan assumed power, a trickle of Turks moving to northern Cyprus became a torrent. He shipped thousands of semi-literate, devout Muslim peasants from Anatolia, offering them free land and illegal occupation of northern Cyprus territory and homes. Turkish Cypriots are horrified by this. This action has forever changed the demographics of the island.

I like walking to work through the back streets of Venetian Lefkosia. I move the office there in anticipation of the Ledra Street crossing opening and as an encouragement to Turkish Cypriots to visit us by walking from the north half of the city across the Green Line.

Glyn Hughes is, arguably, the pre-eminent artist working south of the Green Line. Glyn is best known for the huge energy and drama of his work as a colourist. His painting and his bold use of colour, often on huge canvases, are cousins of Matisse and Howard Hodgkin. But it's uniquely Glyn, inspired by the sunlight and other conditions of the island's environment, politics and culture, which he first came across during his National Service in the 1950s. And where he returned to live for more than fifty years in Lefkosia.

Glyn has been, for decades, at the centre of cultural life in Lefkosia. An artist foremost including murals and batiks, he's also active in stage design, art journalism and lectures on painting. Occasionally, in the evening, we sit on our outdoor terrace under the lemon trees and drink beer. He and Lauren bond quickly as, decades apart, they'd both studied at Bretton Hall, an interdisciplinary arts college under the umbrella of Leeds University. He's a wise informant and commentator on life in Cyprus. He tells me, for instance, that it's the Parliamentary Under Secretary who knows more about culture than the Minister of Education and Culture, while the Minister himself is more interested in education.

WITH THIS ADVICE in my ears, I'm on my way to meet the Greek Cypriot Minister of Education and Culture. His office is housed in a 1970s concrete office block. The staircase and balconies running along one side are open to the elements, and the Minister's on the top floor. There's a lift, but I prefer to walk. I've come on my own for our first meeting, so no one will take notes. As I climb the stairs, I admire the silvery, rust-coloured, peeling bark and green waving fronds of the rustling eucalyptus trees.

The Minister – a large, distinguished-looking man with a rolling ocean of grey hair – is seated behind his desk with towers of paper files on it. There's an old school computer on the desk with the screen blank.

'Welcome to the Republic of Cyprus,' he says, easing himself into a favoured armchair. 'I understand you know Greece.' His civil servants have done some homework.

'That's right,' I reply.

'That's good,' he nods approvingly. 'But not Cyprus?'

'No Minister, not Cyprus. Not yet anyway.'

He smiles. 'It is not the same here.' He pauses 'But you would like coffee?'

'Thank you. Yes, please.'

He's silent for a moment. 'Do you prefer Greek or Turkish coffee?'

I pause. My first test. 'I'll have whatever you have, Minister.'

He laughs 'Good! Good! You know, of course, there's no difference between them.'

It's the start of a fruitful professional relationship shot through with mutual respect and warmth. George Pefkios studied architecture at the University of Sheffield returning to Cyprus just before its 'independence' in 1960. He set up his own practice and has been Minister for two years before I arrive in Cyprus. He dies unexpectedly of a heart attack two years later. I attend his funeral.

Cyprus is the only place we work where we already knew both the Head of Mission and the Deputy. Lyn Parker, the High Commissioner, had been the Political Counsellor in New Delhi a dozen years before. A lawyer, he's collaborated intensely with David, now Lord Hannay, on the Annan Plan to re-unite Cyprus.

WE'VE ONLY BEEN on the island a few weeks when the most opulent of the annual Embassy parties takes place: 4th July, US Independence Day. Everyone's there including the President, Tassos Papadopoulous, who studied law at King's College and trained as a barrister at Gray's Inn. He returned to Cyprus in 1955 ten days before EOKA's first armed rebellion against British colonial rule. In 1960 with Cypriot 'independence', still only twenty-four, Tassos became the youngest ever Cypriot Cabinet Minister. A record that still stands.

It's my first introduction to the Cypriot President not in favour with UK politicians or European liberal circles. I quietly admire the statement he'd made when elected President in rejecting the UN-backed proposal: 'I received a state. I will not deliver a community.' He has the most piercing blue eyes and when he fixes them on you it's easy in that moment to forget how short he is. We become acquaintances on the ceremonial and conference circuit. After this introduction, he always knows exactly who I am and what we're up to.

Against the trend of the time, I make and win the case in London to move the British Council offices from the anonymous 1970s office block into a restored Ottoman Inn in central, Venetian Nicosia near the Green Line. I'd spotted the stone building being renovated just off Ledra Street, the spine of the Venetian citadel.

To some British individuals' disapproval, I persuade Papadopoulos's private office to open our new premises. At the ceremony, he tells me he regularly came to the building as a child when it was a halloumi factory. I show him one of the stone vats used to make the cheese and which I'd insisted was retained during the restoration. It sits below an Anish Kapoor globe from the British Council art collection. Though my favourite piece hangs in my office: 'Burnt Books', a Holocaust-inspired sculpture by Rachel Whiteread. Beyond which, from my window, is a view of a Byzantine church

We soon become fond of the Syrian Friendship Club opposite the US Embassy. It's a restaurant with an outdoor garden and some of the best food in central Lefkosia. Flatbreads arriving so hot from the wood oven they're expanded like balloons: *fattoush* – a salad with parsley and lemon; *yalanji* – like Greek dolmades using chard, not vine leaves; and, my favourite, *muhumarra* – a red pepper and walnut dip given depth with pomegranate molasses. The Syrian waiters are immaculately turned out, highly educated university graduates who speak excellent English. It's an open secret that this is a low-level intelligence-gathering hub close to the US Embassy.

In the US Ambassador's garden, Lauren delights in going to one of the several bars and asking loudly for a Cuba Libre, a drink she likes, but it has an added frisson ordering one on

US diplomatic territory. She later interviews and becomes good friends with the Cuban Ambassador, a talented artist and intellectual. We're introduced to Kyriakos, the editor of the *Cyprus Mail*, the leading English language newspaper on the island. After some banter with him and his English wife, Tracey, I move on, but Lauren remains. I return twenty minutes later and she's still in animated conversation with Kyriakos and Tracey. I hear him say to Lauren, 'If you can write like you talk, I'll give you a regular column in the paper.'

Within a week she files her first five hundred words. It becomes so popular Kyriakos asks her to produce two a week. Anything from high politics to low life, from the life cycle of the cockroach to different cultures' attitudes to marriage. Several of our trips and elements of our domestic lives feature in these pieces. One of the most memorable is our discovery of a small but heavily fenced port not on a map in the heart of 'Ndrangheta country in southern Italy. It's for drug shipments from South America. Another is in the James Joyce pub in Athens where she falls into conversation with two young men from a superyacht docked in Piraeus. The stories she hears about onboard drugs and prostitution feature in one of her columns. Though she doesn't name the yacht, it's clear to those who know what she's writing about. It's Abramovich's superyacht, 'Eclipse'. A few days later the paper receives a flurry of calls and emails demanding the details of who's written the piece. Admirably, they stonewall and after some weeks, the queries subside. She adopts the last name O'Hara, with its Irishness and its association with *Gone with the Wind,* one of her favourite films. Its *Irishness* distances her from the *British* and my job.

Lauren has stumbled on an occupation – columnist and interviewer – which suits her perfectly. She writes about the Danish cartoonist, Kurt Westergaard, whose cartoon of the prophet Mohammed with a bomb in his turban provokes controversy in the Islamic world. She defends his right to publish the cartoon and is invited to an international conference on media freedom where she meets Westergaard. She's been a very good teacher of Politics and Sociology A-levels and the International Baccalaureate 'Theory of Knowledge' paper. She's enjoyed teaching, but it's a relief from the routine of terms, timetables and marking. Live, observe and bang out five hundred funny, shocking, reflective, quirky, unexpected words; you never know what angle or tone she might adopt. She doesn't know herself, I think, until she's in the act of writing.

She loves our old-fashioned house with its generous terraces and balconies, its ornate wooden doors, the abundant lemon trees and the deafening churring of cicadas. We trek in the pine forests of the Troodos mountains of northern Cyprus. A nearby destination is Bellapaix where, in 1953, at the start of the agitation for Cypriot independence, Laurence Durrell bought a house. He abandoned any incipient career in the British Council, Argentina, or Foreign Office, Yugoslavia, and came to Cyprus to concentrate on his writing.

In his memoir *Bitter Lemons*, Durrell makes his sympathy with Greek and Turkish Cypriots clear. But he might have been wiser not to accept the role as Press Advisor to the British Governor. He's there to polish the communications of policies which he has no say in shaping.

WE DRIVE NORTH through the Green Line at the Ledra Palace hotel crossing by the walls and dry moat of Venetian Lefkosia. It's a journey I make several times a week to see my Turkish Cypriot colleagues in the British Council office there. I'm known to both Greek and Turkish Cypriot Green Line soldiers, and they wave us through without checking our documents. We're heading directly east out of Lefkosia under Turkish control towards Salamis, Famagusta and Varosha thirty miles distant on the east coast of Cyprus.

We find much of the site of Salamis, principal city of ancient Cyprus, forested with pine and eucalyptus. We wander through a ghostly mix of Roman, marble columns and statues decimated later by Christians. We drive down the coast to Famagusta where Shakespeare set *Othello* based on the Governor of Cyprus, the Moor. Like Salamis but later, Famagusta had its share over centuries of occupiers, owners, builders and destroyers. It became one of the richest cities in Christendom with scores of churches testifying to its wealth.

In the dying decades of the Ottoman Empire, Cyprus was sold to Britain in 1878 as a protectorate. When Cyprus won its limited independence in 1960, it was only fourteen years before the Turks re-occupied Famagusta. In that short period, the suburb of Varosha was developed by the British as a glamourous Mediterranean destination. In 1974, Turkish tanks roll across the central, dusty plains of Cyprus to Famagusta, which they also bomb. As they occupy the city, it completely empties of Greek Cypriots who flee south. Dozens die alongside holiday makers already grilled in the August sun.

The Turks fence off Varosha and when we visit in 2007 it's a ghost town not under control of the UN Peace Keeping Force but the Turkish military. We walk alongside the rusting chain-link fence peering through to abandoned, decaying hotels, jewellers and restaurants; weeds and bushes push through pavement slabs and cracked tarmac; trees grow through houses and shops. High-rise apartment blocks crumble, their windows blown out, their balconies hang slack-jawed. There are guard towers and helicopters circling overhead. A dystopian cityscape still in limbo after the looting Turkish soldiers had taken everything portable.

We walk the impressive mediaeval citadel in Famagusta, including Othello's tower, renamed to attract visitors, with its winged lion of St Mark, symbol of Venice, prominent over a doorway. The cathedral of St Nicholas, constructed in the fifteenth century, was, following the Ottoman conquest, converted into a mosque. It's still recognisable as a Gothic cathedral with twin towers and three huge doors. To one side is a minaret which climbs higher than the original Christian construction. Its green roof, a thumb in the lemon sky, is raised in the jubilation of victory. We sit at a plastic table under an umbrella and drink Turkish Efes beer. Famagusta has clearly seen much better days but, unlike Varosha, it's open for business.

On our return drive west to Lefkosia through the dustbowl plain, we're puzzled passing what look like enormous aeroplane hangars. We learn that they are, in effect, huge brothels with girls brought in from Bulgaria, Romania and Moldova to service the huge, under-occupied, army of Turkish troops with nothing to do other than be present as a deterrent.

WITH A POPULATION of barely more than a million, it makes no sense to have two offices operating on either side of the Green Line resulting in considerable duplication and inefficiency. It means there's limited knowledge and interaction between separate Greek and Turkish Cypriot colleagues. The British Council – dedicated to international understanding and partnerships – has allowed itself to mirror the distorted world of a divided Cyprus. How could we expect others to co-operate across the Green Line if we couldn't?

I decide we need to change the attitudes and behaviours of our Greek and Turkish Cypriot colleagues. We run a number of workshops exploring how they as individuals and as two different groups viewed 'the other'. I have young colleagues in my office in tears because they're going to have to work, manage or be managed by someone from 'the other side'. Most weren't born when the Turks invaded in 1974. The emotions they show have been transferred to them by their parents or grandparents who've told them stories of bombing, shooting, looting, rape and murder. I'm asking them to work with 'the enemy'. It feels like an enemy they've adopted out of deference to their elders.

The few Turkish Cypriot colleagues born before 1974 were children when Turkey invaded and bear no responsibility for whatever actions Turkish or Turkish Cypriot adults had taken in the short war which divided the island. The most mature member of staff, a Greek Cypriot who had been an adult in 1974 and directly involved in the fighting, tells me he'll resign rather than work alongside Turkish Cypriots. I ask him to take time to reflect on his position.

He requests to see me a few days later and comes into my office looking down at the floor. He doesn't want to look me in the face. From his demeanour, I already know the substance of what he's going to say. He sits down, still not looking at me.

'I'm sorry,' he says. 'Sorry, I can't do it.' He looks up at me. His eyes are glistening. He slowly shakes his head. But remains silent. I wonder what awful scenes he might be remembering. I can't know. I leave him alone for as long as he needs. After what feels a long time, he finally nods slowly and whispers in the croaking voice of a heavy smoker, 'Thank you.' He passes his stained orange hand over his face, stands, stares and leaves.

I USE A touch of reverse psychology when Lauren's showing some resistance to the idea of moving to Athens. 'There's always Tokyo,' I say. 'They'd like me to put my name forward for that too.' (It's true, the CEO has called and asked me to apply.)

'If you go to Tokyo, you go on your own.'

Which I have no intention of doing but it lessens the impact of a potential move to Athens. I persuade her to come with me on a work trip. She isn't happy with the notion of living in an apartment after the lovely lemon-treed house in Lefkosia.

But there's a Steinway in the main entertaining room, and from our private living space a magnificent view of the Acropolis with, ten metres from our balcony, a wild hillside where tortoises shuffle between the boulders. I can walk to the office in ten minutes.

She's sold. The Steinway isn't just a piece of furniture. Lauren's first instrument was the clarinet, which she played in the Middlesex County Youth Orchestra, but she's competent on the piano and often plays her childhood keyboard, which we've brought to Cyprus after its adventures in India and Sao Paulo.

The Steinway is going to come in handy.

RICHARD WALKER

IN 2004, WE drive back to Athens from the Peloponnese, where we'd been on holiday and looking for somewhere to buy a house. This is before the motorway from Athens to Kalamata reduced a tortuous journey on hairpin mountain roads from seven to four hours. Whenever I drive over the Corinth canal and swing south with the massed rock of Acro Corinth on the right, my heart races. The rock towers sheer at two thousand feet with ancient Corinth in its shadow on the coastal plain.

Crossing over the Corinth canal is where you transition from the civilised to the wilder and more profound. The mountain peaks of the Argolid, the first region in the Peloponnese, recede into the distance. They guard some of the most important ancient sites in Greece: Mycenae, Epidaurus and Olympia. Their teeth at the mouth of the Peloponnese never fail to inspire excitement and wonder in me.

It's our fourth trip with the same mix of exploration and relaxation. This time we think we'll strike lucky though it isn't a great start. We fly into Athens from London on a cold February afternoon. We're driving over the mountain roads into the dusk, then dark, high winds and whiplash rain in the cheapest tin can available. We're desperate to make our destination before the tavernas close and, out of season, we lose the chance of something to eat.

It's a seven-hour drive to Pylos on the far southwest coast of Messenia. We can see little of the town and its surrounds when we arrive after nine at night. We find our hotel in an attractive neo-classical building in the town centre and at once ask about food. 'Down the hill on the left. By the harbour. Maybe he's still open.' I'm not optimistic but keep quiet. After thirty seconds in front of the mirror, Lauren's her customary, cheerful self. 'Great! I'm really looking forward to some wind and souvlaki!' We set off down the hill in the rain and wind. Lauren's wearing open toed sandals. I point at them and, in a futile gesture, throw up my hands. 'I thought we were coming to sunny Greece!' she shouts laughing.

I can't believe our luck. Our table is in prime position by a vast open hearth constructed to chest height. Other tables are still occupied with customers finishing their food or nursing an *elliniko* – Greek coffee – or an ouzo. It doesn't take long to figure out why our table is unoccupied. It gets the full blast of the fire. But we're happy to be safe and warm with the prospect of food. We take off our coats, pretending it's the summer that Lauren's sandals suggest.

As the waiter prepares the table with a paper cloth over the cotton one laying up glasses, water and a basket of bread with cutlery inside, I ask him to bring *'ena miso kilo krasi, kokkino, parakalo,'* a half-litre of house red, please – which will come in a carafe drawn from a barrel in the bowels of the taverna. We look at the menu, which is several pages long, knowing they won't have half the things listed on it. You can spend an age poring over its endless possibilities and concocting an elaborate variety of complementary dishes to find that many of them are seasonal and not available. After topping up Lauren's small tumbler of wine, I finish mine and pour myself a second. 'I'm just going to ask him what's good. Something hearty and warming.' As if to punctuate my decision, a gust of wind throws the rain against the windows in a rat-a-tat-tat. She nods, 'Proper glasses,' she says, grasping her tumbler made of thick glass – a few tavernas have started to use more standard wine glasses with stems, trying to impress foreign visitors or Athenians.

The waiter returns. 'What's good?' I ask.

'Everything is good,' he says smiling.

I try again. 'I mean what's really good. Special here. What do you recommend?'

He trawls through the usual list: *horiatiki* – Greek salad, salty feta, black olives exploding the tang of home-grown tomatoes; *fasolakia* – green beans simmered slowly with tomatoes served warm not hot; *tsatsiki* – creamy yoghourt with cucumber sharpened with garlic and lemon juice; *gemista* – tomatoes and peppers stuffed with herb rice and slowly baked in olive oil; *skordalia* – cold, mashed potato bursting with lashings of crushed garlic; *fava* – cooked broad beans like hummus; *briam* –aubergine, tomato, potato, onion, okra drowning in their own juices and oil; *horta* – wild steamed greens like spinach, hot or cold, with oil and lemon.

It's curious that you don't get powerful aromas with most Greek cooking. It's all in the flavours of the fresh produce. The cooking uses herbs and spices but is not so pungent as its neighbour Turkey, where 'the East' in culinary terms kicks off.

'*Souvlaki*?' asks Lauren.

He shakes his head, indicating not tonight.

'Meat?' I asked tentatively, Oliver Twist-style though I haven't yet had anything at all.

Kotopoulo me lemoni – lemon chicken; *horino me selino* – pork with celery.

'The lemon chicken with roast potatoes for me, please,' says Lauren.

'Anything else?' I ask. A dog begging for a bone.

'*Ena lepta*,' one moment.

He disappears into the kitchen and returns quickly. 'We still have *stifado*. Very good,' he grins.

'Great! I'll have that please.'

I pour more wine. An hour ago, we were sitting in the tin can with rain hammering on the roof, praying we reached our destination. Now we're by a roaring fire, with red wine and food being prepared. All's right with the world again. It's something we love – still do – about Greece's ability to surprise and delight in the simplest, most profound things.

My *stifado* looks like taking things from good to great. Those who only visit Greece in the summer when it's too hot to eat casseroles and stews haven't experienced another side to Greek cooking quite different to its salads, vegetables, seafood and fish, however delicious. *Stifado*, or stew, is more commonly served today using beef. To my delight, this *stifado* has been prepared with its original main ingredient, *kouneli* or rabbit. A Greek rural dish with tomatoes, shallots, garlic, red wine, olive oil as essential, and any combination of spices like cumin, coriander and cinnamon available. If simmered, for about three hours, it can be stunning – it's the tomatoes locally grown in the taverna's or a relative's garden which add the rich depth to this and other Greek stews. This one is just that, its flavours magnified after our tortuous journey and the miserable gale. Lauren feels the same about her chicken, lemon and roast potatoes. Another half-litre of red and the heat from the fire move us closer to bliss. This feeling is capped when the owner insists on our drinking a *tsipouro*, a clear white spirit, on the house.

Tsipouro is similar to white spirit drunk across the Balkans, and some Mediterranean countries like Italy where it's called *grappa*. It was initially a by-product of fermenting wine from dark grapes. In Greece, this is thought to have been developed by the monks of Mount Athos, where no women are allowed. In Cyprus it's called *zivania,* Bulgaria *rakiva*, Turkey and Crete *raki*, and Lebanon a*rak*.

Holding on to these minor differences is a way of saying 'ours' not 'yours' and sometimes leads to challenging questions of identity and nationalism. Take the decades-long dispute, settled for the moment, over the name for the territory north of Greece: since 2019 called the Republic of North Macedonia. Many Greeks are unhappy about it. After all, they have a region called Macedonia pure and simple. Think of the Republic of Ireland and Northern Ireland. Not pure and not simple.

All this is a long way away from that wet and windy February night, which for a while has become a Greek winter paradise by the fire with a *digestif.* It's no surprise we sleep soundly.

WHAT AMAZES US the next morning is primrose sunshine and a warm day. The shutters open to reveal the harbour at Pylos below and, stretching into the distance, the Bay of Navarino. Pylos and the Bay have a distinguished ancient and modern history, but right now we're enchanted by the harbour scene, an islet in the bay, and a stroke of yellow sand on the far side of the glinting, mica waves.

It feels like were getting close to where we want to be. Long before we'd contemplated buying land or property in Greece, we'd spent holidays in pure, interested idleness wandering around and between the Greek islands. But why are we now considering buying a place, and why in the Peloponnese?

I'm approaching fifty years old, and my British Council career is going really well. I'm in a new role as the first Regional Director for all our work in East Asia. We've returned from Brazil to our house in Haslemere where West Sussex, Surrey and Hampshire meet. I'll be based in London for five years, albeit travelling several months a year for at least two weeks to East Asia from Japan and Korea in the north through China, sixteen countries finishing in the south of the region with Australia and New Zealand. I'm professionally content, not to say busy.

Lauren is happy to be back in England teaching at the local sixth-form college. Rowan's finishing Modern Languages and European Studies at Bath University; Will's boarding at Charterhouse, just down the road, finishing his GCSEs until he leaves for Godalming Sixth-Form College. They're developing through the cycles of teenage years and early adulthood.

But what's my next personal challenge? I suggest to Lauren I'd like to learn to ride a motorbike.

'You're not serious!'

'Mmm, perhaps.'

'Do you remember your other idea?'

'Which other idea?' I say, looking in the classified ads for a bike.

'Buying somewhere in Greece,' she says.

'Oh, the olive farm.'

'Sort of. Not exactly, but . . . ,' she trails off.

I put down my coffee and look at her for the first time in the conversation. 'Really? I thought you weren't interested.'

'I don't want to be an olive farmer, but perhaps somewhere by the sea might be fun.'

It's true that at one point, I'd sent her links to sprawling half-abandoned olive farms in the hills, miles from anywhere with derelict dwellings and collapsing sheds.

'But you can't do the motorbike thing too.' She's serious. She doesn't want me to ride one. She's right. Not only is the chance of death high with a bike, she knows how frustrated I get with machines. If something electrical or mechanical doesn't work instantly, even if I've wrongly assembled it, a red mist descends on me. Fucking useless!!

When we start to rediscover and explore Greece further on our return from Brazil, we head to the areas we know: the Cyclades and the Dodecanese. We have a vague notion that one day we might buy something, somewhere. How we discover what we want is an organic process nurtured out of sight until it becomes visible to us both. On one of these early trips to Lipsi, a tiny island north of Patmos, someone ask if we'd ever visited the Peloponnese. We can barely say it correctly, let alone spell it. We log the suggestion, and the following year make our first visit to the east coast of the Peloponnese.

This time in Pylos, in the far southwest of the peninsula, is the first night and day of our fourth trip, and we've decided – without discussing it – that something will happen this time. As possible candidates, we've targeted the Messenian towns of Pylos, Methoni and Koroni, all south and west of Kalamata. We think that if you like a place in February, it has something beyond its obvious summer attractions.

'Modern', that is neoclassical Pylos is attractively set in a bowl of hills with a hairpin road looping down to the harbourside. It was laid out by the French in the early nineteenth century. Fishing and pleasure boats shove and jostle alongside the *plateia* (πλατεια) or square. The handsome town faces westwards over the Ionian Sea towards Italy. Elegant neo-classical buildings stand to attention, one housing the birthplace of a local athlete who won four medals in the recreation of the modern Olympic Games.

The capacious main square of Pylos is flanked by arcades: grocer's, a wine shop, a butcher's, baker's, cafés and restaurants. It's home to some magnificent sycamore trees under which you could while away an hour over coffee or more for lunch.

'Let's walk up there,' says Lauren pointing to a side street that leads off the neo-classical shopping arcade. I guess what she's looking for. The square with its cafes and one-way traffic around it is bustling, the traffic in a slow queue even in February. She's after somewhere quiet but in easy reach of this πλατεια.

The name of the square is *Trion Navarkon* (Τριον Ναωαρχον) or Three Admirals, who were British, French and Russian. In 1827 their governments had instructed them to work together to blockade the Ottoman navy occupying Pylos. Their defeat of the Ottoman navy is a key event in the liberation of Greece from Ottoman rule and is commemorated by a monument in the square.

We walk to the crowns of two hills; the views over the rooftops to the harbour and bays beyond are charming. The neo-classical buildings lend an air of solidity and prosperity. There are orange trees on the pavements, but few houses have even a small garden. Everywhere we walk there are cars passing and we can still hear the traffic humming in the square. Lauren doesn't need to say anything.

We climb into the car and drive round Navarino Bay a few kilometres north of Pylos to one of the most important nature reserves in southern Greece. The Gialova lagoon is home to more than two hundred and fifty species of birds, many of them protected and on a migration route to and from Africa. It's the first place they stop having flown over the Mediterranean or the last before flying south 'back home.' Some overwinter there. We plan to stop only a short while. We stay longer fascinated by a small group of flamingos with their unique mix of stillness and elegance, their graceful necks and heads, then those sudden jerky movements on long, painfully thin legs, skeletal fashion models of the avian world.

On that February day of our search, we're astounded by Voudouklia (Ωοιδοκλια), one of Greece's most photographed bays with a perfect horseshoe of white sand. The Greek letter Ω. It's a picture you might draw if you imagined a child's fantasy bay.

WE HEAD BACK towards Pylos, passing by Nestor's Palace, where in the 1950s hundreds of tablets were found which showed a version of Greek, Linear B, six hundred years older than scholars had previously discovered. We resist it for now. A dozen clusters of men are having their morning coffees and ouzos as we drive around the square and head out of Pylos. The road rises towards and swings past a sixteenth century *neo kastro*, new castle. I slow down, and Lauren sees me looking at the side road towards the castle.

'Not today,' she says firmly. 'We have work to do. And I'll want some lunch soon.'

I'm about to say that getting to know a place *is* part of 'our work,' but think better of it. 'I like Pylos,' I say as we drive out of the town, on our right a set of stone arches, an impressive stretch of Ottoman aqueduct which once supplied the castle's water.

'Me too,' she says. I knew she was thinking something that she didn't say.

Methoni approached by road from the north is not enticing. It's flat, flat, flat. It's deserted and in hibernation as we drive through the customary Greek mix of low-rise apartment blocks, mostly shut up. There's a scattering of handsome nineteenth-century neo-classical houses looking unoccupied and closed for the winter. Most shops and places to eat are closed. A solitary, crooked woman in black shuffles along the pavement. We park next to the main square by the sea.

As we turn around, we're stuck by the reason for Methoni's fame: its castle. The moat and body are constructed right up to the coastal cliffs, and to what is now the edge of the town. But there's a long extension into the sea ending in a prominent tower, it looks as if the tower's floating on the blue-grey, ruffled-silk sea.

We stroll up the track looking down into its dry moat, opposite the stone walls and battlements and cross the arched, stone bridge through its impressive gateway. We walk between the high walls of the Venetian-Ottoman fortification, which leads us through into a vast expanse of land – more than twenty acres – which had housed an entire town. Now it's dotted with the ruins of Ottoman baths and the foundations of other unknown buildings. Through some of the crevices in the walls, fig trees have pushed their way and are still growing, levering the huge stones apart in their unending quest for sunlight while the buildings disintegrate around them. The Venetian winged lion of St Mark is embedded in a huge block of granite at head height.

On the far side of the castle's ruined town, we peer down into the Ionian, dashing its waves against the rocks from which the walls rise perpendicular. The occasional spray is gusted up into our faces. We imagine waiting for a ship to come sailing south from the Republic of Venice tacking east round this tip of the Peloponnese with goods to trade in Egypt and the Holy Lands, tradesmen or pilgrims or crusaders, or all three. Methoni, with its sister town Koroni, *E matia tou Venetiou* (*Ι µατια τοο Ωενετιοο*), the Eyes of Venice, were crucial refuges and lookouts in the sea traffic between Venice and the near East.

Three hundred years later, we could have been in the same spot and watched a galley bruising the waves. Miguel Cervantes, an Ottoman galley slave and later the author of *Don Quixote*, might have been one of its oarsmen.

'Do you think they let him out to have a look round the town?' I ask.

'Look at that,' Lauren points towards a pile of fire burned stone and brick that might have been a fireplace. 'I bet the Ottomans gave them pizza after the Venetians had lost but left their ovens here.'

The mention of pizza reminds us we were hungry. Back in the modern town of Methoni we can't find anywhere open that we like. So we head back to the car. Without saying a word, we know we won't look further for a place here. Apart from the vast and impressive castle with its photogenic tower, the *Bourtzi*, on a rocky islet at the end of the causeway, Methoni doesn't create a good first impression on a windy February day. But like many first impressions, it's only that. It's a rare year when we don't go back and slowly uncover what it has to offer with patience and enjoyment.

IT'S HARD NOT to like Διονισιος Σιπσας, Dionisios Sipsas. He has a smile that rises from his heart, and the lamp in his eyes is always lit; he's tall and good-looking with an easy, languid manner. He drives a mammoth 4 x 4 on metalled and unmetalled roads at the same high speed with the accelerator flat to the floor, its tyres scrunching, dust and chips of stone flying everywhere. After the first ride, Lauren refuses to go in the front seat, but from the back cranes her head forward: 'Dionisios, if you don't slow down, we won't look at anything more with you.'

He laughs, 'Lauren. Trust me.' And continues driving with his foot to the floor.

That phrase, 'Trust me,' becomes his. A mantra he uses only when he judges we're genuinely concerned or anxious about something. We'd emailed him from England, and he's expecting to show us some land and properties in the town and area of Koroni. By the time we arrive at his house on the edge of the town, it's late afternoon; the temperature has dropped, the sky's grey, and it's going to rain. He offers us, free, an apartment adjacent to his own house.

'We will look in the morning,' he says. 'Now or later, you go and see Koroni. I think the best place for you to eat is Bogris. See you tomorrow.'

Despite the threat of rain, we'd spent enough time in the car and walk into town. The topography of Koroni is an arrowhead where all roads converge and narrow down to the Venetian castle at the apex. Most of the town – its housing, squares, shops, tavernas, churches, the secondary school – slopes down to the harbour on the east side. On the other side, the land falls away facing south with a sprinkling of houses in larger plots, orchards and green spaces fronting a two-kilometre long, sandy beach.

The numerous paths on the east side wind down to the quayside and the two main streets. They're all steep, some precipitous, mainly cobbled, and a maze that sometimes confronts you with a pile of tumbled stones and no route through. Elsewhere, you pass immaculately plastered, white-painted neo-classical houses with black wrought iron balconies and courtyard gardens with orange trees. Mopeds and small motorbikes are commonly used for shopping or transport.

We know none of this when we set out and get enjoyably lost while heading down to the harbourside. It's dusk when we reach a main street running parallel to the harbour. There's still some bustle with the bakers, a fish shop, a small supermarket, the chemist, the banks, the wine and hardware shops, people of all ages going about their business.

On the front street by the harbour, we find most of the tavernas, bars, restaurants, ice cream shops and other places for food and drink, from the humblest *ouzeri* with blue metal tables and wooden chairs to the swanky bar with cool stools and high tables. Some cafés and tavernas are open, and the waves are splashing against the harbourside, threatening to soak the outdoor chairs and sofas. A colourful assortment of fishing boats is tugging firmly on ropes and chains. Cocoons of fishing nets are piled on deck or quayside.

On one corner stands an exquisite two-storey Venetian

building with stone arches. It's shut up and in need of restoration. Its flaking plaster, with patches of seaweed green, is being swallowed and digested by salt and wind.

It's too fresh to sit outside, so we opt to go inside the *kafenio*. Unwittingly, we've entered the heart of rural and small-town Greece. It's loud, and we can barely hear the young waiter behind the bar gesturing us to enter. A horseshoe of men clustered round a suspended television are shouting at a Greek football match; one group's playing cards with onlookers shouting advice, groaning when it isn't taken, and the hand's lost; others talk politics gesticulating to make a point. Two are playing backgammon with spectators urging them on while they smack down the wooden pieces as loudly as they can. One man in a corner reads a newspaper, oblivious to the cacophony.

The waiter's shouting out orders for coffee, ouzo and beer, or serving small plates of *piklia*, literally 'a variety' of snacks: black olives, cucumber, tomato, feta, anchovies, cuts of roast chicken or pork dripping fat, and hunks of snowy bread.

Overseeing everything whilst he pours drinks, prepares coffee and food is the owner. No one apart from the waiter says anything to us, but it's clear we're the only people in the *kafenio* who don't know everyone else. A couple of older men acknowledge us with a slight tilt forward of their heads in our direction. It's a matter of courtesy and curiosity. What are we doing in Koroni? Why are we in the *kafenion*, café, in February? The waiter takes our order, for Lauren *ena tetarto lefko*, a quarter carafe of house white, and for me *mia birra*, Mythos, a beer.

Two things strike us by their absence and presence: women and smoke. The *kafenion* is traditionally a male preserve for coming together over anything from football to politics, to the size of Yiannis's catch that morning, to the parcel of land for sale over the hill. When there are Greek and foreign tourists in the summer, a woman will occasionally be seen, though she's likely to be younger.

We're instantly engulfed in a fug of tobacco, coffee and fried food. The smoke has wreathed itself every cranny of the room and its furnishings. The high ceiling is a deep mahogany. The extractor fans are wheezing with the fumes from gas hobs frying food and no capacity left for tobacco smoke.

WE PAY OUR *λογαρισμο*, our 'logarithm' or bill, then exit from the fug and taking a deep breath head, as suggested by Dionisios, to the restaurant, Bogris.

In warmer months its courtyard garden, planted with mulberry trees, offers a canopy of piebald shade. The mulberry tree is common throughout the Peloponnese as the staple food of the silkworm. The Peloponnese was a major producer of silk in the eighteenth and nineteenth centuries. The Greek word for mulberry is '*μουρια*' or '*mourea*', and the medieval term for the region now called the Peloponnese is The Morea. The industry and the silkworms have disappeared, but the white mulberry trees remain with their glossy, dark ivy leaves deflecting the sun or rain.

What's become a dark and chilly February night means the courtyard isn't in use. It's a traditional family restaurant that takes great pride in fresh, home-prepared food. The mother is visible in the open kitchen doing the cooking, the son waits on the tables with enthusiasm and energy while the father oversees operations. As the son is laying up our table, he gestures towards the kitchen fronted by a glass cabinet with eight or ten dishes already prepared and reels them off including: *brizola sto fourno*, pork chops with roast potatoes cooked in the oven; *stapodi stifado*, octopus stew; *moussaka*, moussaka; *psaria me saltsa ndomates*, fish baked with fresh tomato sauce; *gigantes*, giant white beans cooked in fresh tomato sauce; *kolokithakia*, fried courgette or zucchini. There's an open fire and with a half-litre of *kokkino*, red wine, we're soon content.

IN HIS SILVER whale, a pick-up truck marked with his name and business details, Dionisios had gone into real estate and property development two years earlier. He shows us three houses he'd built, the quality of the construction and workmanship seem good, but they're in places where you'd always need to be in a car. He takes us to another half-completed house whose purchaser has gone bust. He can finish that one for us. It's in an attractive location on a hillside overlooking a bay, but it's a steep walk down to the deserted beach and back, and you'd still need a car to get any provisions.

He changes tack, and we career ten kilometres inland from Koroni up into the hills on dirt tracks through clouds of dust. The views south-east over Koroni and across the bay of Kalamata to the Mani, the central digit of the Peloponnese, are spectacular. We're in olive tree territory.

'Here,' says Dionisios.

'Here what?' says Lauren.

'Here. This is where I build your house for you.' He smiles expectantly, holding out his arms, showing the estate as if we're already the lord and lady of its acres.

'Great views,' I say. A part of me is attracted by the idea of a house surrounded by olive groves. There's something eternal about olive trees that appeals to my sense of continuity. As Keats' 'Ode on a Grecian Urn' has it:

Happy, happy boughs! that cannot shed
Your leaves, nor ever bid the Spring adieu.

I already know Dionisios is living on borrowed time with this suggestion.

'Too far from the sea, too far from the town, too far from anywhere or anything,' says Lauren. For an instant, I think she might have upset Dionisios.

'There are other places.' He smiles.

The next place we see is slap bang in the centre of the old Koroni with its tumbling streets and cobbled pathways. It sports vivid pink, red and white geraniums in recycled olive-oil cans;

waist-high ceramic pots are painted in primary yellows, aquamarines and crimsons; twisted gourds are decorated with fantastical dolphins and sea creatures. Up the narrow lane behind the house is one of the gateways to the Venetian fort whose battlements look down on that east-facing side of the town.

The exterior plaster on this ramshackle house has been lovingly whitewashed every Easter for at least two centuries. There are no straight walls or floors. The ground floor must be the original flags, not one the same size as any other, all sloping at different angles. The beams and upstairs floorboards are an equally eclectic lot of timber, some as thick as a fisherman's biceps, others as wide as his shoulders, perhaps hauled up through the lanes from a shipwrecked vessel.

At the front of the house, from the small windows with sills deep as a sailor's chest, there are spectacular angles and views over the lanes below; a succession of brick red, clay-tiled rooves cascading down the hill, a Cubist painting made in three dimensions. The eye is drawn down to the harbour by the new jetty, jutting out into the sea for a hundred metres, at a crooked angle to the harbour wall and piled up with gigantic slabs and slices of rock, conglomerates two and a half million years old. It's a February afternoon and the sun has disappeared behind the house over the shoulder of the castle behind.

'You want in the town. You have in the town. Everything is here, the supermarket, the restaurants, all the shops,' says Dionisios enthusiastically.

I nod slowly. I know what Lauren's thinking. Too dark, especially in the back of the house; even in summer, the sun disappears early. The beach below, five minutes' walk down the steep hillside, is rocky and pebbly. It isn't clear how clean it might be adjacent to the harbour and houses with their nineteenth-century plumbing. It's charming with the rolling dice of houses tumbling down the hill, wrought-iron balconies with views across the bay of Kalamata to the coastline of the outer Mani. Lemon, orange and fig trees grow through collapsing dwellings. We're by the doorstep straight onto a lane. Cars can't pass but one's parked tightly in a tiny space on the cliff edge.

A moped chugs its way up the steep cobbles with provisions in its metal basket. The driver brings it to a halt where we were standing, its engine, bronchial lungs, still wheezing. A weather-beaten face pokes out from under a battered cap and arthritic hands clutch the throttle and brakes. The driver greets Dionisios so they exchange the stock courtesies.

'*Yassou Michalis. Ti kanete?*' Hello Michael. How are you?

'*Kala eimay. Esi.*' I'm good. You?

'*Kala, poli kala. Ta leme sintoma.* Good, very good. See you later,' says Dionisios, bringing the ritual conversation to a close. Then before we can say anything he says. 'Let us go and take a coffee.'

The rhythm of his speech shunts me back to that great modernist poem, 'The Love Song of J Alfred Prufrock':

Let us go then, you and I,
When the evening is spread out against the sky
Like a patient etherized upon a table;

I learned it by rote more than fifty years ago, captivated by the melancholic monologue of its modern Hamlet, an impotent bystander watching the tsunami of the First World War crash onto the shores of Europe.

WE SIT OUTSIDE across the road from a restaurant owned by Dionisios. He tells us he inherited it from his father. His section of the quayside is distinguished from others by glass walls and partitions shielding us from the February breeze. Other cafés have hard plastic which chatters loudly when the wind blows.

The coffee is served: cappuccino for Lauren, espresso for Dionisios and Greek for me. He looks mainly at Lauren not at me.

'So, you don't like the townhouse either? I know. You don't need to tell me.' He angles his head very slightly to one side like a blackbird or thrush when he's concentrating. It's a characteristic gesture I'm beginning to recognise. 'You don't want to renovate this place we have just seen. You are right.' He smiles. 'You don't want to build in the hills. Or be away from Koroni in the car.' He shrugs.

'We thought we'd like to renovate something old near the town but not in the town,' I say.

He slowly shakes his head once. 'It doesn't exist. Or, if it exists, it's a goat shed or a boat store. You must knock it down and start again anyway.' He pauses, asking if he can light a cigarette. We allow him to draw on his tobacco while we watch the fishing boats nodding. He leans forward towards us with a slightly conspiratorial air.

'I have something special. I think you will like it. But not today. Tomorrow morning.'

'We need to see somewhere tomorrow,' I say. 'Or it'll be too late on this visit.'

Then: 'We'll pay for the coffees when we leave.'

He tut-tuts, meaning 'Already paid.'

He stands, I stand, and we shake hands. 'See you tomorrow morning. Trust me,' he says and is gone.

We look at each other wondering what Dionisios has up his sleeve. We'd googled and read. We'd spoken to Greeks and foreigners who knew areas we might not otherwise go to, and we'd visited most of the likely places over four years. The Mani pointing south on the eastern exit from Kalamata was the most obvious place.

We can see it now through the glass partition on the other side of the bay of Kalamata. The peaks of the magnificent Tageytos mountains including the highest peak in the Peloponnese are still covered in snow. Geographically-geologically it's a spectacular region with the mountain range running south, the tail of a lizard ending in a network of caves. The furthest point south is Cape Tenaro, where we'd stayed and seen the cave which is the entrance to Hades. This area, the deep or inner Mani, is beautiful in its brutality. Little grows in the patches of barren ground between rock and stone.

When I became the British Council Director in Greece, we mounted an exhibition of Islamic art at the Benaki Museum in Athens featuring the life and work of the seventeenth-century Turkish travel writer, Evliya Celebi. He visited the area and wrote: 'It is in truth an unpitied place. The inhabitants are dark-skinned, small in stature, with large heads, round eyes, with voices like sheepdogs, wirily built with large feet they leap from crag to crag like fleas.'

The Mani is best known for its settlements of stone tower houses each with its own mini fortification of battlements and ramparts. In many places, these abut each other so you can almost reach out and touch the next tower. But vendettas were rife and families in adjacent houses were enemies for decades with family members kidnapped, stabbed or shot. Many of these tower houses are now desolate, mirroring the bleakness of the landscape. As if the stone had decided to collapse and crumble and rejoin the scattered boulders flung across the hillsides. The Mani has always had a fierce sense of itself. Whether it was the Venetians, the Ottomans or the French who captured and controlled different regions of the Peloponnese, the Mani kept much of its independence. We'd been there exactly one year earlier and had walked through snow on the higher peaks.

The first Greek writer to win the Nobel prize, George Seferis, writes in 'Mycenae':

I've raised these stones as long as I was able
I've loved these stones as long as I was able
these stones, my fate.

KORONI, WHERE WE'RE sitting by the harbourside, is in Messenia, the region with the most westerly land mass in the Peloponnese that points southwards from Kalamata on the western side of the bay. It's infinitely more fertile and greener than the Mani. We applaud its bounty. We'd had our share of primitive bleakness with our stone cottage in Yorkshire. Later, we'd lived with some unforgiving, unyielding stone when we renovated a labyrinthine Elizabethan/Georgian pile on the lower slopes of Dartmoor. Somewhere in a corner of my heart, despite all my travels or maybe because of them, I'm still a soft landscape (Surrey woods/Sussex downs) boy.

Unspoken, this feels home. We've instinctively settled on Koroni and its landscape as the small town we'll enjoy visiting in all seasons. As we're finishing our coffees, there's a gale of shouting and laughter blowing along the main street. The secondary school or gymnasium, which sits in a low-rise yellow block at one end of the harbour, has finished for lunch, and its teenagers are spilling into the streets. It's confirmation that this town has a life of its own, and it'll continue its life regardless of the season and whatever we do or don't do.

Dionisios' last name, Sipsas, is, as we discover to our benefit, threaded through Koroni though it originates in the adjacent village of Vasilitsi. His father was a prominent jeweller in Koroni. He has two establishments on the waterfront. One, a trendy place where the local youth hang out fantasising they're in Athens or Mikonos. The other Flisvos, is the restaurant where he's brought us for coffee. Even on the back of a cursory stroll through the town, it looks the most upmarket restaurant on the quay. We eat there a couple of days later and the seafood is excellent. If ever there were one word which incorporates being a coastal Greek, it's *flisvos*. English needs 'Sound of the waves on the shore,' to capture it.

Just along from Flisvos is a mini-market. Above the door of the mini-market is the name of its owner, Constantine Sipsas. That family again!

THE NEXT MORNING the clouds have lifted, it's gloriously bright and, for February, warm. Dionisios has sent a message to meet him by the primary school at the top of the ridge. Opposite the school, there's a mini-market, someone's front room, with refrigerators outside for cold drinks and frozen items. Five metres to one side of the shop and its pyramids of crates is a stone tower, seven or eight metres high, a little less in diameter with window openings. It would've had a wooden roof except most of its timbers had, like its internal staircase, rotted away. On the ground a small fig tree, thirsty for light, is shoving its way through one of the windows. It commands an unsurpassed view of the harbour of Koroni and the entire arc of Kalamata Bay sweeping across to the Mani and the Tageytos mountain range. To the south, the Mediterranean is visible where vessels once sailed from Venice, Genoa and Sicily. To the east you might have spied Ottoman vessels sailing from Izmir, Bodrum or Alexandria. A couple of mopeds are propped against its wall. I stick my head inside and above, open sky glimmers, crisscrossed with rusting cogs and axles confirming it'd once been a windmill.

With a thunderous roar coming up the steep, narrow road the silver pick-up truck announces the arrival of Dionisios. He swerves the vehicle to one side of the road and stops. He uncoils himself from behind the wheel and holds out his hand.

'I hope you slept well. And are feeling strong?' Another smile flows out along with that characteristic momentary bird tilt of the head. 'We go down,' he says indicating a concrete path dropping round the corner of the school.

Turning the corner, we're hit by a spectacular view of the Mediterranean four hundred metres down the hill. On the headland to our left is a nineteenth-century sandstone church, Panayia Eleistra, facing down the coastline and fronted by a bell tower. Through the pine trees above it, we can see the battlements of the Venetian castle. The concrete path leads winding, sometimes steeply, down to the right. We're descending with the sea first in front then on our left and on our right a scattering of houses in large plots set back from the path and framed by bougainvillaea and olive trees. On our left the path falls steeply away with a huge open field sloping down to the sandy beach fringed with tamarisk trees, their wispy foliage fluttering in the breeze. In the flat area of the field, the orange trees dance in the sun with globes of fruit glowing in their branches. As we reach the foot of the hill, the path takes a sharp left down to the beach fifty metres away through a bamboo grove. We walk on for another twenty metres behind Dionisios, who stops where the path ends in a grove of olive trees and says, 'Here.'

It isn't clear where 'here' is, in amongst the olive trees. The ground at this point is still gently sloping down towards the beach. Fifty metres up the slope to our right is a sandstone cliff. Down the slope a little is a ramshackle house with a collapsed dwelling and storeroom to one side. Dionisios sees me squinting through the olive trees and vines at these structures. 'Baba Tassos,' he says quietly and puts his finger to his lips signalling us to be quiet. *Baba* is a Persian word referring to an older gentleman and can be loosely translated as 'father, grandfather, wise old man, respected sir.' It's used in Greek in all these senses.

Below where we're standing are extensive olive groves, then fields edging the beach. There are no more buildings for more than a kilometre. We walk back a little to where Dionisios had said 'Here.'

'You buy this land and build your house here. No one can build in front of you or to the side. This is the last place you can build a house in the town zone by the beach.'

We're stunned. We'd set out expecting to convert or restore somewhere. We hadn't considered building from scratch. But we've both fallen straight away for the location. We hear the waves on the shore and feel ourselves being dragged out to sea by the undertow of its caress on the shingle. We have to stop ourselves from drowning in its emotional pull.

'There's a lot to think about,' I say.

'I told you, you would like it,' Dionisios has already seen through us and knows how we're feeling. He knows we have to process, check and calibrate our emotions.

'Can we stay here for a while on our own?' I ask.

'Of course, take your time. I will see you later. At the restaurant about five o'clock.' He starts to walk away, and Lauren calls out, 'Dionisios!'

He stops and turns.

'Please don't show it to anyone before then.'

He smiles. 'Trust me, Lauren.'

We're left alone with early-season wildflowers under the olive trees and the gentle whoosh of shingle on the shore. The sun's out. It's so warm I have to take off my jacket. We hear the light drone of a bee. It's late February, we don't want to spoil the moment and sit enjoying the sun on our faces. Lauren eventually speaks.

'How will they build it? There's only that narrow path. And it's steep.'

'We'd need the house high enough so you can see over the olive trees and get the view of the castle and church.'

'And across the bay to the tip of the Mani.'

'How do we know no one can build in front of us or nearby?'

'What about getting stuff down here?'

'And Baba Tassos?'

Our questions wheel on and on. But we both know that barring some unsuspected obstacle, we're committed to the project if the price is manageable.

Were we seduced by its tranquillity, its romance and its beauty? Yes. But there's a foundation of reason too. Since we'd begun scouring Greece for somewhere to settle, we've winnowed to the essentials. We don't want to be in a car every five minutes going to a beach, doing the shopping, driving to eat and drink; we want peace and quiet but not isolation. We want a summer house including spring and autumn, for short or long breaks, but we don't plan to live there full time. That said, if we visit in winter, we want somewhere that still has a life. We prefer swimming in the sea to a pool. We'd like some history on the doorstep – not difficult in the Peloponnese. Other cultural stuff isn't essential.

Now Dionisios has brought us five minutes' walk down from

the edge of the town and seven minutes up. The town's small but large enough for all the things you might need for longish holidays. It's a working Greek town going about its business, profiting from Greek and foreign tourism but not hostage to it. Its residents are sufficiently accustomed to foreigners to know what they need or the kind of challenges they have, but they manage their lives and businesses without being overrun by them. It still has a pleasantly antique sense of reserve, courtesy and good manners. The presence of both primary and secondary schools is an indicator of a healthy community. There are two fishmongers, two bakers, an adequate minimarket, a chemist, a post office, two banks, a cobbler, hardware shops, four churches, an optician, a health centre, several tavernas, restaurants, bars with plentiful outdoor seating on the harbourside.

There are fishing boats, and an occasional yacht, but there's no trace of a marina. The battlements of the Venetian castle seen from our balcony will support the sun rising over the Mani, and, at night, thirty kilometres away we'll see pinpricks of lights winking from its settlements. The rose-pink or tangerine dawn will creep over the Venetian battlements, at night we'll see a fiery globe rise from the sea, the moon catching the last rays of the sun and growing paler as it rolls up into the dark blue, velvet sky. The fishing boats will chug round the headland from the harbour at dawn, daytime and dusk. We'll start with a few olive trees and plant the rest of the plot with lemons, oranges, pomegranates, bananas, bougainvillea, plumbago, oleanders, geraniums, hibiscus, the deepest damask fattest roses you've ever seen. We'll swim in the Med less than a minute's walk from our house. We'll be happy. No! Ecstatic! We stroll out from under the olive trees back onto the path. It's then that we have our first sighting of an elderly man we assume is Baba Tassos. He's in a small field with what looks like a Second World War flamethrower strapped to his back. He's spraying the low-rise vines with a liquid from the antiquated contraption, a snail shell, strapped on his shoulders. Bent over and concentrating on his work, he doesn't see us as we walk past. This seems to be perfect for our first 'meeting'. His vines are, quite rightly, more important than we are.

We head down to the beach to get another perspective. It's pale brass flecked by a few flashes of small shingle at the sea's edge. There are twenty metres or so between the tree line and the sea. Small hillocks of what look like black seaweed squat in coils, squid-ink tagliatelle, washed up in heavy seas during a storm.

As we head back up the hill, it's clear that Dionisios has saved all this, his trump card, until the last hand.

WE'VE JUST SAT down by the harbourside when Dionisios glides by in his silver whale. He stops in the middle of the road and leans out the window with a huge grin. 'You order what you like. I come in a minute,' and drives off. It's half an hour before he appears. Contrasting with the warm, sunny day, on the distant peaks of the Tageytos mountains there lies frozen, glistening snow. Lauren's taken one of her sketch pads from her canvas bag and is concentrating in a way that signals, 'please do not interrupt me unless the house is on fire.'

I amuse myself by going and standing at the edge of the harbour. In the clear water, I see shoals of fish swimming in that mysterious, unified formation, where one darts and the others follow, mirroring how birds wheel and swoop in the sky, one indivisible and harmonious movement. A long dark eel, foreboding, disappears in the shadow of a rock.

Two days later, from the same spot, we see a seal in the outer zone of the harbour. This is *Monachus monachus*, the Mediterranean monk seal, which, as its name suggests, is the only seal to live a solitary existence. With an estimated five hundred pairs globally, they are seriously endangered, more than half survive in the Med. I've never seen another.

Dionisios finally appears and joins us. Without waiting for us to speak, smiling, he says, 'So you like it,' a statement of fact, not a question.

Lauren holds out her sketchbook. 'Something like this,' she

says. It's her artist's impression of what the house might look like. Before either of us has a chance to say anything, she turns over another page with a crude floor plan, not to scale. 'And this might be helpful,' she adds.

Even the measured, unflappable Dionisios is surprised but delighted. 'Good, I take these', he says, pointing at Lauren's sketchbook.

Lauren shakes her head, 'You don't need this one,' she points at her artist's impression. 'I'll draw another copy of the plan for you.'

Dionisios nods, impressed. 'You have some questions?' he asks us both.

'What about the land?' I ask. 'Who's the seller? How much does he want?'

Dionisios smiles. 'Baba Tassos.' The bent figure we'd seen in the field with the snail shell strapped to his back. 'You will have to meet him before he agrees to sell. It will not be a problem.'

'And the cost?' I repeat.

Dionisios gives us a figure which doesn't seem unreasonable, though I've prepared to wince and be surprised whatever he says. To do my bit of haggling.

'The cost is fixed. There is no negotiation. I know you think everything in Greece you can bargain. But not this,' he smiles. 'It's a fair price. Trust me.'

We all pause for a moment and neither challenge nor accept the price before he adds, 'When you meet Baba Tassos, it is not about the price. It is about you. You agree the price with me and then he will meet you.'

I nod. Lauren asks, 'How will you build it?'

'We bring everything along the beach. We need permission from the *Dimarcheio*.'

'The Town Hall?' I confirm.

'And from the owner of the land in front, by the beach.'

'How long will it take?'

'We start all the things for the legal agreement this week. You see the lawyer; you see the accountant. You go to the bank. I start to get the permissions. Organise everything. Then we wait for the end of the summer. September probably. We need to wait for the turtles. Then we start. Your house is ready next year. Spring.'

'Turtles?'

'We cannot bring anything on the beach with the turtles. They finish September.'

It sounds now a highly ambitious programme, to bring all the materials to build the foundations and a four-bedroomed, two-bathroom house pretty much by hand, as nearly everything will need to be brought along the beach. The nearest metalled road stops abruptly by the only taverna three hundred metres away. And then they'll still need to bring everything up the sloping field a hundred metres inland to the plot we hope to buy. It's a tight schedule. But Dionisios' confidence takes root and grows in us.

'What about the price for the house?'

'I tell you tomorrow. Latest day after,' he replies. 'I see you in my office tomorrow morning. And then we see Baba Tassos after.'

It's the first we've heard that Dionisios has an office. 'Opposite the church. The main square. See you tomorrow at ten,' he pauses then laughs. 'I will be on time.'

He sees me getting out my wallet, determined this time to pay for our coffee. 'You don't pay for the coffee, but you give the waiter a small tip if you like.'

We spend the rest of the evening mulling over what we've heard. The price of the land doesn't seem unreasonable given its location: walking distance from the town, not isolated but with a small scattering of dwellings in large plots mostly hidden by bushes and trees. It wouldn't suit everyone that they couldn't drive to the house. For us, it'd be part of its peaceful charm, encouraging us to buy only essentials.

THE NEXT MORNING, opposite *Eglesia Ayios Georgios*, St George Church, at the foot of a steep hill, we find Dionisios in what looks like a Venetian-built, ground floor office. He pulls out enlarged photocopies of a plan of the plot. The approximate area is nine hundred square metres, about a quarter of an acre, more than enough for one house with large plots surrounding it and open fields down to the sea. There are some rough pencil sketches on one copy. He points to an area well to one side from the centre of the plot where I suppose any house will be constructed.

'Here is where you build your house,' he says.

'But it's not in the centre of the plot. That would make more sense,' I say firmly.

Dionisios raises his chin a little followed by his eyeballs as if being told by a doctor to look at the ceiling then he brings them down to meet mine. 'If you build here to one side, later you can build another, smaller house for your children or other people.'

'We only want to build one house. We don't need two houses,' I reply.

He smiles and shrugs. 'Maybe now you don't. Maybe in the future. Or maybe someone wants to buy your house and build another one. You don't know the future, yes?'

It's my turn to shrug.

There's a lot to do in only two days. Open a bank account at the National Bank of Greece opposite the church. Set up an appointment with the accountant, Pantelis Kritikakis. And be distracted by the view of the harbour, boats, Kalamata Bay and the Mani from his office window – the best office of any accountant I've ever met. Go and see the lawyer, Maria Baggelinou-Gialleli, opposite Rachel the baker, then the only place to buy brown bread in Koroni. In the end, we need three meetings with Maria, one with a translator for legal reasons, although she speaks good English. But first, we need to meet Baba Tassos.

He's wearing what might have been a pinstripe but is now a very faded, grey jacket. He'd nicked himself in two places shaving, though his small white moustache still makes him look dapper. He's wiry with the gnarled hands and weather-beaten face of someone who spends most of his time outside by the sea. Later we find out that he'd owned all the land around – including where a Swiss architect had built his house nearby. He'd sold it off slowly, a plot here and there, every decade or so. It was peaceful still, but it must once have been solitary, at least after his wife died. He's been on his own for two decades.

His house is on the left on the way to the plot he's selling. If it goes ahead, he'll be our neighbour. His home has seen better days and needs re-plastering and painting, but it's screened by orange and lemon trees. There are enamel bowls on the concrete outside where he feeds cats and their kittens. It's never clear whether the cats originally belonged to Baba Tassos or they've attached themselves to him because he puts out food. Further along stands the tool shed and a smaller house, unfinished internally. They are largely invisible from what we hope will be our plot, hidden by a mix of olive trees, vines and bougainvillaea.

This first meeting with Baba Tassos is a little stilted but not difficult. We stand in a rough circle among the olive trees and shake hands in turn. After each handshake, he puts his hand to his heart. He has glinting grey-green eyes. Dionisios does most of the talking and translating explaining who we are and that we we're ready to offer the price that's been asked.

'He wants to know if you are going to plant anything,' says Dionisios.

'Flowers, λουλουδια', says Lauren. *Louloudia* is one of her favourite Greek words.

'Some trees,' I add. 'Orange, lemon, pomegranate. Like Baba Tassos has.'

'He wants to know if you are keeping the olive trees,' says Dionisios.

Lauren replies, 'Of course! We love the olive trees!'

It's evidently the right answer. Once this is translated back to Baba Tassos he smiles and relaxes.

Dionisios explains Baba Tassos is entitled to claim some euros for each tree he owns, though I suspect there's sentiment too at work – he'd planted the trees with his father. Though we're hoping to buy the plot that's his, he'll continue claiming his subsidy for the dozen trees, and who are we to disabuse a bureaucrat in the Ministry of Agriculture?

'He wants to know why you want to come here,' says Dionisios.

Lauren and I look at each other, agreeing with our eyes she should answer first. 'It's beautiful. It's peaceful, the olive trees, the sea, the church, the castle.'

I add, 'We've visited many places in Greece and have lived all over the world, Brazil, Thailand, India. Nowhere is better.'

Baba Tassos listens to the translation carefully. He stands a little straighter and holds up his hands at head height, turned inwards with their scarred knuckles facing us, partly obscuring his face and speaks with a wry smile. I hear the word, '*doulia*', which is 'work.'

'He says it is very hard work but welcomes you and is happy for you to come.' Dionisios speaks to him briefly and then Baba Tassos holds out his hand, to Lauren first this time. He speaks in Greek while looking at her and shaking her hand.

Dionisios laughs, 'He says you're lucky to have a beautiful wife; with blue eyes.'

Baba Tassos turns to shake my hand, holding on for a while longer than necessary, bows his head and says, '*O Theos borei na einai mazi sas.*' God go with you both.

This blessing makes even more sense when, in following years, I see him early on a Sunday slowly climbing the steep, concrete path up to the ridge. Even in summer, he wears the threadbare suit and a tie to church. Baba Tassos becomes a presence of our early years in this beautiful place.

We're left alone in the olive trees to discuss some details with Dionisios. I'm determined the first floor of the house is built as high as possible to ensure it has a panoramic view of the headland and bay. In the foreground, I crave an uninterrupted view of the nineteenth-century church, *Panayia Eleistra*, with its bell tower and up above it the white domes of the convent, *Timiou Prodromou*, dedicated to St John the Baptist. If the house is high enough, we'll see the battlements of the original Venetian castle extended by the Ottomans. And beyond, the lizard tail of the Mani.

When I sit on that imagined balcony, I sketch in my mind's eye the details of those interiors, particularly the convent with its beautifully tended flower beds and citrus tree orchards. I conjure its neighbour, the Byzantine eighth-century *Αγια Σοφια*, Saint Sophia church, partly ruined but with its roof and walls still standing. There's something sensual as well as spiritual about Byzantine brickwork. It breathes the labour of love and devotion. Without these views of the ancient buildings, the perspective of the sea and landscapes I know our house would be missing something, a connection with its environment. I must have repeated variations on this theme so often that Dionisios finally said, 'Trust me, Richard,' which signals the end of the discussion.

In addition to the height of the house and its balconies, we have to agree with Dionisios other key features of the house: the size and design of the windows, their shutters and the front door, the type of ironwork for the balcony railings, the size of the open fireplace we want in one corner upstairs. Some of the larger decisions like the open rafters showing the roof timbers inside are easier. We've seen them in one of the houses Dionisios has built so we say, 'like the house near *Paralia Peroulia*,' Sea Horse Beach. We discuss the shape and appearance of the house together and grow confident we understand each other. Dionisios says he'll be advised by a mechanical engineer on the foundations and core structures; that it isn't necessary for planning permission in Greece to involve an architect. We're content to cut any unnecessary cost.

In the following weeks back in England, when we tell people what's happening they remain tight-lipped. Or they say we must be mad buying land and trying to build a house in Greece at a distance. And without an architect we're just increasing the risk of something disastrous happening or nothing happening at all. With the house built from scratch, it's the detail that takes time. The exact position of the outside shower head, the curve of the concrete path from what would become the front gate, the size, colour and design of the floor tiles. Most crucial of all – in Lauren's view, and she's right – is the exact colour and shade of the shutters and external doors. That's where the soul of the house will rest. It's branded in my brain. You might think, 'traditional Greek house' plus 'blue shutter' would be easy to pin down. But it takes us an age to find the right colour in a catalogue. And then we have it! It belongs to a small group of words and numbers that will be the last to leave me. One day you'll hear me repeating to myself 'Amorgos Number 74.' Amorgos is a stunningly picturesque island, one of the main sources of the archetypal, Cycladic sculptures which so influenced early twentieth-century Western art. Here it refers to a unique blue imbued with a shade of slate grey. In the Eastern Med, 1974 is notable for the Greek military junta supporting a coup in Cyprus prompting Turkey to invade and partition it. This hastens the Greek military junta's fall in July '74 when democracy is restored. In Koroni, 74, at least for me, is a shade of slate-blue in a paint catalogue. Before we leave, we agree to the purchase of the land, pay a deposit for it and set in motion the full payment through bank transfer. We sign several documents plastered with brightly coloured postage stamps. I recognise our names and my and Lauren's fathers' names, which have to be included. A signifier of how patriarchal Greek society remains. For all we could decipher the Greek text, we might be signing to buy a herd of donkeys.

We pay Dionisios a small deposit for setting permissions in motion, contracting builders and so on. He agrees he'll ask for no more payments until the foundations of the house are built and the roof is on. We'll come back later in the year and see it. How can we trust him? He has a lot to lose. Most of all his reputation in the small community where he still lives. His family name, Sipsas, is at stake. The restaurants, the supermarkets, his father's cosmetic and jewellery shops and now this business, new to him, of finding land and project managing a build for foreigners. He's recently started on this venture; has done enough to show he can deliver a quality house at a fair price, but he's still eager to impress. We're playing a role in creating his portfolio for the future with other foreigners. His and his family's other businesses will suffer if he lets us down on this project. He doesn't. He's as good as – no, he's better than his word.

IN 2007 WE arrive in Athens from Cyprus for my new role as British Council Director in Greece. (The Directors in Israel and other countries in Southeast Europe report to me too.) The mobile refuse bins are emptied daily but are still full to overflowing. The bins are battered and bruised by arguments with concrete walls, trucks, or each other, like oversized, dented dodgems stuffed with rubbish. They provide temporary homes for stray, one-eyed, three-legged, scarred and skeletal cats. The mangey, ungroomed dogs envy the cats these shelters, the brief sanctuaries they offer with their relief from screaming cars, popping motorbikes and lumbering buses all belching fumes with the lead hovering heavy over the ground. Sometimes the cats find a takeaway on offer: cooked and uncooked fish heads and skeletons, bones with threads of meat hanging, or an overripe, burst watermelon with its flaring vermilion flesh a slushy drink – they have the skill and patience to nibble round the embedded, black melon seeds. The dogs aren't agile enough to get into the bins or to show such technical finesse; they wander round aimlessly in packs of half a dozen, occasionally snapping and snarling at each other like drunks. They're like all the desolate, abandoned and uncared for who hang out together.

Kolonaki Square, where the British Council office is, and its environs has a range of bars where sounds pump out so loudly that conversation, if it happens at all, has to be whispered fiercely and directly into the ear. Athenian twenty and thirty-somethings are there to hang out, to be seen and to see, not talk. At the other end of the range come cafés straight from a 1960s Fellini movie, where the women over fifty and younger have had extensive facial and other bodywork inflicted. They visit the *peluqueria* for their coiffure two or three times a week; in the cooler times of the year, they wear fur – not fake – and are draped in ostentatious necklaces and bangles; on their gold rings diamonds predominate, though rubies, emeralds and sapphires are common enough. The men favour carbuncular watches, toads squatting on their wrists, and not infrequently, their hair is also dyed. They wear suits and ties that are not quite contemporary but were once very fashionable and expensive. A woman friend visiting from England asks why the women are dressed like someone's mistress from a bygone era, and the men are posing as ageing lovers or gigolos. Just down the road are the branded shop fronts: Gucci, Prada, Fendi, Dolce & Gabbana, Versace, and the rest of the bling.

Into this confusion of rubbish and bling-filled zones of the city, the British artists, Gilbert and George, are invited by a private gallery that's selling their work. Greek ship owners and other wealthy Greeks are great collectors and supporters of contemporary art, sometimes through their foundations. I know the gallery owners and agree with them that the British Council will find an art critic who'll interview Gilbert and George on stage at the Benaki's Museum of Modern Art. It'll be a free event open to the public. After the conversation with the critic attended by four hundred younger Greeks, I host a dinner at our apartment for Gilbert and George. There are buyers of contemporary art and a sprinkling of artists, academics, writers on art and some of the great and the good. It is, for some, a bibulous dinner with five round tables positioned in the main room, which includes the Steinway.

Without warning, George gets up from the table where I'm seated and meanders to the Steinway. He starts leafing through the songbooks piled on its lid. Then, as far as he ever strays out of his brown-suited phlegmatic character role, he becomes animated and starts waving a songbook at Gilbert. It'd been given to

Lauren by her grandad, Pops, as a child and is one of her favourite possessions. She'd been introduced to opera by her Fabian Pops, but this is a book of *Best British Pub Songs*. After whispering with Gilbert, George beckons me over.

'Do you play?'

'Lauren's the pianist.'

'Your wife?'

'Uh ha. Yes.'

'Please . . .'

She's already on her feet gliding on the parquet towards us.

'This one first, please,' says George.

I have no idea what the Athenian glitterati make of two men in sober suits though far from sober, are doing singing 'Roll out the Barrel'. It was a Czech song, originally an instrumental with words added and translated into several languages. It was sung by soldiers in many opposing armies in the Second World War.

Roll out the barrel, we'll have a barrel of fun.
Roll out the barrel, we've got the blues on the run.

The Athenian art world listening to these songs has no idea how subversive they were. 'Underneath the Arches' – a song popularised in 1932 by Flanagan and Allen at the depths of the Depression in Britain in 1932 – focused on the unemployed and homeless sleeping rough.

The Ritz we never signed for
Savoys they can keep
There's only one place that we know
And that is where we sleep
Underneath the arches.

The railway bridge arches were in Derby where the unemployed and homeless slept.

And another from the First World War which ends: 'Take me

back to dear old Blighty.' 'Blighty' is a Hindu word meaning foreign or British. The first professional soldiers in the First World War brought 'Blighty' back from the crown jewel of the British Empire. 'Blighty', a term I will forever associate with those East End, Spitalfields boys of British art, Gilbert and George. Except, of course, Gilbert – the short one – was born in northern Italy, and George in Plymouth, Devon. Very self-consciously, ironically, they'd taken on the personas of working-class stereotypes and played with them, both profiting from and undermining the stereotype. They're deeply conservative, and like their buyers, supporters of high capitalism, the Conservative Party and Brexit. They're still humming and half singing some of these pub songs when I show them down in the lift to where their car's waiting.

DURING THE FOUR-PLUS years of our time in Athens we are, of course, regularly visiting our house in Koroni. It's a marked contrast between the glitz, often fun and interesting, of life in Athens and the simpler pleasures of small-town life in Greece. The restaurant, Bogris, where we ate on our very first night in Koroni before we even saw the land we bought, becomes year on year part of our food and cultural landscape. It's steadfast in its adherence to a traditional way not only of sourcing, preparing and cooking local food but in its way of managing itself as a family business. The young man who served us on that first February night is still doing some waiting, but his father slowly withdraws. He will occasionally appear in a corner with a coffee or, in summer, under a mulberry tree with a beer. But his son is now in charge. The father never appears to interfere in the running of the place. Still, he is there, an icon reminding us of something intangible which is handed down. The mother is still doing the cooking, though she has more help.

It's at Bogris on one of our summertime visits to Koroni that we experience authentic Greek dancing and plate smashing. We appear early-evening looking for a table. The place is heaving; laughter and good-humoured shouting echoes under the mulberry trees. A huge wedding party for the son or daughter of some local notable is in full swing. It's been on the go since mid-afternoon. The celebration has completely taken over the restaurant, and it's closed in the sense that it isn't taking orders for food. Instead of being told this is a private party, we're welcomed in and offered a drink. In the courtyard, the tables under the trees have been pushed back creating a space for dancing.

There are four musicians in one corner: *ena klarino*, an older style of clarinet with fewer keys and a more plaintive tone not used in modern classical or jazz; *i violi*, the violin introduced to Europe by Arab musicians, with three but now four strings, sharing the melody with the *klarino*; *ena laouto*, the lute related to the Arab oudh but with a longer neck and more cheerful voice, mainly used for chords and rhythm; *i defi*, a percussive tambourine on which the skin can be tightened and tuned. The musicians are in their late fifties or sixties except for the younger lute player, who's the singer. They're dressed in their own white shirts and dark waistcoats. As soon as they strike up, the place reverberates loudly, mixing with the cacophony of guests shouting from one table to another, plates of food and carafes of wine banged down on the tables, regular cries of 'Yammas!', literally 'to us!' The clash of tumblers overlaid with children laughing and crying make conversation impossible.

Sometimes children, teenagers, younger and older adults all mix in together dancing. Some children wear a version of Greek traditional costume with floppy red hats, *foustanella* or pleated white skirts for the boys and blue and white waistcoats, white tights and trainers; the girls are in ankle-length skirts, mainly pink, and white blouses, red tops with gold tassels and lace ruffs.

The adults range from the smartly attired in suits and dresses bought in Kalamata especially for the occasion to the dusty, oversize suit with huge lapels that an aged widower wore for his own wedding decades earlier. Another wears his clean, Sunday shirt tucked into his trousers – held up by string – in which he normally digs his potatoes and onions.

Some dances are in rounds with the dancers holding each other's shoulders in a human chain. A few dances are sedate, only holding hands. Some seem to be taken more seriously where only those confident with the steps take part. Others seem more of a free for all, with children pulling elders from their chairs into the dance space, dragging them round with peals of laughter. The instrumental music is mainly up-tempo, but if it starts quietly, it invariably ends in a frenetic and crazed crescendo.

The musicians take a break. It makes no difference to the volume of the shouted conversations and jokes being tossed around and across the tables. 'Hey, Yiannis, where's your donkey? No, I'm not talking about your wife!' followed by screams of delight from the woman in question, replying, 'At least he still knows how to ride. I hear you haven't been able to mount anything for at least ten years!' More guffaws. 'Pavlos, my friend. Where did you find that suit? *Sto skiato?*' – on the scarecrow – 'Protecting your vegetable garden from the wild boar?' To which the response is, 'The boars know where to find the best vegetables in Messenia. *Sto kipo mou!*' In *my* garden!

The musicians reassemble. They start very quietly, unlike anything they've played earlier. The shouts, the jokes and the laughter all fade and concentration is on the dance space where one of the older men of the wedding party has arrived. He starts to turn and weave slow half steps and curves, balancing on one bent leg while the other makes a crescent around his twisting but still upright body. As the rhythm picks up a little, so do his movements, the arcs of his hands and arms in the air swerving and diving, swallows in slow motion.

First, the fingers of one then the other hand brush the floor lightly while he keeps moving rhythmically in a figure of eight. His knees are bent, and his trunk remains upright when his fingers brush the flagstones of the courtyard. The tempo of the music picks up, and he spins faster while the guests clap time and cry out in support, cheering him on. The song reaches a frenetic climax, and abruptly the dancer stops; the intensity of all the instruments playing flat out dies away with a plangent *klarino* passage finishing the movement. The dancer balances and turns on one foot slowly, a child's doll on top of a music box but with both arms and hands raised in supplication. He's holding a moment of prayer, and the wedding guests are holding it with him in the short silence of the pause in the music. It's the Greek dance, traditionally performed only by solo males, called *sembekiko*.

Then all pandemonium breaks out: the music has started up fiercely, piles of plates are being dashed down on the flags of the courtyard to cries of *'Opα!'* Hey! Even the destruction of the plates is a skilful not a random or careless act. The fragmented shards of the porcelain remain within the area of the dance. The origin and significance of plate smashing are still unclear. One notion is that it symbolises throwing away the old and marks the couple's new start together. Another is that it wards off evil spirits. My own is that it displays how wealthy the bride's family is: it can afford to smash precious items of crockery.

ANESTI AND RAZIA are Albanian immigrants who come to play a very different important role in our Koroni lives. They are recommended by a Greek, ex-archaeologist neighbour and friend in Koroni to look after our house and garden. They clean the house, do odd jobs and tend the garden under Lauren's supervision. The one task in the garden Anesti can do unsupervised is to prune the olive trees around November. He takes the sacks one at a time on his moped to the top of the hill, where they're collected by a truck and taken to the local olive press a few kilometres away. They're inspected, weighed and cold pressed. The number of litres of oil we get depends on how many kilos of olives we send. Depending on the crop we get anything between forty to sixty litres of olive oil. Anesti gets to keep half. Their two children have been raised in Koroni, are in the local schools and fluent in Greek. They already speak good English while their parents' Greek isn't as good as mine and their English is very limited. But we muddle through, increasingly, with the support of their eldest child, Paris.

In contrast another Albanian I meet in Athens in our first year is Gazmend Kaplani, a lecturer, journalist and writer. His book, *A Short Border Crossing*, has recently been published in Greece to some acclaim. It's being prepared for an English translation on which I'm invited to comment. Gazi's is a fascinating story, and he's a very considerable character. As a political activist against the Communist regime of Enver Hoxha, he had to flee the country from the secret police when he was twenty-four years old. He learnt Greek from scratch, took a degree in philosophy, and completed a PhD in political science and history. As well as teaching, he's a journalist on the left-of-centre newspaper, *Ta Nea*. The News

One conversation I remember is about similarities and differences in the Balkans. 'Those differences are what Freud called the narcissism of small differences.' For Gazi, that difference of a place of birth neighbouring the one where he's studied and made a success of his life against the odds, becomes too heavy a burden to bear. Right-wing groups in Greece threaten him, the police are unhelpful, and government officials can't say when, if ever, his application for Greek citizenship might succeed. I help him network to a couple of EU conferences in which we're involved around issues of identity and migration. I hope this might help him find a contact or open a door somewhere in a British or other European university. It doesn't. Eventually, more I think in sorrow than anger, he leaves Greece for the US, where he now teaches and writes in Illinois.

MANY OF THE special times we have in Koroni feature the natural world. One late summer afternoon, I'm sitting on the balcony of the house looking across the olive groves to the Med. I see three, large, ragged birds land and perch, shoulders hunched, on the tamarisks by the shoreline. Through my field glasses, I watch the wrung-out birds, heron size but thinner, with snaking necks and deep chocolate brown feathers, furs on their shoulders. They flutter on and off the trees for an hour or so, then take off with a stuttering flight. When I see them land, I consult my *Collins Birds of Europe*: purple herons just arrived from Africa. They're gathering their strength before making their creaking wing-beats to the lagoon wetlands at Gialova forty kilometres away. Another day from the balcony I see flocks of Eleonora's Falcons circling over the castle battlements. The Greek coast and islands have about two-thirds of the world's population of these falcons. It's a medium-sized bird of prey which, unusually, breeds in colonies late in the season, and specialises in capturing other birds on their first migratory flight.

But Zaga Beach in front of our house is the main focus of interest, for there in summer anytime from May loggerhead turtles, *Carreta carreta,* nest there. In our first few years the nests total around thirty to forty every season, now there are well over two hundred nests each year. The female turtle returns to the beach where she was born every two to four years, and well above the waterline scoops out a nest about seventy centimetres deep where she lays a hundred plus eggs and covers them with sand with her flippers. No more than one in a hundred of the eggs – I've seen much higher figures, one in a thousand – will mature to a full adult turtle which can live a hundred years. We fund some of the young volunteers who come from across Europe to help protect them during the nesting and hatching season. Occasionally at dawn, I walk the two-kilometre length of the beach with them to look for new nests signalled by the tracks of a female's flippers. After covering the nest she heads back down to the water leaving a characteristic trail of flipper markings in arcs brushed onto the sand in a symmetrical pattern. When a nest is discovered, an experienced volunteer carefully scoops the sand away with their hands until they reach the eggs. The depth and width of the nest are measured and recorded, then the eggs are covered again. They make a lattice frame from bamboo which is laid over the nest to protect it. Sometimes instead, they use a light, spaced metal grid that they've brought with them. Either way, a bamboo tripod is erected, marking the corners of the nest, and placed over the grid around waist height. It's tied with red and white tape as at the scene of a crime or an accident. Finally, a large smooth pebble or a piece of wood is inscribed with an indelible marker giving the date when the nest was discovered and numbered in sequence.

The nest date points to an approximate period when hatching is likely: seven to ten weeks later, depending on the temperature of the sand. A few times, I've discovered a nest myself in advance of the volunteers and waited for them to arrive. Once I go for a late-night swim on my own. Coming out of the sea as I'm about to step up the gentle shelf of shingly sand onto the beach, I spot a female turtle near the line of tamarisk trees. I ease back into the water and float a few metres offshore. Twenty minutes later, she lumbers, a metre long, comical and ungainly down the beach. As she slips into the water only four or five metres away, she's transformed into a graceful creature plunging to fly in its depths.

FROM OUR MAGNIFICENT apartment with its view of the Acropolis, we descend the steep steps and pavements with flags jumbled by tree roots rupturing them into the air, landmines under the glowing oranges. We almost have to stop ourselves from sliding or running down the hillside into the bowels of Exarchia, the notorious anarchist quarter of the city. A descent some might think to Hades. We're heading for a favourite fish restaurant. Suddenly, from out of the dark, we're in the middle of a riot, dozens of people running, shouting and throwing stones, a few with crowbars or hammers trying to smash bank or shop windows. A couple of Molotov cocktails shatter nearby without catching fire.

Then two refuse bins are rolling across a sloping *plateia*, square, in front of us, each pushed by a cluster of rioters. The bins or their contents are on fire – doused with petrol – and, as they pick up speed, they're deliberately rammed into parked cars and a shopfront. We're hit by the pungent, acrid smell of smouldering tyres. A dozen anarchists are rocking a stationary police car from side to side trying to turn it over. I hope it's empty.

Then almost as instantly as we'd found ourselves surrounded by the mob, they disappear. We hear their distant shouting and footsteps clattering and fading down the cobbled streets and pedestrian alleys. There's a long silence punctured first by the wail of police sirens. Then the traffic and hubbub of the city resume, preparing for its Friday night: customers coming out to eat, drink and be entertained in one of the numerous clubs, bars or tavernas.

'Did you hear that?' says Lauren.

I nod. 'Italian and Spanish definitely. Maybe French as well as Greek,' I say.

It's our confirmation that some of the rioters had arrived from outside Greece to join in, to stir up or even to organise the trouble around us. It's mid-December 2008. Exarchia hunches down in central Athens, cheek by jowl with the upmarket Kolonaki district. Some cautious guidebooks and British Embassy advice warn you not to venture there. I do the opposite. When I get the chance, I enjoy the contrast to my working days and evenings. If not busy, I walk through its graffiti and bohemian scruffiness early on a Saturday morning to go to the fruit and veg market. Sometimes I sit in its main square for a while where a sprinkling of the homeless, drug addicts, alcoholics and bohemians are in residence along with pigeons and the detritus of a Friday night. Earlier in December, a fifteen-year-old student, Alexander Grigoropoulos, was shot dead by the police in one of Exarchia's narrow streets. There'd been trouble brewing in the days before he was shot but his killing hugely ratcheted up the tension in Athens and other cities throughout the country. And internationally.

During December and into 2009 there's a recurrent but unpredictable river of demonstrations, protests, incendiary cocktails, burned-out cars, overturned vehicles and smashed shop window fronts from supermarket chains to tiny independent businesses, none are immune. Serious, 'professional' anarchists use the student and wider population protests as cover for shooting at police officers stationed outside public buildings. They have Kalashnikovs and Magnums. One officer needs intensive care and, fortunately, survives.

Masked demonstrators firebomb my colleagues at the French Institute on the fringes of Exarchia. They spray on its walls, '*Etincelle a Athenes. Incendie a Paris. L'insurection s'approche.*' Other graffiti read, '*Gallia. Ellada. Exevresi Pantou.*' France. Greece. Uprising everywhere.

More than once I have to close the British Council office as a precaution, with a demonstration heading for *Plateia Syntagma*, Constitution Square, where the Greek Parliament stands in its nineteenth-century, neo-classical, royal palace. We sometimes close because tear gas wafting into the building threatens to engulf our students, visitors and staff.

It's a coincidence that this sequence of rolling riots all kick off in the month of December. I don't read or hear any commentators drawing direct parallels, but in December 1944, sixty-four years earlier, in these same locations around the Grande Bretagne Hotel, there'd been even greater demonstrations and deaths with the future of Greece in the balance. Then it was an even more perilous position than the start of the global financial crisis we're witnessing, which leads to the EU, and Germany especially, strangling the Greek economy and its citizens to the point of suffocation.

PARENTS. CHILDHOOD. SECURITY and comfort. Love. Desire. Marriage or not. Or divorce. Becoming a parent. Friendships. Work, a career. Boredoms and excitements. Achievements, successes and failures. Self-discovery. Creating a path. Unearthing that passion. These are some of the commonplace tropes by which we define and measure our lives. The final one is: if we have some agency in it, how we manage dying and death. I think I'm going to die. I'm on my own in the penthouse apartment. Lauren's away on an English language examinations trip to the lawless heartlands of Mexico. It's eight o'clock on a Sunday morning when I wake shaking. I can't stop. But it isn't me.

Our double bed's juddering like a Dakota clattering down the runway – a childhood memory from Ghana. A free-standing dressing table and its stool waltz over the parquet flooring. Coming down the hallway from the kitchen, I hear the glasses and porcelain chattering in their cupboards. Then a black and white photograph of Lauren in a deck chair at the Edinburgh Festival tumbles off the wall and smashes as it hits the floor, shards skittering everywhere. Oh, fuck!

I think I hear water running in the kitchen. I don't have time to check. I grab shorts and a tee-shirt, pull on trainers, grab my phone, keys, wallet and hurry out the front door. The building's swaying rhythmically from side to side. Shit! My glasses! Go back! I fumble the key into the lock. Not in the bedroom, not in the bathroom. Here in the snug! My heart's pumping. I'm shaking with terror. I bound down the stairs. I expect to see others doing the same. I might have to slow down. Will I pass or help them? Will I die crushed under crumbling masonry or suffocated with the dust of the collapsing building. It's a parallel universe where I imagine ways in which I'll die while my body's doing its best to escape them all.

But my descent is solitary, which makes it more intense and strange. Am I the only one desperate to escape? I reach the ground floor and wrench open the main entrance door. There's a small knot of younger residents in the street shouting and smoking furiously. I say '*kalimera*' and walk straight on down the hill. I can't bear to face a crowd in a state of agitation. I have my own to deal with. I need calming solitude to absorb and dissipate the waves of fear rolling through me. But I'm out!

I wander, dazed and dislocated around my immediate neighbourhood. I pass the magnificent 'icing cake' – a perfectly proportioned neo-classical building. During their occupation of Athens, the Nazis chose it as their headquarters. I pass it walking to or from the office only ten minutes away. It never ceases to bring a chill wondering what awful things happened behind its ice-sugar façade. Now in a state of shock, it morphs into a skeletal bone-white. Death seems everywhere.

Athens is the only place where a British Council Director has been murdered. I'd been advised during my security briefing to vary my timing and route to the office. The murder is a case of mistaken identity. Ken Whitty, father of Professor Chris Whitty, a late fixture on our TV screens during Covid briefings, is going to the office by car and is shot dead at some traffic lights. The Palestinian terrorist thought he was the defence attaché.

I stumble down the steeply stepped hillside in a narrow lane just off *Odos Skoufa*, Skoufa Street, to one of my favourite cafés. There I can sit outside under some olive trees away from the building itself. It's early, and the café's just waking up. I'm the first customer, and despite the quake, the staff inside are preparing to open. Over my coffee, I read the news on my phone. There's a breaking item about the quake. Early reports suggest it registered 5-point-something on the Richter scale, just short of very serious. Nothing yet in my messages from the Embassy. Nor have I seen any evidence of the quake other than my furniture dancing and the building swaying, both graceful and terrifying. The nonchalance of the café staff turning up and working as usual relieves my anxiety a little. When I ask the waiter he shrugs, '*Ti na kanoume?*' What can we do?

I send Lauren a message saying I'm OK, so is the apartment – so far – and not to worry, that it isn't yet clear how extensive the damage is. I don't want to return home until the overall picture is clearer. I decide to walk to the top of Lykavitos, the highest point in central Athens and accessible by foot from Kolonaki. It's no more than a forty-minute brisk and, in places, challenging walk where the path up through the pine trees is very steep. Some take the funicular railway there from Odos Plutarchou.

The focus and energy needed to make the climb offer a release and distraction from the previous hour. By the time I reach the chapel of *Ayios Georgios*, St George, my body is not exactly purified or cleansed. But the exercise has released its endorphins. It's dispelled the stress of waking with the laws of physics up in the air in a dancing mockery of how solid objects and structures should behave.

I sit outside the gleaming white chapel and gaze directly across and slightly down to the best panoramic view you can have of the Acropolis, and its place in the city. The Parthenon columns are rooted in the *'Akro Polis'*, literally 'rock of the city', the building like an ancient olive tree with some limbs missing but surviving. The city buzzes around the rock in a blue fug, a swarm of grumpy ants scurrying on their ceaseless business. On the horizon is the smudge of Piraeus and beyond lie the islands of Hydra, Aegina and Agistri, flecks of white foam floating on the Aegean.

It's only then that I cry quietly and inconspicuously – there's no one else around – realising what might have been and how lucky I am. And so is almost everyone else in Athens that day. In the afternoon, I hear there's been some limited damage to buildings and one reported death. It was less than five minutes between my waking, realising what was happening and my exit from the building. A highly concentrated time when the intensity of every microsecond counts, a hundred-metre race, heart pounding, an agonising surge to the line.

The irony is that Lauren, at the same time, is in far greater danger of sudden, accidental death in Mexico. She's staying in a provincial town where there's a gunfight between competing drug gangs in the square outside her hotel.

Still outside the chapel I look down to my right where there's a three-thousand seat amphitheatre constructed in an old quarry. The highest performance space in Athens with spectacular views of the city. Around the same time last year I'd walked from our apartment up to the theatre to see Nick Cave and the Bad Seeds perform there. For a while I'm in the thick of the echoing, hollow wooden temple block and doom-laden song 'Red Right Hand', the divine vengeance from Milton's *Paradise Lost*. Then the encore of the gig overtakes this sombre mood and I'm uplifted by the sounds of salvation in human love with Cave's 'Into My Arms'. I'm safe from the earthquake now.

LATE JULY 2011 in Athens, we have our final breakfast at the St George Hotel, Likavitos. Like our apartment, it's situated on the upper slopes by the last road which circles the hill and its final steep ascent to the chapel of St George. The highest point in urban Athens. Then we descend in the lift to the basement garage and drive out of Athens, me for the last time as British Council Director Greece, heading west along the motorway through the forest of oil refineries. We drive over the Corinth Canal and continue heading west – not south to Koroni – this time with the Gulf of Corinth on our right until we reach Patras. From there we take the ferry to Ancona on the east coast of the Marche and drive north-eastwards through Italy to stay with some friends in Burgundy. My next British Council assignment is about to start based in Brussels. It's a brand-new role and I'm not taking over from anyone. We have to find somewhere to live. In the end, it's an easy decision. We can't turn down the option of living in Rue van Eyck, named after the great Flemish early-Renaissance painter Jan.

We soon visit 'The Adoration of the Mystic Lamb' in Ghent Cathedral. It's overwhelming, literally, a huge work. There are twelve panels on one side, the interior panels which hold the main narrative and can be folded out and closed as required. Originally opened only on feast days for contrast and excitement compared to the more sober and quieter outer panels painted on the back. The structure is 5.2 by 3.75 metres. That's twenty square metres of highly wrought and immensely detailed painting across twenty-four distinct and complex scenes showing in total hundreds of figures on wood. The technical term for this work is a *polyptych* from the Greek, *poly* meaning 'many' and *tych* meaning 'fold'.

Today when most visitors aren't attending for religious reasons the panels are semi-permanently open during visiting hours, so that you can see both sides. As first-time visitors all we can do is extract from the avalanche a few details: the lamb upright on a dais with a gaping hole in its chest pumps blood into a golden chalice; the toes of Adam's right foot appear to step beyond the frame of the panel; the floral design of the blue and white tiles under the feet of the angels playing the organ; above Eve's head, Cain batters and hacks Abel to death with an animal jawbone; date palms and cypresses flourish in Flemish landscapes with towers and cathedral spires.

Only later, when we look at and read the book we'd bought on this masterpiece, do I begin to understand some of its overall design and structure as a work of art for public display in a place of religion for believers. Jan van Eyck's only known such work. 'The Arnolfini Portrait' at the National Gallery in London is much more typical. A man and a woman in a domestic interior. Whilst equally fascinating as 'The Adoration of the Mystic Lamb', its human, domestic scale makes it more easily accessible on first viewing. Though, despite its simple beauty, 'The Arnolfini Portrait' still retains its sense of intrigue and mystery.

On this first visit alone, we park the car in a side street not far from St Bavo's Cathedral. As we stroll in its direction, we're both astounded. It's the first time we've seen, outside central Amsterdam, women sitting in shopfront windows advertising themselves as available for sex. It's around noon on a grey Saturday. The time when busy working people go for their weekly shopping. Bizarrely incongruous some might say, others that it was 'normalising' the business of the sex trade. We're still trailing the surprise of that scene when we take our line in the queue to buy tickets for 'The Ghent Altarpiece'.

The second time we visit is with friends from England staying with us in Brussels. Lynne and Richard are some of our oldest and loveliest friends. They're regular churchgoers. I make sure this time that I drive to a municipal car park on the far side of St Bavo's Cathedral, from where we'd stumbled on the sex-for-sale scenario. I don't want to deflect from their experience of 'The Adoration of the Mystic Lamb'.

OUR HOUSE IN Rue van Eyck has a restrained façade for the swish neighbourhood in which it's located. A couple of steps up to a large front door and to the left a front window two metres long by three metres high. From the pavement, you can see two floors of windows above ground level while there's a further floor set back that's invisible. Nor can you guess from the outside at the catacomb of cellars which house everything from several washing machines and driers to wine racks that could hold a thousand bottles.

On the ground floor, the main sitting and entertaining areas along with the dining room can be used as one through space onto a small terrace that leads down into a tiny but delightful courtyard garden. The decoration and furnishings are high kitsch. Upstairs some of the bedrooms, one of which becomes my study, are varying shades of purple swirled around with vermilion, crimson and ruby. Lauren negotiates an entire internal repainting of the house, some new kitchen equipment, and the removal of all the main furniture so we can start again in the amazing spaces with ceilings nearly three metres high throughout the house. The owners, who live in the adjacent house, are clearly delighted to have the British Council as tenants and don't refuse a single request as the condition of our taking it. We pass a happy afternoon in the storeroom of the British Council Art Collection in London choosing several canvases, drawings and photos to cover the huge wall space.

We spend our first Christmas in Brussels with Rowan, Will and Sarah – by this time Will's fiancée. We have fun with skating, oysters and champagne. The second Christmas we spend at home in Haslemere. For New Year we fly to Greece because we're missing our house and the sea. We walk along the beach with the surf crashing and collect driftwood to burn in the open hearth. One night an intense electric storm strikes when incandescent forks spear the boiling ocean. In the juddering light, the olive trees, the beach and *Panayia Eleistra*, Our Lady of Mercy church, all dance in some wild, late-night stroboscopic rave.

On New Year's Eve, we're invited to dinner by our friends Priya and Yiannis. We have to leave the dinner party before midnight, as Lauren isn't feeling well.

Act 5

Last Dance

Lauren and Richard at the Temple of Aphaia, Aegina, 2009.

It's five o'clock on a Monday morning in January 2013, when I roll over in bed and decide I won't be getting the Eurostar back to Brussels. Intense pain has kept Lauren awake most of the night. She needs no persuasion when I say: 'I'm taking you to A & E. Those doctors at the health centre have no idea.'

She's been going to our local health centre in Haslemere for months. She prefers dealing with a familiar medical system. She'd seen a private doctor in Brussels shortly after we arrived there. He'd diagnosed a cracked rib from a fall in the bath, but it was a stab in the dark. The GPs at the local health centre aren't any better. They've been throwing darts blindfolded – maybe gallstones, perhaps appendicitis – multiple blood tests but nothing firm's been identified even though the pains in her abdomen, trunk and lower back have become more acute and frequent. There's no suggestion that she needs a thorough examination by specialists.

We drive up the A3 through light rain in the cold and dark to the Royal Surrey Hospital at Guildford. The road's surprisingly busy before six in the morning, with traffic heading into London trying to beat the rush hour but creating another jam instead. As she's finding it difficult to walk, I drop her right outside the entrance to A & E where the ambulances unload their patients.

I park then hurry inside, but Lauren's still sitting in the outermost ring of the galaxy of the A & E department.

'Has anyone seen you yet?'

'They asked me to complete this form,' she holds up a clipboard.

I take the form and board from her and go to the reception desk where I speak firmly but quietly, 'My wife's in a lot of pain. Is someone going to see her soon?'

No doubt the receptionist has heard these words thousands of times. She ruffles through her papers. 'She's fourth in line.' As if she's waiting to be anointed.

'How long will that be?'

'I'm sorry, that's impossible to say.'

How that stock question and answer echoes in the reception room and down the corridors in the days, weeks and months to come. That day elongates in my memory into one extended wait punctuated by intense flurries of activity: temperature taken, blood pressure measured, two pills in a paper cup, two doctors each giving Lauren a physical examination with the curtain drawn round the bed. 'Does it hurt here or here? How does it feel there?' Being wheeled on the trolley bed where she lies for a scan. Later a second scan and more questions: 'How long?' 'When?' 'When was it first?' 'What about eating?' 'What about your mother's history?' 'Your GP?' 'What about the health centre? How many visits?'

I think and want to say, but I don't: 'Yes! What about that fucking health centre!?'

More time is spent waiting to see someone or for something to happen than happens. There are long stretches of Lauren dozing, me trying to read *The Guardian* or going to get a coffee or salad from the Costa implant in the hospital. I email the office in Brussels saying I won't be there that day and I'm not sure when I will be. I message Rowan and William to tell them we're in A & E and Lauren's having some tests. I'll call when there's any news. I speak and message them later in the afternoon saying we're still there; it's looking like they've found something or something's up because it's taking a long time. It's all a blurry, weary jumble of trite, unremarkable moments. Then twelve hours after we've arrived, we're told that Lauren should get out of her hospital gown and get dressed. It feels half normal, comforting to see her back in her own clothes. 'You'll be seeing the consultant in a minute,' says one of the junior doctors. We sit and wait for fifteen minutes outside an office where we hear voices whispering. Out of character, I agree only Lauren will ask and answer questions. I will listen and take note of what's said.

The door opens and we're asked to come in by the consultant who's on her feet but behind her desk. She's an upright woman with blonde shoulder length hair and high cheek bones. I guess in her mid-forties and in quiet control. She invites us to sit down and introduces two other people in the room: a young, male doctor and an older woman nurse. Once we settle, she introduces herself mentioning she'll be looking after Lauren from now on. Then she says:

'Mrs Walker. Why didn't you come and see us sooner?'

'I've been going to my local health centre for months.'

Silence.

'Mrs Walker. I'm sorry to tell you, you have advanced ovarian cancer. Stage Four.'

Time's suspended and in that moment we're all frozen. There's no, 'We think you have,' or, 'It's probable you have.' The medical world only delivers such certainties when it's one hundred percent sure. When it's a fact from which it cannot retreat. Or unsay.

Lauren breathes deeply and looks straight at the consultant. 'How long have I got?'

'That's not easy to say.'

'I don't need it to be easy to say. Or to hear,' says Lauren. 'I'm asking you to tell me how long I've got.'

The consultant almost imperceptibly shrugs and repeats, 'That's difficult to say.'

'I know it's difficult to say but I want to know.'

'There are so many factors.'

'We can talk about the factors,' says Lauren. 'But I still want to know.'

'It depends,' said the consultant.

Lauren doesn't take that bait. 'I want to know how long I've got. I'm not leaving this room until you tell me. You're the person in this room best qualified to make an educated guess.'

The consultant glances at the nurse and it feels as if she wants to sigh, but she doesn't. Then her gaze is on Lauren. 'Mrs Walker.' She pauses. 'Six, nine months. If you're lucky, up to a year.'

Lucky! How can you say you're lucky to be told you have up to a year to live?!!

The only person who can speak next is Lauren, and she keeps us waiting for what seems an eternity. No doubt it's much longer for her.

'Thank you,' she says humbly.

THE DAY AFTER her diagnosis Rowan arrives and we go to the Noah's Ark at Lurgashall where Lauren orders half a cider. She takes only a sip and leaves the rest. One of the first things she says is, 'I want a dog.' Our peripatetic life had inhibited us from committing to one. Rowan and William come and stay, we go to a labrador breeder in Petworth, and Lauren chooses the black runt of the litter. His pedigree name is Macguire. He soon becomes Mac. I manage to keep on top of being available for Lauren, Mac and my job. Occasionally, he goes to stay in Oxford with Will and Sarah to give me a break. I'm ready to give up my job straightaway. But Lauren sees no reason for that to happen. I speak quietly to the consultant who'd given us the news. She's an admirable Polish woman. She confirms that unless Lauren's asking me to stop work, in her view, it isn't necessary. 'Lauren wants everything to remain normal, as it was before the diagnosis.' Which, of course, is impossible for both of us, at least in our heads. But I understand what the consultant is saying. The external routines and rhythms of life maintained, as far as possible, as they were before the diagnosis

I spend most of my time at home in Haslemere, especially when the first cycle of chemotherapy begins. Within a week we understand that the coming months will be dominated by chemotherapy, likely to be followed by major surgery then followed up with more chemotherapy. The first of six sessions start within ten days of the diagnosis. A session lasts a full day including travel. There's always a hassle over parking at the Royal Surrey adjacent to the Cathedral. It's not the cost, but often there's absolutely nowhere to park. I want to be walking into the hospital with Lauren not waiting for a free space while she has to negotiate alone the queues, the forms, the blood tests before the chemotherapy itself begins. Sometimes there'd be a mess up in processing the order for Lauren's unique mix of chemicals. Carboplatin plus Taxol adjusted for her. Then we might have to sit for ninety minutes or more before Lauren can be connected to the drip. Often the junior nurses fail to get the cannula into a vein, and we have to wait until the Irish sister's free so the infusion can begin. The black lounging chairs the patients sit in for seven hours are comfortable enough with retractable legs and footrests. The room with a large plate glass window down one side is light but it can't be opened so it's often stuffy and overheated. There are around fifteen patients, most with a partner or friend, so the room's always crowded. Occasionally, it's so crowded that some of us have to sit in the corridor until a space becomes free. Lauren sometimes dozes late morning and always in the afternoon.

The six one-day sessions are three weeks apart. We discover and adjust to the cycle of how Lauren's body reacts in these three-week cycles. She's bad for the first five or so days and I work from home then. Fatigued and nauseous with the chemicals, she has to take another chemical against the sickness. Sometimes she has numbness in her fingers or toes. The second week she's good and the third week she's her old self. We try to make the third week the period when I take some days off and we go away or do something different. In some of those weeks, she's able to play tennis. The most upsetting side-effect of the chemotherapy is the hair loss. She tries a cold cap, but it doesn't work and clumps of her curly, red-gold hair, autumn leaves fall in the shower. A woman recommended by MacMillan comes to the house and she has two wigs made.

I make occasional work trips to Brussels, London or other European cities, organising those visits at times when Lauren's well enough to go and stay with Rowan in Finsbury Park or Will in Oxford. Occasionally, they come and stay in Haslemere. Some months later we give up the house in Rue van Eyck, packing up and returning to England. I continue in the same role for our work in Brussels and Europe, but do it from home and London instead of Brussels. I turn down the proposal that was made just before Lauren's diagnosis of my leaving Brussels and going to Paris as the British Council Director there.

The surgery happens five months after the diagnosis in January. We discuss having private treatment, but it would be the same surgeon as with the NHS. £30,000 is a high price for fresh flowers in a vase. Lauren doesn't need to think twice. She was always sensible with money. I hold her hand while she's on the trolley in the dark green gown and the anaesthetist places the mask over her face before she's wheeled into the theatre.

I wander aimlessly around the Tesco supermarket next to the hospital then drive home. I have a number to call. I try after six hours, but she isn't out. She's in the operating theatre for over eight hours. I'm allowed to see her very briefly in intensive care that evening. She's awake and conscious of her surroundings. I call Rowan and William from the car to tell them their mum's fine though shattered.

The hospital allows her to be home recuperating for six weeks, at the end of which she's on the tennis court and we stroll on the Sussex Downs. Then the cycle of chemotherapy starts for another six sessions over eighteen weeks. We know the switchback of how Lauren's body will respond. The only time I ask Rowan to attend one of the sessions with Lauren is when I have to go to Venice for a conference I'm chairing at the Art Biennale and the dates have been fixed years before. I feel guilty enjoying it without her.

Apart from the sip of cider the day after the diagnosis she

never touches another drop of alcohol. And she's someone who'd enjoyed her gin and tonic and wine. She's far from self-pitying or miserable. Her mantra is Eric Idle's Monty Python song: 'Always look on the bright side of life.' She's rarely been extravagant and has been careful in her choice of anything material from a house to a car, from gigs and opera tickets to holidays. We've always eaten healthily, but now she focuses on paying even closer attention to her diet. We don't stop having fun.

Lauren decides she doesn't want to dwell on the periods when she has to have debilitating medical attention and invasive procedures. Thinking about these will be kept to a minimum and blocked in the diary as necessary. We'll make absolutely the most of times when we know she's going to be strong and well enough to enjoy travel and new adventures. These will be the times when we feast on new experiences with each other squeezing the most from the days left. We're determined not to dwell in the shadow of her illness. We'll glory in the light of the other person and celebrate the days as special, each one an anniversary of loving presence. We'll capture daily a holy, human memory for as long as we have a shared memory. What follows are the scenes of this marvellous mystery tour which we construct for ourselves, and I share with you as we experience it.

WE WAKE AT dawn and draw the curtains of the restored boathouse on the banks of the Afon Teifi. It's New Year's Day 2014. 'Look, look, there's one!' Lauren whispers fiercely; and shortly, in the rippling wake of the waves a second brown, whiskered muzzle, the head dips then surfaces, and we catch sight of its white throat. Probably a mother and pup. The males swim solo marking out the territory for their mate and offspring, though that's the only contribution the male makes to raising the young. We're seeing what we hoped to see but never dreamed we would.

They are both graceful and powerful, pocket-sized submarines especially if you're a fish, their main prey. In the mouth of the estuary are *Lutra lutra*, two European otters.

Later we sit on pews in the nave of St David's Cathedral under the unique oak ceiling pendants carved in 1540. The notes, the prayers and the souls of one thousand five hundred years of continuous worship echo, humming silently in our heads.

WE WALK THROUGH the front arched gate and down the slabs of the path between the rose bushes in the full bloom of a perfect, warm English summer's day; the lawns are well cared for but in need of rain. The mellow limestone house with its double gables over the front porch, oak seats on either side, welcomes us onto the huge flagstones. The temperature drops by two or three degrees. They were laid in 1571 and have been burnished by five and half centuries of boots, shoes and sandals. One sitting room has parquet flooring from a later period. It has a panelled box bench seat under the diamond leaded windowpanes. Three armchairs are covered in the same fabric, which is lighter and darker blue with a touch of pink, the intricate designs feature foliage and broad-leaved plants entwining mythical, long-necked dragon birds. The rug on the parquet mirrors the design. The woodblocks cease, the stone flags reappear in front of the grate. The predominant blue of the fabric and rug is picked up in the geometric design of the tiles on either side of the hearth. Blue tiles that would look at home in a Spanish plaza or a Portuguese church. We call it the Blue Room.

This house is where Gabriel Rossetti spent a whole summer with Jane Morris and her children while William was in Iceland. In the first chalk study he made of her, she holds a small bouquet of pansies for love and remembrance. In the sumptuous, finished oil, her lips glow scarlet and she holds a wreath of willow branches for sorrow and longing. The house itself is the backdrop to her portrait, known as 'Water Willow'.

Fringing the Morris' four-poster bed we read the script woven in blue punctuated by tendrils of leaves and flowers: 'The night is a-cold ~ and Thames runs chill ~ twixt mead & bill ~ but kind and dear ~ is the old house here ~ and my heart is warm ~ midst winter's harm ~'

We're quietly excited, this is the house, Kelmscott, which inspired and where William Morris wrote his novel, *News from Nowhere*! Following Sir Thomas More's coinage of the English word *Utopia* from the Greek ου-τοπος, literally 'no place', *News from Nowhere* is often referred to as 'utopian'. William Morris's entire life, as evidenced by the house we're visiting, was spent trying to make his ideal world happen. Morris's The Kelmscott press printed *News from Nowhere* with a frontispiece picture of the front garden which we've just walked through. Its alternative title, not often quoted, is *An Epoch of Rest*.

IT'S LATE OCTOBER, early winter sun, bright and on the edge of warm. We stroll along the beach then find a café where we buy a takeaway Earl Grey for Lauren and a small bottle of Moretti for me. We take them back to the beach, where we sit on concrete steps beside Montalbano's balcony from where he takes his daily swim and sits for lunch or dinner cooked by his housekeeper, Adelina. We're secretly waiting for her to arrive and clean his apartment. The Rai TV series of the fictional detective, *Il Comisario Montalbano*, is one of our guilty pleasures. The pleasure is partly scenic with the stunning baroque towns and dramatic landscapers of Scicli, Modica and Ragusa in the Val de Noto.

Early that morning, we'd sat in the main square at a café opposite Montalbano's police station. From the balcony, the blue and yellow-starred EU flag flutters alongside the red and yellow Sicilian flag. This has a striking three-legged figure, at its centre the head of a Medusa. It symbolises the three points of the island; the design found on silver coins in Syracuse from the fourth century BC. The flags remind us how Sicily has been a magnet for successive waves of migration and assimilation from corners of Europe, North Africa, the Near and Middle East, and over hundreds, thousands of years. Medusa on a flag! We like them because they're telling us they're European and global as well as uniquely themselves. They wave at us with multiple identities.

We're staying in a small house with eighty deep steps up to the Duomo di San Giorgio, the patron saint of Ragusa Ibla. There are eighteen World Heritage buildings in this town alone. We enjoy wandering the narrow streets of the city rebuilt after the earthquake of 1693. In the twisted lanes we pause, admiring the wrought-iron balconies which almost kiss in front of their wooden shutters. Inhaling the scent of basil, plants and bushes spiral in green tresses down the primrose, limestone walls, which are streaked with rust from the outdoor AC units.

'Look!' I say pointing at the tangled loops of wires overhead. 'Just like *bucatini* but with electricity not *salsa di pomodoro*.' In the clouds of laundry drying overhead, one wash catches the eye: seven pink and black football shirts emblazoned with an eagle, the kit of Palermo FC. At night, the cast-iron lamp posts flick out their shadows, darting tongues, on the plaster crumbling from the walls.

Negotiating the damp cobbles of Castelbuono through the November evening mist we enter Nangalarruni, one of the best restaurants in central north Sicily. It's named after a local mouth instrument like a Jew's harp and is famous for its seasonal foods. Its foyer is a brick cavern steeped in olive oil, red wine, thyme, crushed garlic, lemon zest, countless litres of home-grown *salsa di pomodori* and *aubergine caponata*. Though we're here for something else. The bricks are smoky red from the fire banked high in the corner hearth; the vaulted timber ceiling blackened. Scores of wine bottles, all Sicilian, mainly red, stand to attention on shelves and cupboards.

Earlier in the day, we walked through nearby valley forests of holm and cork oak, chestnut, cherry and ash trees. The ash are carefully managed and farmed. As in rubber production, small cuts are made in the bark, a sweet sap leaks out and is collected for use as a natural medicine and in confectionery. It's called *manna*. From heaven indeed. It's these forests that produce the food we've come to enjoy.

'There! Look, over there!' Lauren whispers as we're led to our table. She's pointing to a large wicker basket on the floor which is an olive pannier for a donkey, though we aren't looking at olives. These are the fruits of the forest floor. *Funghi porcini*. *Porcini* means little pig. A reference to the plentiful wild boar we'd heard but not seen on our walk earlier. Inside, the pannier is a riot of colour and shape, anticipated flavours and textures. These are the organs of the forest floor. In a butcher's shop, you might think you were looking at offal: lungs, liver, heart, kidneys, ears.

A waiter picks a selection from the pannier placing the magical plants with gills in a small trug and brings it to our table. 'You choose, we cook. You like this one,' he says pointing to a mushroom that's a blackened ear. 'We cook with *spaccatelle*. Or this one,' he points at a delicate long white stalk ending in the standard lampshades of our childhoods, buff speckled with snow. 'We cook with *busiate*. I come back.' He leaves the trug with its glorious profusion of wild mushrooms.

We giggle over one that is a man's penis with the foreskin drawn back. We never learn its proper name. It's forever the '*prick porcini*' for us. Here is one with a thumb, a thick white stem funnelling out into a dark mouth wide open, the King Trumpet. Here's another with its chestnut frilled edging and symmetrical black marks on its rounded cone; underneath it has spiky gills, the Hedgehog Mushroom. Now we have, looked at from the top, a pink-saffron fried egg, the Pine Mushroom. What's this? An orange mushroom, the size and shape of a small new potato, name unknown. Here's one reminding us of the bakers of our childhoods, a bulbous stem with a round, symmetrical head toasted light brown, glossy and sticky, known in England as the Penny Bun.

The dishes arrive one by one with time between each to savour multitudes of pasta sauces complementing the mushrooms we've chosen. The last plate is the *occhi de lupo*. When we leave the warm embrace of Nangalarruni, the glow from the lampposts is weak in the dark and mist as we navigate back to our limestone house overlooking Ventimiglia Castle. Never mind, we don't stumble. We've eaten wisely, the *occhi de lupo* help us to see. They are 'wolves' eyes'.

In bed we feel deeply connected through the stone of the castle built in the early fourteenth century with its cubes of Arab architecture, Norman and Swabian towers, respectively round and square. Castelbuono has a profound history built over the ruins of a Byzantine settlement. 'Wherever we are,' I say, 'It always comes back to Greece,' and fold her, a moth gently closing its wings, in my arms in the dark.

EVERYONE HAS LEFT, lugging their elongated multiple photo lenses, light meters and tripods, clothed in multipocketed, olive-green jackets and dark waterproof trousers with heavy boots and leggings. They whisper fiercely at each other like parents shouting at their children not to shout. The clamour and clatter of scientific, militaristic endeavour leak away and we're left alone in natural silence. Which is not silence: the wind is chattering loudly through the reed beds which nod in agreement with what they're being told. We're elevated at two metres in a wooden hide at Minsmere on the Suffolk coast of my schooldays with a view two kilometres distant over the reeds and the waterways that flood through them. Though noon the light is grey, the reed beds, old people hunched, are bent low, and the water is ruffled, corrugated iron. Two marsh harriers dipping and swooping in the lead sky – reconnoitre the just departed convoy – but the wind whips away their high-pitched calls and they slash the sky in silence.

Through the reed beds we've glimpsed splashes of cream topped by the persimmon bills of mute swans; in the middle distance a deceit of lapwings clothed in a faint shimmer of purple-green beats slowly over the reeds, crests flattened in flight. From a sandbank, the sentinels of the marshes, the redshanks, dart on ballerina-thin blood-orange legs, the blood-orange repeated in the bill as it drills the mud for molluscs. But these and other sandpipers, ducks, foreshore, marsh and sea birds are the supports for the main act that might never turn up. We've tried once before and failed. *The shadow* hovers above us, a dark raincloud. 'Probably your last chance,' it says without speaking.

'Let's give it another twenty minutes,' says Lauren, while I punch my fists into my palms trying to keep my fingers warm.

I nod. 'OK.'

The sudden whistling call of the light Japanese motorbike, a kingfisher, as it accelerates low over the water flaunting its tangerine and electric blue feathers is a temporary distraction. But we've come for the elusive buff bird, not the many-coloured dandy.

It's over a metre long, but *Botaurus stellaris*, the Great Bittern, is one of the least visible of all birds. Think of it as a compacted, squatter heron with its neck often jammed into its shoulders making it look hunchbacked. It breeds, feeds and lives in wetlands, marshes and in these reedbeds. Its regular and irregular patterns, striped, barred, streaked, mottled, black, brown, buff, tawny, rusty and dull yellow are ripples of the water, the reeds and the play of wind and light on its chameleon plumage.

We're listening as much as watching. Under the cocktail party chatter of the siskin and the harsher babble of the warblers' committee room discussion, we hear the male bittern once, twice and then on the third stroke, we're sure. Tuba notes rising quickly and falling in slightly slower time played from somewhere deep in the earth, muffled as they break, and call in search of a mate. This foghorn of the reedbeds booms out in five or six-second intervals alerting us to something, but we don't know what it is or why. Cannons in the distance. Over the horizon, just out of sight, Sizewell B splits atoms where the intense heat in a pressurised water reactor converts to steam to drive the turbines that spin out electricity through a generator. And beyond, from the shingle beach, through unfathomable intricacies of machines and wires to work our washing machines, refrigerators, televisions and to illuminate our lives.

We've heard it! The bittern's boom! That's all that matters for now!

We descend from the hide, the spell of the bittern's boom from the core of the earth still resonating in our heads. On a stretch of cut reed bank, fifteen metres away we see a Great Bittern in the open; five or six seconds is enough before it runs down a ditch and into the reeds.

In the nineteenth century, in season, thousands of bittern eggs were sold weekly in London markets. The bird's habitat, under huge pressure and threat, has for the moment been saved, and the bittern has taken a short flight back from the cliff edge of extinction in Britain.

'We're so lucky,' says Lauren. 'So lucky.' And links her arm through mine.

THE GALICIAN FARMHOUSE is still working but has four rooms and a small swimming pool for its guests. Heavy, dark furniture, brass, lace, the spider-web varnish of oils, black and white photos of agricultural labour before the tractor are an entire provincial museum. Outside a blizzard of cherry blossom avalanches down the sloping ground in all directions. We've been here two days scouting the area and the city with our rented car. Now we're ready for some more serious footwork. Dressed in shorts, we pull on and adjust our trainers for the way ahead. We've set a maximum of ten kilometres and estimate our walk will be eight. I have a small rucksack with water, cereal bars, sweaters for the cooler evening. We're setting off after mid-afternoon when any heat is a gentle brush on the cheek not a punch to the head. More than half the walk is a track with a slight downward incline until it reaches the city's skirts morphing into the mediaeval centre. I know Lauren is apprehensive. This is the longest walk she has tried since *the shadow* fell across our path. 'Don't forget to put in my sketchbook and pencil case.' Even the invisible bruising of the shadow can't distract her from drawing, though the periods of her concentration are shortening as the time left shortens.

'It's huge,' she says. We're looking at a stone, barn-like structure. But it's a metre above ground level. It squats on two rows of stone toadstools, more than twenty metres long, four metres high with a pitched roof topped by a stone cross over one gable. But the cross is a distraction. It's not a church or chapel. It's the stuff of storing life. *Uno horreo.* A granary for fruit and seeds. Raised above the rats, mice and other vermin to hold food during the winter season when nothing fruits and to supply the next spring's planting. In its way, it's as impressive as the destination of ancient pilgrimage we are walking towards: the Cathedral of Santiago di Compostela.

As we trudge through the suburbs and deeper into the old city, we converge with others streaming towards the cathedral and funnelling into *Praca de Obradoiro,* Galician for Square of the Workshop – the Gallego dialect sounds a mix of Spanish and Portuguese. This brings us alongside hundreds of pilgrims and others milling about as we join a long queue outside the Gloria Portico. The seated, stone figure of a neatly bearded St James sculpted more than eight hundred years earlier leans forward over our heads welcoming the pilgrims at the end of their journey. He has a scroll in his right hand, *Misit me Dominus,* The Lord has sent me, and a staff in his left. His bare feet protrude from under the folds of his garment where a small lion emerges behind his left leg. The halo circling his head supports scenes from the three temptations of Christ after forty days fasting in the desert:

> *turning stones into bread to satisfy your hunger;*
> *throwing yourself from a church spire to prove the angels*
>   *can save you;*
> *gaining control of all earthly powers if you agree to worship*
>   *the devil.*

We shuffle in through the Gloria Portico. There are a few older Spaniards and foreigners like us, but the majority are much younger Europeans and North Americans with clusters of Koreans huddled in tight knots. A mass is just about to start. 'Let's join it,' says Lauren. We sit about halfway back from the altar on wooden chairs. There's a buzz of agitated whispering. Bees swarming.

A miked voice is reading and reverberating around the cathedral. It takes us a little while to realise this is a list of names welcoming the pilgrims who've registered their arrival and the places they've come from: Mainz, Lyons, Plymouth, Ghent, Montpelier, Graz, Turin, Prague, Valencia, Krakow, Salonica, Cluj, Munich. A call that rolls across Europe for ten minutes or more. Then the silver censer is swinging suspended from somewhere in the cavernous roof with a thick twisted rope secured by four chains. We see the clouds of incense before they wreathe around our heads. Sweet and cloying. This is one of two *botafumeiros* – smoke pushers – used in the mass. Originally to cover the stench of the pilgrims and fumigate for disease. It's the smaller one, *La Alcochofa*, the artichoke in the shape of a small woman's torso. Her wide hips are swinging from side to side in an ecstatic dance.

I'm concerned Lauren will start coughing, but she seems fine and happy to rest, with the mass partly inaudible and unintelligible echoing in the vaulted arches. We're lulled by the drone of the service and the heady incense into a light trance. Then suddenly Lauren is on her feet and in a small line at the front by the altar. She kneels and holds out her palm for the wafer, her thumb pressing down to trap it and dissolve it on her tongue. After she takes a sip of the wine. The priest is careful and none of it spills. He runs a white cloth around the rim of the chalice before Lauren stands, bows her head, and returns to her chair fortified and radiant. It's her first and will be, we silently assume, the last Catholic communion she takes. Another step on her unknown, indeterminate journey.

Outside it's chilly in the evening air. We pull on our sweaters and find a square where we order seafood, and I have my more minor epiphany. I taste my first glass of the Atlantic wind and waves, the nearest you'll get to drinking the sea without salt: it's a light, slightly tart lemon. We're in the origin and home of the Albarino grape. *Albarino* is Galician for 'whitish'. It ghosts over my tongue and palate

The next day we drive to the ends of the earth. *Finis Terrae.* Cabo Finisterre. The last peninsula, rock digit of the western world for the Romans and their Spanish colony. The water is freezing, a few children splash at its edges with occasional adults in black, seals bobbing in the waves. Lauren dares me to brave them. The moment I plunge I'm lost for words, for breath, for my life with my lungs crushed while she is safe on the shore.

If only.

I come up, a gasping, warm-blooded fish. My head splitting with ice-cold. I lurch and stumble back through the breakers to Lauren who's waving at me from the shore. Waving not drowning. She's smiling with a dark purple beach towel wrapped around her in the bright but cool, late spring sun. She's sitting waving and knows that I know that it's *she* who's drowning, not me. Drowning slowly on the sand while I have momentarily fantasised my life ending in the sea.

But still, she smiles. 'I owe you a beer,' she says.

I shake my head laughing. 'No. No. I want some red wine. It's warm.'

'Aah, yes,' she says pulling the towel closer around her. 'Like blood.'

IT'S A SUNDAY morning in Haslemere and we're lazing in bed with tea and papers. Lauren's phone pings. It's from Rowan. 'I've met him. A party last night. I think he's the one.' Along with Will, we first meet Andrew aka Baz at the O2 in south London. We're

there to watch the top eight men tennis players in the world compete to see who will finish the year as number one. Lauren, still the conductor of souls, has organised this.

Will and Sarah, who've already been together for eight years, are married eighteen months after *the shadow* has whispered in our ears. They've chosen August too, like we did. The immediate family are all residents for the wedding and celebration at Poundon, a Grade II listed neo-Georgian mansion with stables and a five-hectare Oxfordshire estate. It was constructed six years before the First World War by an Eton-educated gentleman cricketer. It remained in the Heywood-Lonsdale family, until the first year of the Second World War when it was requisitioned for use by the Special Operations Executive, known as Churchill's Secret Army or the Ministry of Ungentlemanly Warfare. The SOE was modelled on the success of the IRA in achieving independence for the Republic against overwhelming British military force. Its aim was to disrupt the Axis Powers' operations in Europe and work with resistance groups across the continent.

We motor down the drive passing through double rows of lime trees on either side. The façade of the house is Eydon stone: a mellow, soothing ochre. It exudes reassurance that everything is right with the world, and it will always be so. This is Queen Anne, reconstructed two hundred years after her early eighteenth-century reign. We're going to spend two nights in her architectural legacy, even more immaculate than when it was first conceived.

We unpack in our huge bedroom under the chandelier weeping crystal; the fireplace tiled with blue and white milkmaids, the portrait of a young woman, bobbed hair, pink frock with lace, above it. We're more interested in what's outside: the wide gravel path with its alternating English and French lavender whose scent will later arrest us, the clipped knee-height hedges; three green copper herons caught in mid-act of fishing and flying; a two-metre high burnished copper beech hedge and beyond it a huge willow weeping for joy in its green foliage; the geometric terracing, an Escher garden of form controlling textures and shades of gravel, lawn and lake; pears ripening against a lichened, rusty yellow brick wall; elegant waist-high cast-iron fencing through which the fields of stubble stretch sloping up to the horizon. An English pastoral paradise for the weekend.

The ceremony is outside on the terrace. We're seated at the front and keep having to twist our necks, nosy birds, wondering who else has flocked and alighted here. The registrar explains that while we, the guests, are outside, Sarah and Will have to stand just inside at the open double doors as the marriage licence is for inside the house, not its gardens. John, Sarah's father, has led her up the aisle of gravel and the couple are in full view, splendid in a silver threaded wedding dress from Paris and a powder blue suit from Oxford High St.

I've chosen and read 'Ithaka' – my own translation – by the early twentieth century Alexandrine-Greek poet, Cavafy:

> *When you sail to Ithaka*
> *I hope your journey is wave-tossed and long,*
> *Crammed with excitement, stuffed with surprises.*
> *Don't catch the fast winds, it's good if*
> *Your voyage takes years.*
> *Best to be grey when you reach the island,*
> *Rich with experience.*
> *Don't expect Ithaca to make you loaded, opulent.*
> *Ithaca was the mirage of your voyage*
> *Without Ithaca you wouldn't have left the harbour.*
> *Now her well is dry.*

After the ceremony, we find our way slowly down the steps onto the lawns and gravel paths where there are drinks on trays. Uncle Stuart in his white linen jacket, in his mid-80s, plays croquet with younger generations of nieces, nephews and in-laws. We spot Mac with a golden football which he chases round and round in his blue bow tie. Sarah's grandma, older than Stuart, is elegant and gracious with her blue dress, white shawl and stick, posed happily on a bench with her daughter Claire, Sarah's mother, and her grandson Tom.

There's a distant grumble in the skies growing to a growl and then a thunderous roar. The guests strewn across the lawns stop whatever they're doing; they momentarily abandon the wedding and gaze up into the blue wash searching for the source of the guttural booming. From behind a lambswool cloud a small formation of four planes fly sedately, by modern standards not fast, and low in the sky. We can almost feel the vibrations of the hot metal on our skin and see the pilot in each cockpit. Someone standing nearby cries in a loud whisper of amazement, 'Spitfires! They're Spitfires!' As if we were guests at a choreographed ceremony laid on for Churchill's Special Operations Executive. Mac barks, the spell is broken and we return to the moment of the wedding tinkling with chatter, laughter and glasses.

Inside the marquee, the architecture and design of the decorations and tables has been masterminded to a perfect confection by Sarah supported by Claire. Huge sails, off-white lightly patterned material billow up to a central chandelier. Crystal white pom-poms, a cross between snowflakes and snowballs, are suspended over our tables. Here on a side-table is a plate hand-painted by Lauren with strawberry hearts over a light turquoise wash. 'Will, Sarah, 24 August 2014' inscribed in blue paint. On an upright piano here are photos of our own wedding nearly forty years before and other, earlier family weddings in black and white. The food summit is a five-tier wedding cake, each circular layer, slightly smaller than the last.

After the speeches, the toasts and courses, the tables are cleared and taken away to make space for the dancefloor. The main act are friends of Will's from Oxford, Temple Funk Collective. Lauren doesn't need a wig. Her hair's grown out long enough for her to be her customary uninhibited self, dancing in a shimmering dark blue velvet evening dress with the lightest of straps over her bare shoulders.

Baz and Rowan are there taking it gently as she's heavily

pregnant. Two months later the bright presence of the newborn Scarlett casts our private shadow into a more distant place. As the child grows, her radiance intensifies and minimises the shadow in our lives. Minutes elongate, becoming hours that stretch into days which in turn are as long a week, each week itself endlessly spiralling into months. It's the waiting, the not knowing which makes time slide, slip and vanish, except when brutally punctured by the invasion of chemotherapy.

LAUREN, ROWAN, BAZ, Scarlett and I are surrounded by shades and shapes of green. Olive, pea, emerald, lime, moss, viridescent in curved walls of low hedgerows, bushes sculpted in topiaries of balls, snowmen, towers, doughnuts, arabesques, toadstools. This all-enveloping green is set off by the lilac pouring down the mellowed Cotswold stone on the façade of the house, the kaleidoscopic beds and the golden rain showers of laburnum trees. We hear the rushing of the Avon River through the small valley of the grounds below and its fishponds. We're sauntering through the Abbey House Gardens in Malmsbury where Benedictine monks grew medicinal herbs and flowers in the Abbot's Garden. Now it has the largest collection of roses in Britain. This pastoral scene is a cleansing balm before we move on to the prime reason we've come to stay in the King's Arms in the centre of town.

The car is half-stuck in mud on the edge of a field. We've been asked to pull over, off the track. Other vehicles are being waved past. Lauren's explaining she's forgotten the tickets and is trying to find a way to prove to the lady in a fluorescent jacket that we really have paid for them. Rowan and Baz are in the back of the car with Scarlett who's nine months old.

Rowan's telling Baz a story that is a canonical text in the family history. 'We drove through France for a holiday in Catalonia. The return trip was to take the ferry home from Bilbao.' Her Dad wanted to see Gehry's new Guggenheim Museum before catching the ferry. Mum, Dad, Will, she and her friend Jenny turned up and did just that. We saw the tumbling dice on the waterfront of the River Nervion. The thirty-six thousand titanium plates form the skin of the structure; the material was chosen because it changes in different lights, and when it rains it turns to gold. The curves of the structure are maritime, sails billowing, ships' bows, the swell and the dip of the waves. 'We got to know the outside of that museum really well,' says Rowan. 'I remember chasing Will under a huge spider by the water.' (It's a Louise Bourgeois sculpture.) 'But we never got inside the Gehry Guggenheim. Dad hadn't checked. It was closed on a Monday! Then we drove to the port to catch the ferry back to England. Mum had the time wrong. There wasn't another for three days. We had to drive all the way back through northern Spain and France!'

Then, still in the car, we're rolling down the wet hill sliding in the grass and up the other side to park. It's not raining now but has been much of the day. By the time we've walked up the slope through the camping area and entered the main enclosure our trainers are already soaking and squelching with mud. We take it in turns to carry Scarlett. She has miniature wellingtons and though she can't walk she wants to splash in the puddles. She grasps my thumb with her hand and Lauren's with the other, so we're guiding her through the muddy brown water. We've arrived at WOMAD, a hippier Edinburgh festival of world music, arts and dance, in the Wiltshire countryside just outside Malmesbury.

We spend the next two days as a shifting target of sunshine, rain, mud and world food vans; Lauren and Scarlett whizz by in a blur on a merry-go-round with red and white flowers in their hair. Scarlett wears a rainbow-coloured cardigan knitted by the mum of Rowan's friend, Anushka. She has headphones to protect her hearing as we dance to the Japanese funk band, Osaka Monaureil. We stamp our feet and clap to the English folk-rock band Bellowhead pumping out their song 'London Town'. On stage they produce a glorious, harmonious cacophony driving the songs with bass, rhythm and lead guitars, fiddles, bouzouki, drums, tambourines, broomsticks, glockenspiel, coal scuttle, frying pan, tuba, its cousin the sousaphone, trumpets, trombones, alto and bass saxophones, kazoo. Lauren cries with laughter. She loves this band second only to The Levellers. At the Radio 3 stage, we're mesmerised by the wailing of a Kurdish/Turkish singer.

Ghostpoet is playing 'Be Right Back Moving House', opening slowly on one note then chords, a firm but not loud insistent strumming rhythm, the bass coming in building slowly underneath through the six minutes of the song, 'love, love remains, throughout the pain and strain over the years,' the chorus with its shimmering guitar behind, 'and I am sitting over here looking for the answers . . . working it out one day at a time,' a croaking half singing, soft speaking, a South London lyrical toughness.

Ghostpoet's shaven bald head rising, a distant hill over his huge round dark-framed glasses, wide-eyed like a wise old owl.

One day at a time, one day at a time, one day at a time, one day at a time.

Ghostpoet's is the mantra of our lives now, repeated daily until Lauren leaves.

ROWAN AND BAZ have a registry office wedding at Islington Town Hall. Scarlett is in attendance, a spinning top learning to walk and fall. Baz's parents, Pam and Rodger, Lauren and I are the witnesses. We have lunch outside at The Albion.

Then in late September, they have their wedding party at Chateau de Lisse in Gascony, halfway between Bordeaux and Toulouse. This is a party for their friends, few relatives, with only parents, siblings and their partners invited. Two weeks short of one-year-old, Scarlett's top spins for longer before it falls on the extensive lawns. Guests are accommodated in the thirteenth-century chateau itself, in an adjacent barn and other outbuildings. Laughter and excitement echo through rooms with huge fireplaces, beamed ceilings and children rattling the suits of armour.

Late acceptances lodge in Nerac, where on the first evening guests assemble outside for dinner.

When we return to the Chateau, Baz and Rowan set up an impromptu bar with cocktails and beers on the terrace where the wedding breakfast will take place the next evening. Someone has found the 'honesty cellar' below the kitchen, which holds hundreds of bottles from the Chateau's own vineyards. Lauren says she's going to bed to save her energy for the big day tomorrow. I stay up with a crowd of twenty or so, drinking, joking, laughing, telling stories, smoking. At some point a discussion about the rights and wrongs of eating *foie gras* starts up. It escalates and gets a little heated. In the pro-corner is Will and in the anti-corner one of Baz's friends. Others are chipping in, but Will and Glen are going at it full volume. From somewhere in the dark overhead a woman's voice rings out, 'Will you two shut up?! Some of us are trying to get some sleep for tomorrow,' and a window bangs shut. Ever the one to speak her mind, it's Lauren. It's time for me to join her too.

The following morning, we come down to breakfast. Several guests who'd stayed up too late are asking for more and stronger coffee. I've been detailed to take care of Scarlett for a few hours while preparations for the day unfold and the women, especially the bride, embark on their elaborate toilette and lay out their costumes for the phases of the day and night. I'm told there's a light lunch around one-thirty and the ceremony in the chateau chapel is at three o'clock. 'Be back by one sharp.'

I decide to return to enjoy the picturesque medieval and Renaissance town of Nerac. I push Scarlett in her buggy along the banks of the Baisse and its arched, Gothic bridge, strolling past half-timbered facades. We follow the curving limestone walls of the fifteenth and sixteenth century Chateau Henri IV, which support a galleried walkway under steep-pitched, auburn-tiled rooves. It's quintessential Southwest France. I'd be happy to wander here all day but there's a wedding ceremony.

Now we're waiting outside the Chateau's private chapel for the final guests to enter. Rowan beautiful in a full-length ivory gown with a lace bodice and Baz handsome in a dark suit set off by a white waistcoat with the splash of a salmon tie are stars of the show, and everyone is charmed by eleven-month-old Scarlett in her mini bridesmaid frock. Lauren is in a calf-length dress with soft pink flowers. Sarah is gorgeous in full length blue-black, Will in cornflower blue, me in a darker blue linen. We hear Tom Walker, Rowan's friend, inside the chapel strike up his viola, a signal we should enter soon. There's a crunching and a screech on the gravel as a taxi, travelling fast, brakes in front of us. A slim, red-haired woman and a dishevelled, dark-haired man spills out. 'Tracy! Inigo! You made it!' cries Rowan. We all enter together.

Tom is playing on his viola Bach's First Cello Suite (BWV 1007), an arrangement of 'Salut D'Amour' by Elgar, followed by 'Autumn Leaves' and 'Fly Me to the Moon'. Rich, Baz and Rowan's celebrant, gives a great address. Rowan's brother, Will, offers us all wise words:

'Marriage is a lifelong commitment of two people to each other. It's the final binding of the co-authored, book of loyalty. But it's just the binding, the real story of the love and the family is the pages in-between the covers. And although the book has now been bound there is still plenty of room for you to keep writing or doodling or spill wine over it. But the important thing is that you've now got something that will contain all of your happiness together. The more pages you add and the bigger the story becomes the better the book will be. We've all loved reading the book so far and cannot wait to see how the story unfolds.'

We file out from the candlelight of the chapel into the buttery, late September afternoon sun. Waiters are circulating with drinks on the lawns and parterre. We're serenaded by a punk accordionist playing her instrument with wild concentration like Hendrix played his guitar. I talk to the late arrival Inigo, Rowan's independent journalist friend who works mainly for Channel Four. I'd last seen him five years earlier dancing on a bar top in Tel Aviv. He might not have stopped since. Apparently, his birthday was in London the day before the wedding. He'd said he'd try and make it. He'd been up all night and just got to Gatwick in time to catch a flight to Bordeaux. Tracy, another journalist friend from Rowan's time at *The Observer*, was on the same flight.

We make our way to the round tables on the terrace outside, the glasses and cutlery winking and glittering in the late beams. A stash of wedding paraphernalia has fallen out of Rowan and Baz's car boot on the drive down to the chateau. One of Rowan's bridesmaids, Josy, steps in to organise the seating plans and set up. We know that soon the sun will sink, and we'll continue the wedding breakfast in warm darkness under the fairy lights. A small platform has been erected for wedding speeches. I know I won't have any difficulty projecting in the open air, unamplified, across the terrace to more than a hundred guests. But I want everyone to see me and I'm not tall. At some point during the several courses, I notice a window in the chateau wall located halfway way along the terrace. I go to the loo and check if the window opens. It does and there's a wide mullion where I can stand. When it's my turn to speak I disappear and emerge on the mullion where all the guests can see me. I'm about two metres above the terrace. As I stretch to my full height there's concern I might fall. I try to hide my own nervousness, which is mainly about falling. I start to speak:

'Rowan went to primary school in Bangkok. Lauren and I are with two adult friends on an adventure weekend. Rowan, six, is with us. The cave is half a mile long with a small river running through. It's lit with overhead lamps every fifty metres. Halfway through the lights go out. The generator has gone. It's darker than closing your eyes. All we hear is running water. Bats brush our faces. There may be scorpions or worse. *Nous sommes tous* – excuse my French – *effraye de merdre* – except for Rowan who, quite unfazed, leads us calmly along the river bed until we see the mouth of the cave.

'Little did we know how such determination and bravery was preparation for life in London at *The Observer*. Especially that part when, at five in the morning, she finds herself, after a good night's partying, on some desolate corner in Hackney with no wallet, no phone, no cash, no map, no idea at all about where she is. After the preparation of the jungle cave, life lost in London was easy for her.'

Later that night the wedding party moves down into the cellars to dance to their friend, Peepshow Paddy's, deejaying. Inigo has recovered from his birthday and asks Lauren to help with his make-up. He appears using Paddy's amplification to give us an impressive fifteen-minute Elvis impersonation. Not only the tremulous voice, but the quiff, the dark scowl, the huge collar. Along with other journalists, he and I are the last to go to bed.

Not much sleep. I'd 'volunteered' to be up to look after Scarlett for the first hour or two to let Rowan, Baz and Lauren have a lie in. When I hand Scarlett to Lauren, I know I need a violent shot of something to keep me awake for the next period. Here I am standing by the edge of the reedy lake. I plunge into the dark water, gasping for air; my heart and lungs are momentarily frozen. I can't breathe, then gradually the cold recedes and numbness creeps in. I feel nothing but weightlessness. Then a tingling as sensation bubbles through my limbs, which are mysteriously no longer frozen but vaguely warm. After breast-stroking round the lake two or three times, shaking off weeds wrapping round my ankles and shins, I hear distant shouting. A voice gets nearer. I can hear the shouting and a word distinguishes itself. 'Out!' Then others, 'Dangerous!' 'Drown!' Lauren's with Scarlett in a buggy on a pontoon screaming at me, 'Didn't you see?' She's pointing to a sign by the pontoon. 'Get out before you drown! Fool!' Then she turns and pushes Scarlett back up the gravel. My chest heaving, I clamber up on to the pontoon and stagger down it to read the red words' warning: DANGER *Baignade strictement interdite. Le lac n'est pas sûr pour la baignade.*

Later I tell Lauren it was perfectly safe and the owners probably had to put it up for insurance purposes. She gives me a withering look. I don't tell her my ankle did get caught in the reeds.

Some of us play tennis, including the Italian, Luca – who, having no shorts, plays in his underpants with no top, much to the amusement of players and spectators. He's one of the better players as if liberated from too much clothing. In the afternoon we laze in the glistening blue water of the pool and drink cold beers in a twenty-first century *Bigger Splash* while children's laughter aboard a giant, pink flamingo echoes against the backdrop of the fourteenth-century chateau's towers and steeples.

I HAVE TO go to Budapest and arrange the visit at a good time for Lauren to travel. We stay with Simon, the British Council Director, and his wife, Ann. They will be the last British Council residents of number 70 Uri Utca, which loosely translated means Lord or Gentleman Street. Among other things, I've come to confirm that message with Simon. The British Council can no longer afford to reside in faux aristocratic splendour. We enter through the outer, double doors into what was once a ground level stables and reception for carriages and horses. Cellars for storage. A stable hand or two might have slept here, but the rest of the household ascended a sweeping staircase to its salons for living and dining, its bedrooms and bathrooms. Simon's grand piano perfectly suits this space. His successor will live in a modern apartment. If they are musical, and lucky, they might be able to squeeze in an upright. The interior structure is sixteenth century, its frontage eighteenth.

Facing the house across the tree-lined street stands the three-tier tower of Mary Magdalene church, bombed in the Second World War. The body of the church no longer present, the tower rises still, a long neck with a severed head. In post-war communist Hungary restoration of churches was a low priority. Further down the street is the military museum housed in a handsome square with cobbles laid in circular designs. I walk their dog, Sponj, across them at night and his nails click. The nineteenth-century cast-iron streetlamps cast a fuzzy glow in the mist, and the skittering of Sponj's nails morph into the thunder of horses pulling the heavy canons guarding the museum from their station. There's been no expense spared in the restoration and preservation of Hungary's military prowess. Sponj is a rescue dog from South Africa. The Afrikaans for English 'sponge', which captures the texture and shades of the ageing Dalmatian's coat.

At the far end of the street is the Buda castle and palace with spectacular views over the Danube to the Hungarian Parliament in Pest where we all go – at Lauren's advance request – to the Hungarian State Opera. We're assaulted visually and aurally by the most whacky burlesque and baroque opera production we've ever seen. Arrigo Boito's rarely performed *Mefistofele*, based on Goethe's *Faust*. One review of the production we see: 'An audacious spectacular opera needing an audacious spectacular production. Kovalik threw the entire kitchen sink at it.' It's the only opera to which he composed the music, though he wrote the libretti for two of Verdi's late, great operas, *Otello* and *Falstaff*. When Verdi died in 1901, Boito was at his bedside.

While Simon and I are working, Ann takes Lauren to the National Gallery. She has her sketchbook and stops to draw on its steps. Inside she becomes fascinated by the Austrian artist Carl Moll's technique in the depiction of snow in *Winter Courtyard* (1902). Moll was at the centre of Vienna's cultural life from the late nineteenth century until his death.

Lauren and I visit the Dohanyi Synagogue, the largest in Europe, in the Jewish area of Pest, knowing that more than half a million Hungarian Jews were murdered in the Holocaust; four hundred thousand-plus in an eight-week period when their deportation to Auschwitz started in May 1944. Later we meet Simon and Ann for a meal in a Kosher restaurant nearby. For Lauren and me, the meal is our unspoken memory to what happened.

IT'S MAY 2016 and we go Koroni. It's now more than three years since Lauren was diagnosed with a year to live if she was 'lucky.' Each day now is the water of life which keeps on flowing, endlessly it seems, but we know sometime soon the well will run dry. Lauren doesn't want to stay longer than a week. Will and Sarah went on their delayed honeymoon to Japan the previous summer. Dylan George Arthur Walker was born in early March and our second grandchild is only a few weeks old. I persuade her to stretch our time in Koroni to two weeks. She's convinced this will be her last visit to the house we built and the garden with its original olive trees and vines. Now it has lemon, orange, pomegranate and banana trees as well as hibiscus, geraniums, rosemary, bougainvillea, roses, asters, oleanders.

We sit on the balcony and look out for hoopoes, a distant larger cousin of our English kingfisher, flashing black and white wings and dipping over the olive trees down to the beach. There are usually a couple of nests in the sandy cliffs behind our house. Occasionally, one lands in our garden, pecking at the grass and dust, its pink-brown body nodding its long, black curved bill scratching for insects, its main food. We see one with orange crest fully extended, tipped black and white. Spartan soldiers of the bird world.

We meet our friend Yiannis alone; his wife Priya lost her job in Athens and couldn't find another. She's now back in England with their children. Yiannis taught in the Greek school in London for a while but had to return to Greece to retain his pension rights. He's managed to get a transfer from the primary school in Athens to the one here in Koroni on the ridge above our house. He's finishing his last couple of years teaching here before retirement. It's the school where he himself was a pupil nearly sixty years earlier. He was born in a nearby village, Vasiltsi where we still see women gathered in the square round a huge vat over a fire making soap from olives. His parents are glad to have him back outside the village in the house they built for him and Priya. I once went with Yiannis to meet his father several kilometres along a rutted, dirt track to a piece of land he owns where he grows a variety of produce: potatoes, tomatoes, aubergines, peppers, courgettes, melons, vines. Now Yiannis tells us his father is becoming increasingly forgetful and distracted. Failing to return from his plot an hour after dark, Yiannis tries to find him and fails. The police are contacted. He's finally found in the small hours of the morning asleep under a boat on a beach. It looks like they'll have to take his motorbike away. What will happen to the fruit and vegetables?

WE'VE DRIVEN SEVERAL times before through this gorge into and beyond the Tageytos mountains west of Sparta. The single lane road twists and turns sharply and steeply on both the ascent and descent. One moment we're in the bottom of the gorge, the tarmac following the flow of the river and burrowing, moles, through limestone tunnels and overhangs. The next we're curving round a huge, elevated bowl above the treeline with distant views of receding mountain peaks. As we descend on the eastern slopes of the Tageytos we pass through the tree line: oak, sycamore, plane, shading the road. We stop for coffee at a café where the balcony juts out lending us a view down the valley to modern Sparta on the plain.

We drive to the upper part of the three-tiered site, which tumbles down the foothills of the Tageytos overlooking Sparta. We pass through the enormous *kastro* gate, huge blocks and slabs of stone from the thirteenth century stand to attention. We know the cobbled path to the summit is steep and treacherous. We need to stop at every turn of the uneven path. We take in the view of the mediaeval *hora*, town, below us. Lauren's favourite building rests between cypress trees. This now houses the only inhabitants of the site, the Pantanassa nunnery. As we step up onto the plateau of the fortress at the summit we're at one thousand feet.

There's a spectacular three-hundred-and-sixty-degree view of the Tageytos mountains on one flank and the Spartan plain on the other.

We sit unshaded, except by our hats, on the original construction, the Frankish acropolis built in 1249. In the following centuries this expands down the mountainside with the creation of an upper town, a lower town and an outer town. These are dotted with numerous churches, houses, mansions, fortified monasteries and palaces. By 1400 it's the most important fortified city in the Byzantine Empire after Constantinople; a centre of Byzantine scholarship and art acknowledged as influential in the Italian Renaissance. It still preserves some of the most spectacular and important frescoes in Byzantine history. In 1460 it was captured by the Ottomans who occupied it – save a brief, fifteen-year period when the Venetians took it – until the Greek War of Independence in the 1820s.

We've come to Mystras for what Lauren says she *knows* is her last visit. I refuse to believe she can *know* this. So, we don't speak about it.

With the bare limestone of the fortification around us we're sitting on the head of a white eagle. It's early enough in the season for us to enjoy the warmth of the sun and we laze, stretching our arms out with hands resting on the top of the masonry. 'Look,' I whisper to Lauren nodding down towards my right hand. A tiny lizard, not much bigger than a gecko, transparent light orange tail, has come to sun itself alongside my little finger.

She smiles, removes her hat and rests her head on my shoulder for a while.

Later I read that in Ancient Greece lizards represented hope and a good life after death.

THE WHITEWASHED INN is a long, lowish building with a mop of thatch falling and rising, bushy eyebrows over the deep sockets of its windows. The lane runs directly past the stone steps up to its front door. But there's so little traffic that cottages nearby have pots and plants outside their walls on the edge of the tarmac. The lime-yellow of small laburnum trees called 'golden rain' glisten in the sun. There's a rectangular block of military red splashed on one side of the pub. A box we used to open to talk to others at a distance. Above the inn door is a painted sign of two birds originating in China. They were introduced to Britain by the Romans and had all but disappeared until they explode into the English countryside in the nineteenth century with the invention of the double-barrelled shotgun. Since when no English rural scene is considered complete without them. We've come to stay in The Brace of Pheasants.

We wander through the hamlet of Plush with growing amazement and disbelief which had begun when we stopped for coffee in the village of Piddletrenthide. As if arriving in this parish of West Dorset we'd opened the door into a world where we'd meet Miss Marple solving one of Agatha Christie's English village mysteries.

We climb a steep hill opposite the inn and stumble on the church of St John the Baptist. It's mid-nineteenth century, Gothic, slightly overgrown and mildly neglected. There are benches to sit and enjoy views across and down the valley. We read that it's deconsecrated. Walking down we catch glimpses of a Regency manor. Our guide tells us it was once owned by the great pianist Alfred Brendel and is still in the family. The Gothic church is used for an annual summer music festival produced by his daughter Katharina and led by his son, Adrian, a cellist.

'We'll come and see them next year,' says Lauren, laughing, not believing herself.

We stumble on the stage-set perfection of Plush cricket pitch and ground. The pavilion sits guarded on either side by symmetrically shaped, incandescent copper beeches. The grass under the soles of our shoes is a fabric with a pile which is softer than velvet. Behind the pavilion the bowl of hills holds the sky.

Later in the afternoon, we set off to climb the highest of the chalk hills near Plush. Half a mile away Ball Hill rises to an altitude of two hundred and fifty metres. In earlier years, she wouldn't have thought about it. Now it's our Everest. The steep gradient forces us to stop every ten or twenty metres. I hear Lauren's heavy breathing, her heart thudding, spadefuls of clay thrown and landing in a trench.

'We don't have to get to the top,' I suggest.

She grimaces and stops. 'Yes, we do. We do,' she rasps.

When, at last, we reach the top of the hill and it plateaus, she drops to the ground, laughing and choking. 'We've come to the ball! Ball Hill!' she cries out. Then falls silent, closing her eyes, enjoying the achievement and the sun warming her face. I drop down, lie beside her, and close my eyes too.

In moments, we hear the first skylark song. Then another and another, and we lose count of the flowing trills and liquid melodies threading their notes in and around the dipping flights of their ordinary brown feathers.

She feels for my hand and twines her fingers in mine. Our eyes are still closed, the sun glows on our cheeks and she whispers, 'If I could die here, right now with you, I'd be so happy.'

WE'RE STANDING ON floorboards dark as charcoal in front of an ancient but handsome domestic fireplace. Above the mantelpiece is a painting of a young man. His dark hair cascades in waves to just above his shoulders. It's held back from his forehead by a soft black cap which could be velvet. His gaze is half-turned towards us, but his right eye is central, and that side of his face is lily pale, his left, further away, is in shadow. Both eyes brown and wide-open look clearly at us, confident but not needing to challenge as if he can see the future and knows what he's going to do and become. The philtrum is well defined, the upper lip in a clear bow, the lower lip is full and slightly tumbling. The shadow below that might have a hint of beard but his long neck repeats the swan pale of his face. Only the upper part of his tunic, where his neck and chest merge is a semi-circle of soft, dark material echoing his hat. The dark of his hair and garments is mirrored in the well-dark recess of the hearth below.

We've just come from the courtyard of the mediaeval house. We flit across the brick in herring-bone pattern from the shade of the arches into the light pouring down from the eggshell blue above. A well with its chain, iron grille and plant pots exude the scent of basil. This is where the artist whose portrait we're contemplating was born on Good Friday in 1483. We glide over the red and yellow tiles bruised by six centuries of habitation and pause to examine his pestle and mortar for grinding colours. Under the wooden carved ceiling we're snared by a portrait of a young woman holding a miniature unicorn in the crook of her arm like the woman we'd just seen in a chic café outside nursing a chihuahua.

The Duke of Montefeltro created one of the leading humanist courts of the Italian Renaissance, with its scriptorium and scribes in the palace of Urbino. He was a renowned intellectual, leader and mercenary soldier, financing the growth and influence of Urbino. Raphael's father, Giovanni, was one of his court painters. The Duke's humanistic court and his support for the development of young artists made him a landmark figure in the Renaissance. He was known as 'the light of Italy'. He didn't know that the environment he'd created in Urbino would produce the greatest of all Renaissance artists. He dies the year before Raphael is born, but his legacy ensures Raphael is thoroughly trained and nurtured. Raphael's mother dies when he's eight and his father when he's eleven years old, but by 1500, when he's seventeen, he's become an independent master.

Eight years later he's summoned to the court of Pope Julius II to redecorate the papal apartments; and six years after in 1514, at thirty-two years old, he's appointed the architect in charge of St

Peter's. Though he dies at thirty-seven his output is prodigious, far exceeding Leonardo's and more varied than Michaelangelo's.

'We've seen where it started,' says Lauren. 'We can go back to the countryside.'

She gets tired easily now and needs to rest every two or three hundred metres. She insists we stop in the Botanic Gardens for our final minutes in the womb of the Renaissance. She's determined to explore each of its three terraces cut into the side of the hill more than two centuries ago. They form a spectacular, planted viewing platform on the edge of the small city. She especially likes the medicinal plants – the simples – which are studied and researched by the university.

'Perhaps there's one for me,' she says.

We drive down and away from Urbino with its fairy tale towers through rolling hills with tumbling vineyards in soldierly lines. Lauren asks me to stop on the crest of a hill where there are no vines, some light woods and a panoramic view.

'My last walk,' she pauses. 'Here in Italy.' She smiles.

I want to contradict but I don't. It seems foolishly, naively optimistic when she's almost certainly right. 'Let her be,' I say to myself.

We saunter laterally across the hillside, going down would mean coming up. She hasn't got the strength left for that today. She's twenty metres away when she gives a cry of surprise and bends down. She holds up what looks like a slim, smooth twig alternating dark brown and ivory about twelve inches long. She calls out, 'It's a porcupine. A porcupine quill! It's beautiful.' She's as happy as she's been all holiday.

Later we sit on the private terrace of our vaulted room fashioned out of a ground floor wine cellar. We're surrounded by vines flowing in waves over the hills around us. It's the quill of an African Crested Porcupine. One of the world's largest rodents. Italy is its only location in Europe.

IT'S A WEEK until Midsummer Day 2016. There's been higher

than average rainfall, especially in London. The previous two days have been wet and muddy, but the site has dried out overnight and now the ground is soft but just firm enough to walk without sinking.

We're at the climax of the evening with the headline act clothed in black feathers holding a saxophone. Lauren, as a surprise, has bought us tickets to Field Day in Victoria Park, East London. The standout act in the afternoon and new to us is John Grant, a big man with a beard who sets deadpan, black humour and the surreal, in glorious funk, uplifting melodies. His songs are sly, funny, liberating, his voice sometimes ethereal, sometimes from the bowels of the earth. He gives us the highs and the lows of his catalogue playing the day after a gunman attacked a Florida gay night club shouting allegiance to ISIS and murdering 49 people.

As the evening builds to its climax, dark clouds mass and lightning flashes when P J Harvey comes on stage. For Lauren the set bursts into life as Harvey plays 'When Under Ether' inspired by Eliot's *Four Quartets*. Her haunting voice in a high register floats through her own poetry. *The mind comes alive / But conscious of nothing / But the will to survive.* 'That's me,' whispers Lauren.

It's the first and will be the last time we see P J Harvey together. The dark clouds are a swirling mass of granite overhead. We walk with the crowds flooding away like a river that's broken its banks and, as we stream Underground in the jostle, Lauren takes my hand and whispers, 'Thank you. I'm happy. I feel safe with you.'

EU REFERENDUM DAY, 23 June, is marked by violent storms across London and the Southeast. St James Park records 44mm – a month's typical rainfall in just six hours – and the Environment Agency issues 45 flood alerts and 16 red flood warnings.

The next day, a Friday, I take a photo of Lauren in our bedroom, in bed. She's holding up a poster she's designed with yellow stars. 'I AM STILL A EUROPEAN.'

LESS THAN TWO months later England has its warmest August since 2004. Midmorning on Saturday August 13 we climb into the Toyota Rav, a car chosen by Lauren, and head north out of Haslemere towards South London as the temperature builds steadily. I've managed to secure a prime parking place in a house drive, two minutes' walk from the ground. It makes it much easier for her to enjoy the occasion. We stroll in the sunshine and still arrive early at the gates to the Oval. We want to ensure we're there before the others and there are several tiers of steps to climb. Lauren has to pause at each mezzanine and take a rest to catch her breath, but we don't need to hurry, and she's relaxed, triumphant when she's made it to the top floor of the stand. We have outside seating under cover. Our friend Bernard has arranged this.

'Wow!' she exclaims looking round the stadium at the green outfield and the drier square with its shorn pitches alongside the one they're preparing now. The groundsman is still painting the whitewash lines around the stumps: the bowling crease, the popping or batsman's crease and the return crease to signal wide balls. We're the first of our party to arrive.

'It's beautiful,' she says. And I know she means everything: our privileged seats, the pigeons on the outfield, spectators trickling into the ground which in twenty minutes will become a flood, the white sight screens which help the batsman pick out the red ball and to our left the gasholder with its wrought iron, latticed frame. Gasholder Number One at 135 feet high is the only one to survive. Indeed, it's Grade II listed. Early in the nineteenth century the cricket ground was a market garden with a neighbouring waterworks and two reservoirs. After 1845 when the market garden became a cricket ground, the Phoenix Gas Light & Coke Company replaced the waterworks with five gas holders. They saw the first Test Match against Australia in 1880. As I write this, Gasholder Number One is being converted into apartments, mainly luxury ones. Residents will be encased by the wrought-iron frame of the Industrial Revolution; sitting on their balconies they'll be gazing through the skeleton of the industrial past to the present and into an unknown future.

Someone asks if we'd like a drink. 'Water, fizzy please,' I say.

'Remember our first time,' Lauren says.

I smile. 'Trent Bridge. Summer 1977.'

'After Spain. Before you went to Kuwait and me Bretton Hall.'

'Against Australia. Boycott ran out Derek Randall, the local boy. And went on to make a hundred. We won that Test.'

This is day three of the fourth Test match against Pakistan. In the afternoon Younis Khan scores a double century with a six off Moeen Ali's spin. Pakistan reach 542 all out in their first innings. After England lose their third wicket and are approaching almost certain defeat, which our friends are contemplating, Lauren turns to me with her hand lightly on my arm, 'I don't mind what happens. I never did. It was always about being with you.'

This day, as it unfurls in England's loss, is her last trip out from our home and garden.

OUR SPACIOUS DOUBLE bedroom's on the ground floor. We haven't moved it there from upstairs, it's always been there. It was a bungalow which we lived in for some months between leaving India and going to Brazil. We take the largest ground floor bedroom with its capacious built-in cupboards because there's no upstairs. The second bedroom becomes Lauren's studio and study. We bought the property for its location and plot with a generous garden – third of an acre – the back a secret enclosure with voluminous yew hedges, a spectacular magnolia, its wax-white petals bleeding pink, always in full glory around Lauren's birthday in mid-April. Apple trees at the far end. While in Brazil we have the roof raised and create a second floor with three bedrooms and a bathroom. Once complete, we never bother to move our bedroom upstairs. The metal-framed windows extend across the whole breadth of the bedroom, so we love being in bed with a panorama down the garden. When we go away for more than a few nights fallow deer take up residence there, and in August and September feast on the windfalls.

It's early September and we haven't left the house and garden since the Oval trip. Late afternoon just before dusk and Lauren, in bed, spots a young fallow deer under the trees. She calls me and I sit on the bed with her. We watch as it munches apples, its chestnut brown coat spotted with irregular splashes of white like a decorator's overalls. Its chest and belly are muddied white. Occasionally it freezes, alert, it's heard something and looks up towards the house. Lauren, propped against a stack of pillows, whispers, 'Maybe it knows we're watching. So beautiful.'

The deer resumes its scouring for apples. When I next turn in Lauren's direction, her head has fallen to one side, her eyelids are fluttering gently then stop. She's asleep.

A few days earlier, at her request, I'd given her morphine for the pain. When she comes round hours later, she says, 'Never, ever give that to me again. Even if I ask for it. It was horrible. I was a zombie. I could hear you and the nurse whispering. Some words. I couldn't speak. I couldn't move. I was out of my body; on the ceiling looking down at you. I hated it. My body was alive, but I was paralysed, in limbo.'

I stay with her that evening and night lying on top of the bed, resting, drifting in and out of sleep. Adjusting her pillows. Sometimes cuddling her gently through the light duvet. Getting up to help her reach the bathroom and wait to steady her back. She's sporadically in pain, but only the morphine could help, and she won't have it. Giving her sips of water through the beaker and its hard plastic straw, which Rowan has bought to make it easier for her to swallow. Her sporadic coughing grows more intense and laboured through the night. We scramble onto the shores of dawn, more exhausted than when we went to sleep. The pale green carpet seeps slowly into view with the rug from Iraq warming the room with its shades of red. I get up to make some tea. Does she want any? No. Just sips of water. Back in bed I fall asleep, properly for the first time all night when everyone else is waking up.

When I next wake, Lauren, somehow, has managed to sit up and shift her weight to the side of the bed where she's sitting with her feet on the floor. She's moaning intermittently, punctuated by bouts of coughing, her breathing alternating between heavy and shallow as if she's panicking. I call out to Rowan who's sleeping upstairs. I adjust her nightdress and drape her favourite silk gown over her shoulders. I sit with my left arm around her. Rowan appears. 'Call the nurse,' I say.

She's slowly rocking backwards and forwards, groaning. Twice she makes a slight lunge as if she's trying to stand up. I ask her if she wants help. She can't answer. She tries to speak, half words form, her language expelled from her. I hear only shards of vowel sounds, 'aah,' 'ee,' 'ay,' puncturing the air and building in volume so she's shrieking and then an almost final consonant, 'lars, dah,' 'lars dah,' but her tongue doesn't have the strength to hit the roof of her mouth. And the 't' never comes. Her body contracts and there's an awful gurgling sound rising from her lungs and into her throat. I'm trying to hold her firmly, but the contortions keep coming in unstoppable waves. Blood fills and pours from her mouth, with each convulsion it vomits down her white nightie, onto the pale green carpet and her body wracked with a final, tidal wave fountains blood across the space spattering the cream cushions on the wooden camel bench. Then she goes limp, and I have to hold her very tightly to stop her falling over. I have both arms round her now. She's silent, head slumped, unmoving. Rowan comes back into the room. 'I don't know, I don't know,' I say. And I sit clutching her to me waiting for something to happen, but it doesn't. We're held together in what slowly dawns on me has been our last dance.

When the nurses arrive, I can't let her go. One slowly and gracefully prises my arms away from her body while the other supports Lauren so she doesn't fall. Once I'm detached and near the end of the bed, they lift her legs and swing her feet round, placing her hands on her chest and adjusting her head and neck on the pillows. She already looks more content, more peaceful than she has for many days. As if her release has transferred all her agony into me.

Epilogue

Lauren and Mac, soon after her diagnosis. Blackdown, Haslemere. 2013

L AUREN, WE FOLLOW your clear, written instructions to the letter. Present at the cremation are Rowan, Baz, Scarlett nearly two years, Leo not three months, Will, Sarah, Dylan seven months, Mac and me. There's no service. We play your specified favourites, including Satchmo's 'What a Wonderful World', and read Keats' 'When I Have Fears that I May Cease to Be'. Laughing and crying, we tell anecdotes about you: the bowl of scrambled egg tipped on Rowan's head in our Bangkok apartment; at a Lagos High Commission party the Star beer you pour over the head of a Nigerian woman you think is dancing with me too provocatively; getting cross with Will when, as a Ninja turtle, he karate-chops Uncle Stuart in his groin.

Your ashes are kept for later burial in three places: near our house in Greece, on Blackdown outside Haslemere with the view from near Tennyson's house to the south coast, and Shotover in Oxford where you walked Mac. 'I want to rest in beautiful places where people are happy to sit and enjoy the view with me.'

It's a glorious day. We've booked lunch in the garden at one of our favourite pubs in Sussex, The Noah's Ark, Lurgashall. My radio play, *Crying in the Crypt*, is set in its church. Afterwards, we all drive to Frensham Ponds where Scarlett paddles and Dylan splashes. You whisper to us all, 'Watch out they don't drown.'

Five weeks later, mid-October, we have a celebration of your life at our house with a marquee in the garden. The invite is from noon until 8pm to cater for distant friends, relatives and neighbours. There's music in the evening and the last guests – some are Rowan and Will's friends who love you almost as much as they do – leave or crash in the house at two in the morning.

YOU LOVED THE nunnery near our house in Koroni and always took first time visitors there to its Byzantine church and peaceful gardens. I know you'd be happy there. But I realise the possibility of cultural confusion and misunderstanding will be high. I approach our friend Alexandra who lives fifty metres up the path from our house. She's that retired Greek archaeologist married to The Maestro – the first ever foreign-born conductor of the Greek National Symphony Orchestra, a diminutive Singaporean Chinese. I help Alexandra bring out the gin and tonics onto the balcony of their beautiful house. We sip looking over the sloping canopy of olive trees down to the sea where a black catamaran is moored. She listens to my explanation and suggestions, asking a couple of questions to clarify matters, then says, 'I'll go with you. It's worth a shot but don't get your hopes up. It won't be easy.'

We agree to meet mid-morning on the concrete path below their house. We walk under a mix of purple and white bougainvillea, olive, citrus and pine trees. On our left the caper plants you used to pick clamber over the stone walls. As we near the top, we hear the twittering, buzz and shriek of primary school children in the playground. I'm sure you remember their joy and excitement.

Alexandra is elegantly attired, coiffured and with judicious make-up. I've swapped shorts for trousers, which is my gesture towards looking respectable. At the top of the ridge, we walk along the narrow road between smaller houses and plots, but all with those spectacular views overlooking the harbour or down to our beach side. Huge ceramic pots painted in glowing primary colours or, those with less to spend, use recycled olive oil cans displaying a bold mix of geraniums, roses and honeysuckle. You loved both pots and cans. We switchback down the road, getting warmer but it's September and not too oppressive. We pass under the impressive arc of the Venetian castle gate and soon turn into the convent. At last count seven nuns were in residence. Whenever you used to go there the nuns encouraged you to think about joining. You half-joke you can't think of a lovelier place to see out your final days. Guarded by an eighth-century Byzantine church, Agia Sophia, the convent is spectacularly located looking over the Gulf of Messenia towards the Mani on one side and westwards towards its sister Venetian town, Methoni. The gardens are a joy, just the right balance of formal planting and wild abandon.

It's here in these gardens that I hope I might be able to bury some of your ashes. I'd come here three days earlier, but the nuns told me they had no authority even to discuss the matter and that I should return on Thursday to meet the priest who visits them weekly from Kalamata and 'looks after our worldly needs.' It was then I'd understood that I needed reinforcements and asked Alexandra to come with me. There he sits, impassive, in all his dark glory. Imposing with long black hair tied back under his black, stove hat, which he doesn't take off throughout the meeting nor does he stand up. Alexandra and I are each offered a glass of water. *'Efaristo.'* Thank you.

I say a few words of introduction in my limited Greek, still waiting for him to speak. He lets the silence hang in the air for a while then opens his mouth and a stream of fluent American English pours out. He thanks us for coming. He's pleased to meet us. He understands we have some connection to Koroni. The nuns have told him the purpose of my visit. I reply that I've brought my friend Alexandra as I didn't know whether he spoke any English and, in any case, he might prefer to speak in Greek. Alexandra knows exactly what I'm suggesting, and she can speak for me in Greek if he prefers. He smiles and says, 'Thank you.' The last words he speaks in English.

He then turns his gaze on Alexandra. A torrent of Greek pours forth, which even I understand is not going to help our cause. It's three or four minutes before he allows Alexandra to say a word. She puts up a brave resistance, but he keeps interrupting her. I know it's all over when she looks across at me and signals with her eyes we should leave. We stand, he stands and shakes his head slowly from side to side. I think his black hat might topple off. He holds out his hand. I take it. He doesn't offer the same gesture to Alexandra. He inclines his head a fraction towards us in a slow-motion nod and we leave.

I can see Alexandra's bubbling with pent-up rage. As soon as we're outside the convent walls, she explodes. She's never been so insulted in all her life. The man's a monster. Even by Greek Orthodox standards he's an extremist. He'd told her, a Greek Orthodox woman, that he wouldn't even let *her* ashes anywhere inside the nunnery. What did she think she was doing encouraging a foreigner with crazy ideas of burying his wife's ashes here? I'm mortified. I'd explained to Alexandra that I didn't want or expect any ceremony to take place. I simply wanted to bury the ashes quietly with my own hands in one of the lemon groves or near a bed of roses. I wasn't asking for any marking or sign that they were buried there. She says he fully understood that but had said it was insulting and by coming here she was passing on my ignorance and that was a further insult to him and his sect.

Wow! I continue to feel aggrieved that I've put Alexandra in this position, but she insists his reaction was extreme and she'd never anticipated such aggression. We walk back deflated in the midday sun, its brightness exaggerating our sombre mood. Perhaps I should have paid more attention to the fact that the convent is dedicated to the last Old Testament prophet, John the Baptist, whose head was brought to Herod on a plate.

TWO DAYS LATER I load a rucksack with a box containing some of your ashes and one of those short-handled hoes which doubles as a spade. Rowan is with me. We walk up from the beach along the shaded pathways, gardens and courtyards accessing the entrance to the church where the caretaker's seated. Behind him stands the egret white bell-tower which faces down the beach where turtles nest. I nod. '*Kalo apoyevma.*' '*Episis.*' Good afternoon. The same to you.

We stroll on round the corner of the church past the chapel holding the icons and head under the pines for the lee of the Venetian castle walls. I've chosen a large boulder right near the end of the path where we can walk no further. I plan to bury the wooden box containing your ashes wrapped in plastic under the boulder's head and shoulders. A natural stone casket. It has two smaller boulders on either side, rocky sentinels. The view is directly south framed on the west by pines on the cliff below the path. The rocks tumble down to the sea thirty metres below where the waves dash briskly.

It's important that nowhere in these grounds contiguous with the church is for burial. We won't be desecrating land reserved in any way for Greek Orthodox burials. These happen in a cemetery on higher ground behind and well up above the church inside the walls of the castle.

You remember how we often heard the priest singing solo in the early morning interposed with the summoning bells. On summer evenings piano, violin or cello notes drifted on the breeze to our balcony from a classical trio in concert. Round the corner of the church is that wild area under the lee of the castle wall. Your ashes will be safe once buried there. You'll have a view over the Mediterranean, what one of our grandchildren calls, 'the big paddling pool.'

IT ALL HAPPENS very quickly. I've said for a long time I'll do two things when I stop working for the British Council. I'll go back to Ghana and I'll write a new book. The two aren't necessarily directly connected. Going back to Ghana is instantly easier than writing a new book. It'll put a marker down, a distance between me as Mr British Council and me as Richard. I'll take one rucksack and travel on public transport. I'll go and see my old bungalow and school. Whatever's left that I remember. And I'll do and see some new things. There won't be any meetings or obligations except to myself. And if, out of the trip, which will clear my head of work stuff and the loss of Lauren stuff and selling the family home stuff, I get a short story or two, if it unlocks something and gets me back on the writing bicycle, that'll be good, even very good.

FROM ALL THE images in my head the one which best captures my feelings about Ghana is a bronze statue of Kwame Nkrumah. It stands in the Accra memorial park dedicated to his life alongside his mausoleum. Kwame stands on a black marble plinth barely a metre high, characteristically raising his right hand in a merger between a wave, a salute and a benediction. He's not much more than life-size and feels approachable, one of us, human. He's dressed in a Ghanaian farmer's smock, European-style long trousers with turn-ups and what the 1950s would have called 'sensible shoes'. But something's missing. The thumb and fingers of that raised right hand have gone, the left arm's cut off above the elbow, and the body's been decapitated.

It's early 2019 when for the first time in my life I'm visiting this memorial park and mausoleum dedicated to Kwame Nkrumah, who championed and led that transition from colonial Gold Coast to independent Ghana. This decapitated statue with the head placed alongside it stands as a monument to overarching ambition and violent overthrow. A postcolonial Ghanaian Ozymandias, 'Look on my works, ye mighty, and despair!'

The mausoleum is clad in Italian marble with Ghana's ubiquitous black star alight on its apex as if landed from outer space. For a moment, I think I'm in the lobby of a five-star hotel with its highly polished marble flooring. The graves themselves are set among small boulders in pastel greys with streams of freshwater gushing round and over them. An hour earlier, I'd walked past clusters of women shouting and laughing while they filled empty palm oil tins with water from a public tap. Even in the capital, some have miles to walk home with the tins balanced on their heads.

On leaving the mausoleum, I come across a much taller, glitzier statue of Nkrumah dedicated at the same time as the mausoleum. The black marble plinth alone approaches three meters high. Nkrumah is pointing forward to the future, echoing the slogan of the party he founded, the CCP, and its motto: *Forward Ever. Backward Never.* He's at least double the size of a human figure. The surface is unblemished, golden and gleaming. Nkrumah's attired in full Ghanaian dress with a robe over his shoulder and is striding purposefully forward in sandals. Not in 'sensible' shoes. His right arm is fully outstretched, with his index finger fully extended. He's imposing, overbearing even. He's moved out of the sphere of being one of the people; he's much larger than that, a figure somewhere on his way to superhuman status. The pose and the size are resplendently optimistic in their national mythmaking. No wonder. It was those supremacists of monuments and myths, the Chinese, who funded and built it a quarter of a century after Nkrumah had been toppled.

Reflecting on my visit to the park, museum and mausoleum, I now understand that I'd unwittingly entered the site in the 'wrong' order. I'd first been backstage with the damaged statue that many people never see. I now hold in my mind's eye double images of the maimed, decapitated but still human Kwame and the other glossy, larger than life, mythical Nkrumah. It's clear which statue is closer to my heart and means so much more to me.

I decide to walk to Independence Square and Black Star arch, which I recall from the state visit to Ghana by Queen Elizabeth II in 1961. I stumble in potholes. I dodge, not always successfully, uplifted, cracked or missing pavement flags beside open drains filled with plastic rubbish and creeping sewage. I spend a couple of hours loitering with crowds disgorged by the swaying, overloaded buses. They're attending an evangelical meeting that evening. About half the population of Ghana, 15 million people, are active in churches categorised as evangelical or charismatic. In this crowded place downtown, in a city of 2.5 million, I'm an object of interest. My exception in that time and place is being white. In his travel-cum-memoir, *Black Gold of the Sun*, Ekow Eshun describes the desolation of this space and how it's fashioned on the Soviet model designed for massive rallies. The kind of bleak square that only looks fully occupied when tanks and missiles roll through in the annual, militaristic parade of nationalism.

But this afternoon, the crowds are doing their best to drive away any sense of desolation. With three hours to go, the square is already more than half full and buzzing with vendors selling food, drink, watches, sunglasses, toothpicks, scissors, pillows, lighters, biros, buckets, flip-flops, dishcloths, against a backdrop of thumping reggae and Highlife – the Ghanaian music I used to jiggle to at the Ambassador Hotel with my parents.

That night in the gardens of my hip hotel, *Somewhere Nice*, I sit with a Star beer and think about Kwame Nkrumah and Independence Square and Her Majesty. And how my Dad found himself in this mix. I suppose as far as he was concerned there was no professional stigma in supporting the creation of a professional army in the first black African country independent from Britain. Perhaps the opposite: pride in the recognition of the professionalism of the British Army. In a broader social context, we were leaving a Britain which still had signs in its Bed & Breakfasts saying 'No Coloureds or Irish'. It was only three years before when no white soldier in the Gold Coast would have taken instructions from a black soldier. Then here he was in independent Ghana advising and instructing and taking his orders from these new Ghanaian Generals. They were his bosses who within the decade led the army which overthrew Nkrumah, known popularly as the Osagyefo, or Saviour. My Dad stayed in his job for three years after the coup. So he must have kept his nose clean with both followers and critics of Nkrumah.

IN PREPARATION FOR my return trip to Ghana, I'd spoken to the Defence Attaché in the High Commission in London. I wanted to give myself the best shot at permission to access Burma Camp where we'd made our home and I'd gone to primary school.

The taxi driver who takes me has never been to the Camp, which is a self-contained, fenced-off, township on the edge of Accra. He wants to know why and what I'm doing. I tell him about my childhood in Burma Camp, which I have to repeat several times on this return visit. At the gatehouse an imposing six-foot woman in a light khaki military uniform and highly polished black boots appears. She's languid and unhurried. She explains we need to go to Protocol.

After the paperwork, the taxi driver and I find ourselves at an armed checkpoint to enter the camp commandant's secure area. The display of machine guns and revolvers is somewhat undermined by the guard borrowing my mobile phone to call the office telling them we've arrived. I'm ushered into the commandant's outer office, where three other men are waiting. Like me, they're dressed in civilian clothes. One is asleep. I can hear the commandant shouting on the phone. Suddenly, his office door bursts open, and there's the Commandant in a resplendent navy, senior officer's white uniform. Ignoring the other men, he strides towards me with an outstretched hand and a big smile.

'You are welcome, Mr Walker. We are pleased you have come. This lady,' he gestures towards a junior woman army officer at his side, 'is the military liaison for your visit.'

He turns and gestures again. 'And this is Colonel Boglo. Colonel Boglo now lives in the house where you used to live. Number 23, yes? He will show you round.'

Colonel Boglo looks somewhat bemused. I guess he's only just learned of my visit. After a brief exchange with the Commandant about my father, Nkrumah and my childhood, he disappears, wishing me a good visit.

The liaison officer comes in my taxi while Colonel Boglo goes ahead in his official car. As we drive through the camp, she explains and points out things that have changed since my childhood. The sports complex with a swimming pool. There are now nine schools housed in the camp, the majority attended by civilian children. When Jane and I attended the Primary and Junior High School, it was exclusively for the children of senior and middle-ranking Ghanaian officers. The liaison officer tells my taxi to pull over.

Smartly turned-out in her green tunic and sharply creased trousers with a red belt, black shoes and beret she introduces me to the headmistress

'Mrs Nyarko, this is Mr Walker. Mr Walker, Mrs Nyarko.'

It's charmingly formal. The headmistress is resplendent in a modern cut Ghanaian dress, its upper tunic waisted and falling over her hips above a matching ankle-length skirt. With aquamarine blue and white-pink flowers, she's in glorious contrast to the liaison officer's military kit.

'You are welcome. You were a student here, yes?'

'In the early sixties, yes.'

She smiles. 'We're much bigger now. Nearly a thousand students.' She hands me a brochure from 2018 celebrating the school's seventieth anniversary. I open it at random and see that the first Ghanaian Head in 1970 was a woman and that all of Mrs Nyarko's predecessors have been women.

'All the headteachers have been women, I see.'

Mrs Nyarko looks at the liaison officer. 'The men still run the army. We women are more caring.'

We're standing outside her office by a table where she was working when we arrived. This is in the shade of the walkway alongside the administration block. She'd been working outside because it's cooler out than in her office. Some of the pupils have pulled their desks away from the concrete classrooms and stationed them in the dust under the huge mango trees in the playground.

'We used to do that too,' I say, nodding in the direction of the children at the desks outside.

'Some things don't change,' she laughs. 'Even when my budget can pay for electricity, we sometimes have power cuts.'

It's the same mix of dust and dappled shade where we'd played football or cricket six decades earlier. I can't shake off the sense that pretty much everything is the same – this feeling is an important leitmotif throughout my journey.

'Would you like to see the school?'

All the blocks, classrooms, or offices are much as they'd been, except for a newish computer building that's locked and looks unused. Concrete, single storey, no window glass, light turquoise shutters, no air conditioning, a few ceiling fans and corrugated iron rooves making lessons impossible to hear in the rainy season.

The headmistress is a confident and competent professional woman. Though as soon as the conversation grows potentially interesting the liaison officer is clearly in a hurry to move me on as soon as possible. As the child of a military father, I know that my visit has a schedule that she's expected to follow strictly. But, of course, like schedules everywhere they can be used as a reason for not exploring more deeply. I don't want to make the liaison officer's life difficult, so I comply.

We climb back in the taxi and the liaison officer instructs the driver how to reach my old bungalow. Colonel Boglo commands instant respect. Built like a modern rugby prop-forward, arms akimbo, hands on his hips, he cuts an impressive figure standing on the red-polished steps of No.23 Burma Villas. He's dressed in army fatigues: jungle green, dark and lighter chocolate, a black undervest, shining black boots laced up to mid-calf with knife creases in tunic and trousers. A black beret with its gold insignia is angled on his head; a splash of red dashes the ends of both lapels, and a red cord over his left shoulder marks his rank. He sports a full but well-barbered moustache and wears dark glasses.

Though he'd been surprised by my visit, he's perfectly courteous. He tells me his wife is living in Cardiff, with their daughter who's studying there. Which explains why, though instantly recognisable and essentially unchanged, the bungalow we'd lived in – and he'd been assigned – wears a slightly unloved air. He doesn't invite me in but is happy to show me around the outside and the garden. I don't ask him to show me inside. I'm already unexpectedly invading his privacy. This means that my memories of the inside of the house will be the ones I've carried with me for more than sixty years. This sets the template for the remainder of my trip. Sometimes I'm left with my original memory in pristine form. On other occasions, the first impression is updated while I still hold the first pressing of it in my mind. I'm then left with two memories of 'true' and 'real', like a painter's different sketches of the same scene or landscape.

As we walk round the garden, I see that only a solitary mango tree remains. The pineapples and maize masterminded by Mum have gone. Round the back, where the papaya trees grew which I could see from my bedroom window, are two huge black, plastic water tanks.

'Yes,' says Colonel Boglo in response to my question. 'The whole of Accra including the Camp has a problem with regular water supply.'

I remember the thrill of being allowed to run out into the tropical rain and a hot shower afterwards. No water shortage then.

Nor can I visit the outdoor cinema, which stood only three hundred metres from our bungalow. It's been knocked down. That's OK. My memory tells me John Wayne's shooting up the town as sheriff and monsoon rain is drumming on the metal seats.

HIGHLIFE, & MY OTHER LIVES

I DECIDE TO venture outside Accra slowly, so I opt to stay in a small 'holiday village' a couple of hours west of the capital on the coast. It's in a secure compound with twenty or so huts of various sizes in local materials and design, grass roofs, a private but outdoor shower, a mosquito net over the bed and a ceiling fan. Well-kept gardens, an OK restaurant and a couple of bar areas, all within thirty metres of the Atlantic surf crashing up the steep beach. There are a few foreigners about, but the staying guests are mainly middle-class Ghanaians as are those who turn up for the band – which play almost non-stop from six in the evening until two in the morning.

Beyond its compound is the only place on my trip that feels and is seedy. There are occasional women on the beach touting sex, some crude craft stalls and mock-Rastas trying to sell marijuana with a string of dodgy, basic bars blasting out reggae. They're all clustered round the place I'm staying at and hoping to pick up crumbs from its middle-class spenders. As I discover a couple of days later, reading Afua Hirsh's *Brit(ish): On Race, Identity and Belonging,* this is the beach where she and her Ghanaian husband had been jumped and attacked by a group of men.

On my first afternoon I attempt to swim in the crashing breakers and then retreat to the well-secured 'village' compound where one of the bars looks down the beach. I find myself in conversation with a third-generation Lebanese who has a Ghanaian passport. His grandfather came to Ghana and built a successful construction business. I remember that we used to go to what I now understand were lavish – 'blingy', but the word wasn't coined then – parties held by the Lebanese community. I imagine my father, as an honorary Ghanaian army officer, was invited so he might introduce Lebanese businessmen to senior army contacts for 'mutual benefit.' The limit of my father's perk was, I'm sure, at the level of an extra pack of duty-free Rothman's 555 or a bottle of genuine Gordon's London Dry Gin. The grandson, overweight and in his forties, is friendly – the afternoon beer talking – and is evidently doing his best to enjoy his grandfather's inheritance to the full. He'd been at a prep school in England but loathed it and asked to leave to attend an international school in Switzerland. He likes the current Ghanaian government ministers, who are, he says, 'Very good for business.'

THE NEXT DAY I head further west to Elmina. There's some dispute about the origin of the name Elmina. The frontrunner is from the Portuguese: *Da Costa de el Mina de Ouro*. Literally, the coast of the mine of gold. This tells us what the Portuguese were doing there: it was gold, not slaves, which was the initial magnet. What is now called Elmina Castle is the oldest extant European structure in sub-Saharan Africa

I choose to stay in the Coconut Grove Hotel in the old town of Elmina opposite the castle. From the balcony on the seaward side of the hotel, across the small inlet leading to the lagoon, there's a photogenic view of Elmina. Its outer, perimeter wall stained by sea salt and humidity encloses tiers of iced white wedding cake, a superstructure with red-tiled rooves. On its western edge, it's fringed by a long line of coconut palms. In the morning canoes moored in the lagoon paddle under the bridge by the hotel and set out to fish in the swelling Atlantic waves. The silhouette of the five hundred years-old castle is straight from the pages of an illustrated children's book. But its contents and history are bleak beyond despair.

Elmina is fully geared up for visitors and conduct almost obligatory guided tours. There are fifteen or so of us. At least half are African Americans with a smattering of Europeans, a Japanese couple and me as the sole British visitor. The guide is practised and doesn't pull his punches. He knows where and when to stop for most effect and dramatic interest. I'm always the last to be cajoled into moving on. In the cells I feel cramped, jostled, crushed and bruised by the dark. This isn't by my fellow visitors but by a sense of the bodies of the slaves once held there. I even think I can smell the stench. Our guide confirms that the slightly sticky surface under our feet, like bitumen in the heat, is indeed man-made. It's been analysed by chemists and found to be a hardened composite of blood, urine, faeces, organs, hair, nail and bone. It's many inches thick formed over decades by thousands of feet tramping it down or knees sinking to it in exhaustion. I imagine the haunches and hips and the shoulders of the fever-ridden slaves rolling and tossing on it. And the chests and faces squashed sideways of those who could never lift themselves up again. I hear the echo of the skulls smashed on it.

The women's slave cells open out into a courtyard with narrow high arches on all four sides and a trapdoor in the centre. The trapdoor covers a well. Our guide leads us up two flights of wooden stairs from the courtyard to the balcony where the commander and his men would have stood. We assemble looking down into the courtyard just as the commander and those men would have done. They would have observed the women being led out to be sluiced down with a few wooden buckets shared between two or three hundred slaves at a time. This provided the commander and senior officers with the opportunity to consider and select which women they would rape. The courtyard below us was empty, of course. But in imagining the scene I feel uncomfortably complicit.

The guide leads us from the balcony above the courtyard through a corridor to what were the commander's rooms. Especially beautiful is the hexagonal bed chamber with its parquet flooring. On the three exterior walls, the shutters are open. Through them, in the late afternoon light, I could see the lace of surf on the beach and the waves to the horizon where the sea meets the sky. The stunning views of land and seascape framed by the commander's windows are even more agonising than the scenes – at least in my imagination – I'd witnessed a few minutes earlier.

We climb higher still up to the heavily fortified battlements facing seawards. There had been a much greater threat to Elmina and other forts from the cannons of pirate ships than from the Africans on land. We face the warm Atlantic breeze as we stand on the pinnacle of the fort admiring the view of the rolling aquamarine, and the gold strip of sea-washed, unblemished sand pelmeted with tropical forest. In a whitewashed tower hangs a bell with a rope attached to its clapper. The bell sounded when a ship arrived, tolling, for many, the start of the end of captivity in the cells. Or it might sound on a Sunday when the men and women slaves were assembled outside for a service none of them could comprehend. But, if they were lucky, a breeze would relieve the stench of the cells though they knelt directly on the hot flagstones.

One cell door has a particularly gruesome skull crudely sculpted over it. If it hadn't been so horrific, it would have been comical like a child's drawing of skull and crossbones. But it's the cell that no one ever left alive. It's where slaves who'd tried to escape or rebel were placed as an example to others. They were given no water or food; it was a drawn-out, agonising death.

In an awful and terrible comparison, *The Door of No Return* offers a glimmering opportunity of a future life, however punishing. This rubric is now invariably sculpted or embossed in the wooden doors and over gates through which the slaves walked down to the rocks and onto the beach. They were then rowed on lighters under guard to the waiting slave ship anchored offshore. As we know, but are justly and for eternity bound to repeat, many slaves died on the journey from malnutrition, maltreatment and maladies. If they survived the Atlantic journey, they often died in the early months or years of becoming a captive, working, unpaid slave.

The guide tells us that if the women got pregnant, they were released and allowed to have their babies in the community. After years, these offspring who were so clearly physically different from their peers begin to form their own, separate sub-community. What the guide doesn't mention are the women who boarded the ships, knowingly or not, pregnant. The statistics suggest that of the 12 or so million slaves transported on the Atlantic route about 1.5 to 2.5 million died during the passage. Though for new-born infants and their mothers the mortality rate must have been much higher not only on the voyage itself, but after landfall if they made it that far.

Elmina Castle is much bigger than I had imagined or than it seems from the Coconut Grove across the lagoon inlet. It must cover about the same ground area as a small football or soccer stadium. It's a warren of courtyards, corridors, cells, other small rooms and grander ones like the commander's dining hall and quarters. In places, it's five stories high. It's built right up against and at the highest point of the coastal rocks, so some of the drops on the seaward side are greater than five storeys. In some ways the overall structure recalls an Oxbridge mediaeval college with its series of courtyards and rooms off twisting stairwells – though, of course, there are no lawns and its purpose is far darker. This darkness was signified by the change of use when the Dutch arrived. They converted the Portuguese-built chapel into an auction room for the slaves.

When I leave the castle, I'm emotionally exhausted and drained by the profoundly sobering experience of the continent's oldest slave fort.

MY ROOM AT the Coconut Grove would have been considered quite grand circa 1985. There's a huge television, a super-king-size double bed, and a cavernous bathroom which would now be branded a wet room. Those are possibly the good points. There's a limited supply of water running from the taps when it's unpredictably cold or scalding, a swirly carpet with a kaleidoscope of grubby colours and an ancient air-conditioning unit that rattles asthmatically all night long. The shutters outside the windows won't open for a view of the lagoon or the sea or fresh air so I can't turn off the AC. I start to feel resentful and trapped until I quickly recall what I'd experienced in Elmina that afternoon. The prospect of sitting out on the terrace with a cold beer and eating there is zero. There's construction and refurbishment work happening which, of course, the website hadn't mentioned.

I don't complain, but ask to be moved to the sister hotel out of town on the beach. This is readily agreed. I leave the hotel for a walk coming out onto 'Liverpool Street' passing some impressive but dilapidated with mildew and crumbling plaster mid-Victorian buildings. I head up to the secondary fort on a hill, St Jago's, with panoramic views over the town and entire coastline. There are hooded vultures circling overhead and a few on the ground nearby pecking at refuse. They're ugly creatures looking as though they've just had a bad day at the barbers with shaven pink heads and hunched shoulders over a dirty brown plumage.

WHEN I RETURN to the Coconut Grove my things, as agreed, have been transferred outside the town to its sister hotel on the beach. It's the only night on my entire trip where I stay in an upmarket resort aimed mainly at foreign tourists who do group tours. Here is where I meet the only black people, all US citizens, who are tracing their roots. They're noisy like parakeets and good-humoured as many such groups are. I suppose this North American rediscovery of roots has something to do with the sheer volume of slaves who were transported west to the Americas, as well as the history of slavery there and the much greater distance emphasising the rupture of African Americans from their origins. In Ghana's case as a former British colony, the links between it and Britain are different in nature to those with the United States. There's the occasional notable British writer or journalist like Ekow (Thursday) Eshun or Afua (Friday) Hirsch, who write about their returns to or exploration of Ghana, but I don't meet any Brits tracing their roots in the way of the African Americans.

On the plane from London, I'd spoken to two people and overheard more at Accra airport who were clearly 'going back home' for a visit. Ghanaians who'd made much, most, or their entire lives in Britain but still have family, some of them close family, in Ghana. These are regular visitors still working in Britain, some of them waiting for their pensions to kick in so they could retire 'home'. I suppose when visiting they don't do 'tours' but they stay with family; they still have a contemporary connection with the country. They aren't looking for a buried past.

My own experience is different still. True, I'm exploring elements of my past, but my family were temporary residents in Ghana whose ancestors were in Birmingham and London, not one of the ethnic groups which make up modern Ghana. I'm exploring something more evanescent than roots; how memory works. The surging flame of a candle which burns much more brightly in my mind's eye than the more dimly lit childhood years in Surrey, England. I'd always thought that I'd spent more of my childhood in Ghana, but when I came to look at the record and set things straight for myself, I'd been there less than four years. Yet this intense and concentrated period in Ghana completely overshadows the longer time I'd spent in England earlier. The English Home Counties experience was the norm against which the Ghana experience, though shorter in time, is by a huge factor more vivid in my memory and still present in my life. To an important degree, it set a template for my adulthood. The years away from the Home Counties and London and particularly those spent living – not merely visiting – abroad are the peaks of various heights in my life. While those in Surrey-Sussex-Hampshire ramble on, rolling hills and fields in the landscape of my life. Against which the greater dramas of Accra, San Francisco, Toronto, Seville, Kuwait, Bangkok, Lagos, Sao Paulo, New Delhi, Nicosia, Athens, Brussels and Hong Kong are more brilliantly animated and expressive.

FOR MOST JOURNEYS of any distance, my choice of transport is the *tro-tro*. These are Volkswagen or similar vans with 100,000 miles upwards on the clock and holding a dozen-plus passengers crammed in with battered suitcases or bundles tied up with string. Like buses, they travel between fixed points but wait until they're full before leaving. They claim to have air-conditioning but, working or not, I never travel in one which is effective. The '*tro-tro* station' is often a roundabout or road junction with no signs indicating which bus might go where and when. There's invariably a cacophony of vehicles and street hawkers, one man alone carrying scissors, mobile phones, screwdrivers, torches, plugs, adaptors, calculators, headphones, batteries, footballs, wire brushes, nail clippers and files. Noxious fumes pour from the vehicles playing reggae or Highlife at a deafening volume. Chaotic not just for foreigners but for Ghanaians, all of them shouting at each other. 'Last time I pay two *cedi* for this journey, now you are charging me three!' 'Why are you charging extra cedi for air-conditioning when you know it don't work?'

Waiting on the bus for it to fill up, passengers are prey to anyone climbing in and forcing tiger nuts, OMO detergent or hard-boiled eggs on them. Evangelicals have a captive audience. One dressed in a shirt with pink and orange hibiscus comes aboard and with a microphone harangues us for fifteen minutes. A woman selling bottled water pulls out a slim paperback, *Life Guide,* produced by the Gospel Ambassadors Church. Passengers call out numbers, she turns to the relevant page and reads out an extract. There's laughter or clapping in response. I think she can read, though I couldn't swear she hasn't learned the whole book by rote. Over several journeys, I spend many hours in these buses. I'm an object of some curiosity, people are aware a foreigner's present, but everyone's polite; there isn't a whiff of animosity or its almost opposite, invasive curiosity. Not once do I see another foreigner on the *tro-tros.* Not even one of the young volunteers or backpackers whom I meet at *Somewhere Nice* in Accra where I stayed at the start and will end my journey.

I LEAVE THE final day of my trip unplanned. The night before I arrive back in Accra by *tro-tro* and check into *Somewhere Nice.* It's a Czech-owned hotel-cum-hostel – everything is made from recycled stuff, like the curtains in my room which were flour sacks and are stamped with the logos of coastal mills, or my bedframe which is constructed from disused packing crates. A chair has been assembled from old tyres. Unpainted brutalist concrete and exposed copper plumbing hold sway. The house liquid soap is palm oil.

Here, over a big shared wooden breakfast table, I meet mainly young Europeans or North Americans with an occasional Ghanaian guest. Many are hanging out waiting to see what's going to happen to the health, education, or agricultural projects they've volunteered for and from which they've been displaced for 'security reasons'. Most of the volunteers don't appear too anxious to return to their projects and are enjoying the camaraderie of their peers and the relative comforts of a three-star hotel with a small swimming pool.

On this final day I strike up conversation with an atypical guest: a British woman who's older than the regular volunteer-backpacker crowd. She has the air of someone who has work to do – which, indeed, she does. She's a freelance development consultant who's been delayed on her flight out of Ghana. The consultant is getting a taxi up to Aburi to meet her husband. She offers me a lift. I can get a bus back. Why not?

In the cooler hills of Aburi in the final quarter of the nineteenth century, the British created a sanatorium for colonial officials needing respite from the coastal capital. The land around the sanitorium was cleared, and a botanical garden was created by William Crowther, a student from the Royal Botanic Gardens at Kew. The avenue of royal palms which leads up from the main entrance gate is impressive, but the star of the show is a huge kapok or silk cotton tree, *Ceiba pentandra*, on the sweeping lawns in front of what is now a guest house. White painted script on a blue sign states the tree was planted by Sir Gordon Guggisberg on 23rd March 1924. Its enormous finials morph into roots snaking across and gripping the lawn, the feet and claws of some mythical dragon. Somewhere in its canopy it must be breathing smoke and fire into the sky. Sir Gordon was a Canadian-born Brigadier General from the Royal Engineers – my father's regiment. After serving with distinction in the First World War, Sir Gordon was made Governor-General of the Gold Coast.

I imagine my father in his voluminous shorts and polished brown shoes standing under the kapok tree late on a sultry afternoon admiring another, more distinguished Royal Engineer, before heading to the guest house for a cold Star beer as I do.

RITA MARLEY, A singer in her own right – and Bob's wife – relocated near Aburi after his death and established a recording studio with her home, which sadly burnt down. She's been made an honorary Ghanaian citizen in recognition of her foundation's work with schools and children.

Reading about the Rita Marley Foundation's work with children recalls my mother's arrangement with Barnardo's the children's charity. Before Ghana, my mother worked for Barnardo's in Guildford. After our first eighteen months 'tour' of Ghana, we flew back to England on leave for months. Gwen's former employers must have been in touch with her to ask if she'd help. The day before our return, Jane and I learn we're taking a young Ghanaian girl with us on the flight back to Accra. Patsy, is from one of Barnardo's homes and it's been agreed with her aunt that she'd go and live with her and her family in Accra. Patsy's frightened, terrified. Despite her Ghanaian roots, she's never been to the country and nor has she ever flown.

I remember her holding my hand very tightly and not wanting to let go at any point even once settled on board. Her aunt at Accra airport has a difficult job persuading Patsy to relinquish her grip on me. I'm embarrassed, I think someone will think I'm encouraging her behaviour.Months later we see Patsy with her aunt and family in their home for afternoon high tea. She's in a new frock and has pink ribbons braided in her hair. It's the last time I see her.

I've tried to discover more about Patsy from Barnardo's. I'd like to have been in touch with her, but they've been unable or unwilling to help. They cite confidentiality and privacy as the obstacle. I hope she's living happily in the region of Accra with children and grandchildren of her own to enjoy. I wonder now whether in a role reversal of mine, she remembers anything of her early years in England.

'IT MUST BE so different. So much must have changed,' is the refrain throughout my trip and on my return to England. This assumption about change is both true and not true. Were you a visiting dignitary it would be feasible to think that Ghana had changed. In your air-conditioned limousine heading downtown, you'd pass the impressive new Presidential Palace constructed in the shape of an Ashanti footstool. You'd glimpse small stretches of glistening glass-fronted buildings, a global bank or two, an air-conditioned shopping mall, a well-manicured lawn between royal palms and a pavement which is truly a pavement. Then you'd decant at the five-star Kempinski Hotel with rooms upwards of $400 a night. You'd have an agreeable impression that, indeed, Ghana had driven into the twenty-first century in pole position as an African disciple of capitalism. Hurrah that it's on its way to the nirvana of being branded 'fully developed', as proclaimed by the saints of the World Bank. It would confirm your reading of the financial data that between 2000 and 2019 GDP growth rate averaged 7 percent with a high in 2012 of 25 percent. This is one universe.

There is another: there's shit in the open sewers a hundred meters from the Kempinski. An eight-year-old boy in ragged shorts, no tee-shirt, split flip-flops, cracked heels, stands at the traffic lights in the morning rush hour, the air already blue and heavy with lead fumes; he holds up a battered carton of cheap biros for sale. Here is a woman with a toddler strapped to her back, combing through pyramids of refuse in the dusk; she's spent the day in the bus station, an exhaust-ridden roundabout, with a tray on her head trying to sell hard-boiled eggs. Out in the bush where few foreigners venture, children don't go to school but walk miles with cans on their heads carrying water then work in a field digging cassava. This is a Ghana I saw too, the one that hadn't really changed at all. I know which universe is the place most Ghanaians inhabit.

And the personal motives of my return? What I learned is that everything is still there in my memory. The electric blue Renault Ondine, the children dragging their desks out under the green mangoes to do their classwork, Reuben battering the snake on the living room carpet, my father listening to the World Service at six in the evening, Jerry Orchard's sandals, the perspiration on my mother's upper lip, the hot damp leather smell of cavalry horse saddles, the click and whirr of the fan, the paw-paw trees with their luminous golden fruit.

I learned that life is double-headed literally and figuratively. It is both/and, not either/or. The heads of the Heads of State of Ghana and Britain in their glorious lit up fireworks representing both black and white. Both leaders are now dead, the lady lived longer. But both illuminated heads exist in perfect parity somewhere in me. The backstage figure of Nkrumah, decapitated, exists alongside the perfectly formed, mythic sculpture in front of the mausoleum. It makes no difference whether what I experience sixty years later is visible or not. My school is still there pretty much as it was, and I'm playing the Archangel Gabriel in its nativity play. The open-air cinema has been demolished without trace, but the rain is still beating on its metal chairs. Even if people think things are different, in one dimension, my memory, they are the same. My Mum and Dad, Gwen and George, are right now at the demolished Ambassador Hotel still laughing and dancing to Highlife.

SO HOW ARE things now, Lauren? What would you recognise and what's different in our corner of paradise since you were last there? In Pylos, the most majestic sycamore tree, the mother of them all, where we used to sit and enjoy our coffee with a view of the harbour, has needed propping up. I'm always hesitant in case I arrive, and something more dramatic has happened – it's lost the human equivalent of a limb or worse. Sometimes I dream about resting with my head in a book in its shade, its leaves whispering until they come to take me away.

Not far away, they've constructed a marvellous new viewing gallery at Nestor's Palace so you can appreciate its layout. It no longer looks like a jumble of stones scattered on a hillside. Nearby they've discovered a tomb, the Griffin Warrior's grave, dated to around 1500 BC. Many of the objects discovered are stunning works of art. It's revised the scholarship of the ancient Greek world.

Takis is still in the *kafenio* on the corner of the square in Koroni, but he's bought the building across the road and expanded his outdoor space at the side of the harbour. He's refurbished the inside and some say it's lost its soul, others that it's bright and fresh. He's no longer that eager, young waiter always ready to serve us and offer advice. He's become his father, the owner standing behind the bar directing operations with a perpetual air of harassment and exhaustion. It's a hard, physical slog inheriting the mantle of the family business, and it shows. He hasn't used the joke for years about not having time to find a wife, 'please find me one from England.' He's still unmarried.

IN SEPTEMBER 2019, three years after you left, I'm sitting at the other end of the harbourside in Koroni with a morning coffee. It's the same spot where we saw the monk seal twenty years ago. People are stopping in the street, animated, gesticulating. Customers are on their feet pointing out something in the harbour. A siren grows louder, it's a fire truck which pulls up thirty metres away. Firefighters jump out and start to clear people from the area, sealing off the road and the cafés with red and white tape. A police launch appears in the harbour. I ask the waiter what's happening.

'They think there's a bomb.'

A Greek customer adds, 'From the war. They think it's not exploded.'

At another table is a group of Germans enjoying their mid-morning beers who hear this exchange. One of them calls out, 'Perhaps they will send it back to Germany!'

Everyone laughs, including the Greek man and me. Though the course of the Second World War in the Peloponnese suggests it's equally possible that it was a British not a German bomb.

Later that year I ask around about the bomb, but no one seems to know exactly what'd happened to it. I ask Dimitris at Bogris. He suggests I try the *Limeniko Soma Ellinikis Aktofylaki*, Greek Coastguard. No one's ever mentioned such an office or person. The jeweller confirms it's hidden up a side street by the oldest bakery in town.

It's early evening. I ring the bell to the side of the darkened glass doors reinforced with iron bars. I'm not optimistic since some public offices and private businesses stopped re-opening in the evenings on account of first the financial crisis and then the Covid pandemic. I wait a little while and ring again. I hear someone fumbling at the inside of the door, which opens six inches; a man's voice in shadow asks, '*Ti theleis*?' What do you want?

I tell him.

'*Ena lepta*.' A moment. He opens the door another six inches, and I can see his bulk moving back into the dark of the office. He doesn't switch on any lights. I suppose he's saving electricity. I remain on the doorstep, not invited to enter. I make out two long desks put together in an L-shape with three large computers banked up.

As he starts to punch stuff into two of them, he tells me in a mix of Greek and decent English that he was absent on the day of the curious incident of the bomb in the harbour. But he remembers all about it. He reads out some key sections of Greek press reports, but none of them tells us anything we don't already know except that the bomb was towed far out into the bay of Kalamata and exploded. Then he invites me to cross the threshold and I'm inside. I ask if the coastguard routinely explodes potentially live ordnance without tracing anything about its history. He smiles and shrugs. By this time he can see I'm not a troublemaker. 'Our job is to protect people and boats. We are not historians or archaeologists.'

I mention my plausible theory that the bomb could have been from an English plane trying to destroy the ammunition dump which the Germans had created inside the Venetian-Ottoman castle above the harbour.

'*Isos,*' perhaps. Then he swivels to the third screen, which has its back to me, and begins looking for something which he finds, and I watch him watching it. There's a muffled explosion. 'Look,' he says and swings the screen round in my direction and replays the footage. It's official coastguard film of the bomb being towed out to sea and then exploded at a distance. He shouldn't be showing it to me.

'I'm sorry,' he says. 'We will never know. I don't think the people here care if it was a German or an English bomb. It's not important for them.'

I thank him for all the time and trouble he's taken to share what he could.

'*Den einai tipota. Parakalo.*' It's nothing. You're welcome.

We say our goodbyes, and he closes the door, locking and bolting it. I stop at the bottom of the steps and turn to look at the coastguard sign above the door and take its photo.

And then, Lauren, my eye's caught by some exquisite, arched brickwork at one end of the alley. It's the shape and size of a six-foot-high shed with a tiled roof. It houses a tunnel and a well half-hidden in a bamboo grove. Water's trickling, tinkling through it. There's a sun embedded in its apex. It looks Byzantine. I think about the coastguard's comment on recent history. Yes, I think Lauren, for its people the history of this place is much older and lives alongside them like you entwined with me.

IN LATE FEBRUARY 2020 in Athens, I walk along Panepistimiou Street from the spot in Exarchia where Grigoropoulos, the fifteen-year-old schoolboy, was shot dead in 2008 near our apartment. I'm heading to Plateia Syntagma, where, in 1944, 28 unarmed civilians had been shot dead by the British army and the Greek police. Although it's a late Friday afternoon when the city gears up for the weekend, it's unnaturally quiet with the few people out scampering along under cover of the walls – as if they too think someone might shoot them.

The city is shutting down, and its museums and ancient sites have closed along with the schools. Most restaurants and tavernas are shuttered, a few are still open in the hope of a final customer or two. By eight that night everywhere is shut. Covid has arrived in Athens. The stray dogs have the square to themselves. The interviews I'd painstakingly set up with elderly survivors of the Civil War have to be abandoned on the reasonable instructions of the ageing subjects' doctors. The next day I get one of the last flights out of Athens to London.

In a window out of the pandemic lockdown in September 2020 I return to Greece, but to Koroni and the Peloponnese. I drive north to the marvellous site of Ancient Messene where we went together and with visitors many times. I pass through the huge Arcadian gate with its monumental blocks of stone hewn and polished two and a half thousand years ago and which we climbed. Now I'm heading somewhere you never went, the town of Meligalas. Which means literally honey and milk. Or more freely 'land of milk and honey.' A paradisiacal name which might offer consolation for its horrors.

Meligalas is the location for one of the most notorious massacres of the early part of the Greek Civil War in autumn 1944. An estimated seven hundred to a thousand right-of-centre Greeks were murdered. Right-wing Greeks had – with German backing – formed battalions of roving militia dedicated to the restoration of the monarchy and a monarchist, right-wing future for Greece. These 'Security Battalions' worked hand in glove with the Germans joining anti-partisan operations and participating in the selection of liberal and left-of-centre Greeks for execution.

It was not their defeat but the manner of their death which became for decades a propaganda coup for the right in Greece. After their military action in and around the town of Meligalas, the Security Battalions and their supporters were rounded up by the Greek partisans with Allied support and taken to an area outside the town where they were executed near a well. And many were stuffed down it.

I visit the monument, erected in the 1950s, which marks these terrible murders and is decidedly municipal: a weather-stained, mottled concrete cross at the top of concrete stairs squatting under a heavy grey sky with the sun struggling to pierce the rain clouds. Large areas of the hillside are paved with stone as if to try and stop the dead rising from the ground. Terraces of gravestones are identical, about a metre high and half as broad. A monumental well has been constructed – far too grand to have been the original well – which is freshly re-painted. There's evidence of a ceremony that must have taken place not long before with wreaths of laurel and dying bouquets of orange Asian lilies and white chrysanthemums.

Fixed to a long, stone wall next to a simple but locked chapel, I count sixty-nine tablets listing the names, villages of origin, the ages and roles, where known, of the victims. They're categorised according to their village location confirming how important place is to Greek identity. The oldest recorded victim I find is eighty-five, the youngest is fifteen.

The township of Meligalas is no better than the dreary monument around the well. It isn't even a one-horse town. Its only redeeming feature a hillside chapel with a view through the pine trees to the distant, massive bulk of Mount Ithome, which forms a natural barrier on one side of Ancient Messene. The rest of the town is surly, avoiding my gaze as if ashamed of its role in twentieth-century Greece. No one smiles or acknowledges my presence. I abandon my plan to find a coffee.

THERE ARE TWO occasions after I've driven back past the sombre *Pigadi Meligalas*, Meligalas Well, when there's a glimmer of light. The first when I stop at the junction of two small rivers with a run of stone arches half-hidden by undergrowth. Their foundations turn out to have been constructed on the ancient route from Arcadia to Messene where the Mavrozoumena and the Pamisos rivers meet.

It's a unique construction: a trilateral bridge of nine arches with three arms in a Y-shape. The foundations and lower part of the bridge display the same rectangular, polished blocks of stone as the Arcadian gate which allows entry to Ancient Messene. It was built sometime between the late-fourth and first century BC.

The bridge is in remarkably good condition. Walking on the marshy bank under its arches I spot a tortoise sunning itself on a two-thousand-year-old chunk of masonry; it's half-submerged in the water, sluggish at the end of summer. As I draw closer, I realise it isn't a tortoise. Its dark shell, head, neck and limbs are flecked with what looks like cream-white paint in a regular pattern. The way it slides off the rock with graceful strokes shows how at home it is in the river. It's a freshwater terrapin. The contrast between the ancient bridge and the natural life it supports helps me feel human again.

The second shaft of light is an undistinguished village, Neohori, which means 'new settlement'. There are hundreds of Neohori throughout Greece. This one is halfway between Meligalas and Ancient Messene at the foot of Mount Boulkano.

One of its residents, George Kalogeropoulos, lived there but was a chemist in Meligalas. In July 1923 he took the decision, his wife Litsa pregnant with their third child, to emigrate to Astoria, Queens, the Greek quarter of New York. To her mother's disappointment, it's another girl, and she shows her dissatisfaction by refusing to hold the child until she's four days old. The girl's christened Maria Anna Selina Sofia. Her father George shortens the family name first to Kalos and then in a further anglicisation, Callas.

Neohori is the village of a girl who becomes one of the early global stars of opera, Maria Callas. I'm telling you this story, Lauren, remembering your grandfather who introduced you to opera, and then later you introduced me to opera. I know you loved Maria Callas, but I know you don't know this story.

As I stroll along the street named after her, Odos Marias Kaloyeroupoulou (Kallas), I remember the first time we saw *Tosca* in Jonathan Miller's production at the ENO. The huge bulk of Mount Voukanou looms in the background, a solid brown loaf with heavy dark clouds gathering themselves for a storm. I hear Maria as Tosca singing the opening line of one of opera's greatest arias, 'I lived for my art, I lived for love.' I lived for you.

On the way back to the car parked in the main square a knot of *ergatis*, labourers, is sitting on the terrace of a *kafenion* over the debris of a generous late lunch, bottles of Fixx beer and wine carafes, bread baskets scattered over the table. They've pushed their chairs back and are smoking. One sees me hesitate, deciding whether to go and have a coffee. He waves and gesticulates at an empty chair nearby. So I step onto the terrace and order a coffee. I tell them I've stopped to see 'Maria's Street.' They laugh. I'm not sure they all know who she was.

They range in age from two who look like they're sixty years plus but are probably younger, to youths in school a couple of years before. Any one of them in an earlier generation might have had his name, age and occupation inscribed on the tablets of the wall of the municipal memorial marking their murder in the civil war.

They're good-humoured but not especially inquisitive. They have their lives. I have mine. I sip my Greek coffee slowly then go inside to pay. The owner tells me the man who'd gestured me to take a seat has already paid my bill. I leave the owner a small tip and go back outside. I wordlessly thank the man who'd bought my coffee bowing my head, my hand to my heart.

As I drive off past the café I wave and a couple of them wave back. The next thing I know I'm motoring into a torrential

September storm. The wipers can't cope, and I pull over for ten minutes to let the worst past. At some point in the downpour, I've taken a wrong turning. I have to drive back through Neohori to get back en route. The rain has almost stopped, and the men have left the *kafenion*. As I find the right road, the sun comes out and the tarmac ahead begins to steam.

I'VE BEEN IN Oxford five years now. I think you'd like the house. A Victorian terrace with a kitchen/dining space that has sliding glass doors that open onto a small gravel area, a raised lawn with beds and at the end corner a rowan tree with some decking. Behind is a churchyard, church hall – where we vote – and the church with a green copper spire topped with a weathervane. I look across to it from my study upstairs. Greyfriars is a Roman Catholic church with Capuchin Franciscan friars sauntering round in brown habits and sandals. You wouldn't mind that, I know. You were always eclectic in your mix of religious interests. There are no bells but several times a year, magnificent 'traveller' funerals with white horses and black plumes pulling a glass sided carriage bearing the coffin of the dead. Sometimes these are so well-attended the police have to block Iffley Road and re-direct the traffic. Then there are lots of vehicles with Republic of Ireland plates parked in the streets. I'm less than ten minutes' walk from the river and fifteen or twenty into the centre. Two gastro pubs, The Chester and Magdalen Arms, which we all went to when we used to visit Will and Sarah, are five minutes away; and there's a proper boozer, The Fir Tree, in sight of my study across from the church. The Uni sports ground where Bannister did his mile under four minutes is next door, and last season I saw Oxford Rugby play England U20s there. The health centre and dentist are both ten minutes' walk. St John the Evangelist, decommissioned, is now a music, mainly classical, venue I go to two or three times a year; the Bullingdon, ten minutes away on Cowley, has a somewhat louder, later and younger crowd. The Isis, twenty minutes' walk downriver near Iffley village, we went once, is great outdoors in summer and has the whirlwind who's Noreen as its owner and musical force along with her partner Adrian. I had my seventieth birthday party there. Bizarrely, we saw Noreen with Rowan when she lived in South London play in QuecumBar, that gypsy jazz club in Battersea. I once heard Noreen telling a customer that she didn't play the violin, she played the fiddle and that the violin was an English, imperialist instrument forced on the Irish who don't play violin but the 'fucking fiddle.'

I see both Rowan and Will and their families most weeks, except when I go to our house in Koroni or they're away. Will and Sarah had Josh nearly three years after you left. And your memories of Dylan and Leo both born in the year you died are probably hazy. I guess Scarlett as the oldest is the one you remember best. She's ten, with Nana's and yours and Rowan's colouring still. Athletic and willowy. Mainly I've spent time in Koroni on my own writing this memoir, though Huw and Jo from Athens have stayed, and I see them in London at least once a year. I've become an annual visitor for a few days in May to the jazz festival in Kardamyli. I treat myself to an upmarket hotel for two or three nights, then usually stay up the hill for two or three more with Simon and Ann at their house. You'll remember them from Budapest and, of course, Greece itself. Ann always points out the plants you gave her. Last year I took Patrick and Wendy to the festival from their house in the Koroni castle wall as they'd never been and wanted to go. I'm glad I did. Patrick died, a brain tumour, last September. I brought back some earth from the grounds of Eleistria church, which we see every day from our balcony. It's scattered in Patick's grave – a Greek Orthodox custom transferred to a Catholic burial ground in Oxford.

Rowan and Baz moved out of Clapham shortly after you left and went back to Finsbury Park for another year, then left London for Waddesdon, the village with the Rothschild Manor, forty-five minutes by car from me in East Oxford. Baz is still in digital marketing and goes to London once a month or so. Rowan is with the King's Fund and in London one or two days a week. All of that changed when Covid, a plague, took hold and shut the world down with very limited face-to-face contact allowed anywhere on the planet for a couple of years. Think SARS but everywhere and longer, more intense and deadly. Sarah is still part-time at the Intensive Care Unit at the John Radcliffe. Will has accelerated up the corporate capitalist tree and is at his third consultancy role in energy and IT, a Swedish consultancy with an Oxford office.

And me now? After returning to Ghana and moving to Oxford I really got stuck into this book, which when it started I didn't know it was going to be a memoir of sorts. I've been working on it for five years with support from a great group of writers at the Oxford Centre for Life Writing, Wolfson College. Plus I've had a brilliant mentor/editor, Charlie Lee Potter, working with me throughout.

I still get to the theatre in London regularly. I go to quite a lot of small gigs around Oxford. Seen Nick Cave a few times with Rowan, and Springsteen last year for her birthday. For my seventieth she bought us tickets to see Bob Dylan in Manchester with his first new album in ten years, the excellent *Rough and Rowdy Ways*. For the same birthday, Will surprised me with tickets to the end-of-year men's top eight players now moved from the O2 to Turin. We stayed in a great apartment with distant views to the Alps located in the beautiful northern part of the city by the Po River. Elegant and gracious baroque architecture. The three of us with my sister Jane all went to Queen's this year and met Emma and Kevin too. Jane's husband Brian is not in robust health, he has limited mobility but continues to enjoy cooking and their new motor boat.

The tennis club off Cowley Road is a good standard and I play in the 'C' team in an Oxfordshire league. Lots of walking, the peak of which might have been last year: eight days back-to-back through the Lake District in late June with barrel-loads of rain most days. Three days mountain walking in the north central Peloponnese was fun, as are long days in the mountains of the Mani. You'd instantly recognise Koroni as essentially unchanged. A couple of smarter restaurants and bars, but Bogris is unchanged as is the Venetian house at the other end of the main street, which continues to crumble in front of everyone's eyes.

I've had the entire house repainted outside and another AC downstairs, but otherwise everything is the same, including the garden. Anesti and Razi, our Albanian housekeeper and gardener, stopped looking after the house a couple of years ago. They've managed to come and live in England where the children have established themselves. I have a more professional arrangement now for the house with a Greek property and maintenance company.

I managed finally to persuade my oldest friend from St Peter's, Rob and his wife Sue to come and stay in Koroni. They enjoyed it so much they asked to come again the following year. After Oxford and the early days of his farming career when we occasionally saw him together before he met Sue, I rarely saw him except for a period when we both worked in central London. Yet he's been a lodestone for me. When I think of him I always feel grounded. The year after you passed, I met an English woman who has a house a mile or two away off Zaga Beach. An Oxford classics graduate, then lawyer, interests in sailing, sport, walking, travel and the arts. She's become a good friend, but not a girlfriend. Only one of those of much note in eight years, and it lasted eighteen months: an environmentalist and painter, but the rest is between you, me and sometimes the children.

Most years in April around the time of your birthday we've rented a cottage or house, often in Devon or Dorset with both Rowan's and Will's families. I could continue talking about the ordinary joys and pleasures of life since you left. Of course I've had my dark moments particularly in the first two or three years. But I've come through the worst and am mainly content, though even when I'm perfectly happy at times it's as though the world has stopped and it's just the two of us together with the resonance of things we did, created or shared together: Glyn's huge, glaring, in-your-face painting on the sitting room wall; the wooden bananas from Brazil trailing in chains down a bookcase from Brussels; or the photograph of you I took in a French town square just this side of the Alps with an aperitif before dinner. Quite often, like this morning, something will trigger a memory of a beautiful moment with you and I'll cry gently with happiness.

THERE'S JUST ONE more thing I want to share with you which happened after you left. It was when you were at Bretton Hall doing your Masters in theatre and I was working in Kuwait. You remember I had to fly home after Easter because my Dad had died, somewhat unexpectedly, with no warning of any kind since we'd last seen him at Christmas. And you remember, I'm sure, after the service and his cremation the shock of my seeing my Dad outside in the arbour and then again back at the wake in their flat.

Four or five years after you left, I had a conversation with my sister learning that she'd hit the man who looked like Dad pounding on his chest screaming at him to leave. How dare he find his way, uninvited, into our father's funeral? She regrets she treated him so. After all, George was his father too. But she was understandably overcome by grief in the moment.

Then I learned from my cousin in Australia more about the man Brian who was the image of my father and my half-brother. He didn't exist for the first twenty-five years of my life and, after that brief encounter at the funeral wake, was absent for another forty-five years. In 2023 I went back to my Australian cousin to see if he had any further details which might help me trace Brian. He sent me the last email and phone number he had along with his birth year, 1934. If Brian was still alive, he'd be ninety now. The average age of UK males is eighty-one. Most likely he was dead.

I wrote him a brief email. Three days later there was no

response. I thought about using the phone number. The chance of my half-brother still living at an address with the same landline from a decade earlier was slim. And, if he was, would he be *compos mentis*?

It was a Sunday around 6pm. I punched the landline number. A male voice answered.

'Hello. Am I speaking to Brian Walker?'

'Yes, this is Brian Walker.' The voice was firm and clear.

'Brian. This is Richard. Richard Walker. I think we're related. We only met once briefly. At our father's funeral.'

'Yes. I remember, Richard.'

I continued that he'd probably be surprised to hear from me. I'd like to talk to him, but I was calling out of the blue. He might not want to speak at all or want to think about it.

He was polite and sounded composed. He was preparing supper for his wife who needed a lot of looking after. He'd be happy to talk but not right then. Could we talk in the next few days? We agreed a time and ended the call. I was surprised at how in control he sounded and at the ordinariness of our brief but courteous exchange.

We've had one more brief, and one longer, call since then. During these conversations Brian remained self-possessed as he'd been during my surprise initial call. I learned about his wife to whom he's been married for sixty-eight years and was in an advanced stage of dementia, with Brian her main carer. They have two children. The sixty-eight years marriage was the opposite of how our father had behaved towards Brian's mother, announcing in 1948 he was leaving the marriage. Brian was fourteen.

'He never contacted me or my mum after that. She wasn't glamorous enough for him. She went through years of suffering, and he destroyed her life, even though she did eventually remarry. She became hard and different. His own family idolised him. When I was born, he was stationed in Colchester. We rarely saw him. He was at Dunkirk then served in the Middle East. I respected and idolised him. Afterwards, I tried to do better than him. I joined the army and had three stripes within ten months. After he left, he never once contacted me or my mother. It was very painful for both of us. I have a cupboard full of poems and letters they wrote to each other. But then nothing. Absence. I had my own problems in understanding what'd happened. He destroyed something in me too. I moved from idolisation to hate.'

I listened in shock to this revelation about our shared father and how he'd damaged two lives of people once dear to him. The damage hadn't gone away. It'd been managed but was still present. I could only listen. This man who inflicted the destruction, our father, I loved. I still love him though I never 'idolised' him, a word Brian repeatedly used. I always 'respected' him. I thought I might respect him less because of this behaviour. But this hasn't happened. If anything it makes him more fallible, more human to me. But, unlike Brian, I have nothing to forgive.

In our first conversation I asked Brian if he'd like to meet me. Just once. In our second conversation I asked again how he'd feel about that. He said he didn't see the point. He didn't blame me for anything. Perhaps he feared it might be an unnecessarily brutal reminder of the hurt he's carried with him and kept buried, dormant but not quite dead.

He'd clearly been a successful businessman. 'I have an acre of garden and thirty-five windows in my house. I have no financial worries.' He told me he'd had a major heart attack in 1978 but had been in good health after recovery until he had a new heart valve in the Covid era. He was still driving and able to look after his wife. He didn't relate his own heart attack in 1978 to the death of our father in June the same year. I didn't want to push him on the coincidence. I asked how it was that he came to be at our father's funeral. He said our father's family had told his mother, then still alive. It was she who told Brian and asked him to go for both of them. Brian didn't want to. But he did as she asked.

We finished that second conversation with him saying I should feel free to contact him if I wanted to talk, ask questions, write or email.

'I'd be happy to have that kind of relationship.'

I've been considering contacting him right now as I am right up against the close of this memoir. But I'm not going to. I feel I've done enough. I have to let him go and not trouble him again.

NOW IN OXFORD, whenever we're waiting for the door of spring, ajar, to open fully, I remove the jungle green cover from the bench I bought to remember you. I always go to Koroni in May, and this has been the ninth spring since you left us. As I do every April, I rub down and varnish the bench for the new spring, summer and autumn, then it's wrapped up again for winter. In the centre of its horizontal, upper strut which you lean against when sitting, is a small brass plaque I had engraved. It reads:

For Lauren 1955 – 2016
With us here and in every garden

The bench welcomes in spring and summer in the garden of my Oxford house, which you've never seen. In Koroni, I sit in a deckchair on the balcony of our house surrounded by the stunning garden you created – purple bougainvillea, golden pomegranates, damask roses, lemon trees, deep pink hibiscus, emerald banana trees – in our olive grove. I listen for the popping call of the hoopoe or a glimpse of black-barred feathers in its dipping flight.

It doesn't matter that the bench and plaque aren't here. One day, I won't be here as I've decided to sell the house. Just as one day I won't be in Oxford either. But while I'm somewhere, anywhere:

In every beautiful place I walk or rest,
you rise and fall in me with every breath.

View from balcony of Richard and Lauren's house in Koroni.

Acknowledgments

I'M SO GRATEFUL to my family for all the support they've given me over the years. Rowan and Baz, Will and Sarah, and their families – always, but especially in the immediate years after Lauren's death. My sister Jane, who along with Rowan and Will commented on later versions of *Highlife*. Hugh Walker in Australia for some invaluable family history. Mum and Dad for giving me a starry start in life: fireworks and dancing. No going back!

The friends back at base camp in Haslemere: Lynne and Richard Taylor-Gooby; Di and Mike Keeley; Jane and Adam Phillips; Susu and Mike Sheringham; Aidan and Jackie Heathcote; David (RIP) and Barbara Jeffers; Tony, Beryl, Tom and Antonia Plant; Alan and Lyndsey Barlow; Alison and Peter Wallis; Carloyn and Peter Moore.

Scattered elsewhere: Andrew Hamilton, first friend; Liz and Mike Morris; John and Claire Chettoe; Pam and Rodger Moodie; Sue and Bernard, Ian and Gill Bossenger; Chantal Thompson; Alexander Ashworth; Jennie and Anthony Morris; Peter and Carolyn Moore; Jenny and Robin Bond; Chris and Jeremy Swainson; Cathy Wills; Rob Madge, a harbour of sanity during and since Oxford. Kate, painter and proper person, a beacon when I needed one most.

I'd like to thank Kate Kennedy for introducing me to the Oxford Centre for Life Writing at Wolfson College. Charlie Lee-Potter, for being a brilliant mentor and inspiring facilitator for the evolving group of writers – lovely people, who I'm lucky to have worked and had fun with for five years, including Lizzie,

Helen, Penelope, Ian, Wanda, Margie, Jim, Richard, Jane, Patricia, Ingrid, Carol and Rose.

Special thanks to Jonathan Curry-Machado, my editor, who accepted an earlier draft of *Highlife* without quibbling it hadn't come through an agent.

Huw and Jo, great friends from Athens who combine fun and help in Greece and London. Neighbours and friends in Koroni, including Dionysios Sipsas, Pantelis Kritikakis, Wendy and Patrick (RIP), Alexandra and The Maestro, Baba Tassos (RIP), Wanda and Barry, Takis, Dimitris, Nikos, Roula Katsa, Babis and Sophia Gaitanis, Anna, Gabi, Dave and Sally (both RIP), Dolo, Anesti and Razia, Paris, Yiannis and Priya.

Many writers have influenced me over the years, and I would particularly like to remember: William Golding (who taught me to drink Campari), Ken Saro-Wiwa (activist in human rights and the environment, a special friend, RIP), Barry Unsworth (RIP), Timothy Mo. Caryl Phillips and Mark Townsend (both writers with awards in fiction and journalism, who read early drafts of *Highlife* and whose encouragement gave me the momentum to continue), John Hegley (poet), Leslie Bethell (for a crash education in Brazilian history and culture), Roddy Beaton (for conversations when I was Director at the British Council in Athens, and his numerous writings on Greece).

Thanks also to many British Council and Foreign Office colleagues and friends: Harriet Harvey-Wood, Andrea Rose, John Hanson (RIP), Martin Davidson, David (RIP) and Verena Waterhouse, Roger Bowers (RIP), Nick Wadham-Smith, Michael O'Sullivan, Chris Hickey, Lyn Parker and Jane Walker, Nigel and Lumi Townson, Alan Curry (RIP), Rosemary Hilhorst, Les and Jade Dangerfield, Keith Davies, Rebecca Walton, Jan and David (RIP) Broad, Richard Phillips, Simon Ingram-Hill and Ann Rossiter, Sushma Bahl, Rajni Badlani, Nicholas (RIP) and Sue Fenn, Rob and Julia Fenn, Warwick and Pam Morris, Simon and Marianne Gass, Martin Dowle, Iain Murray, Chris and Mary Gibson, Simon and Jen Gammell, Ian Simm, Jeff Streeter, Tony Buckby, Jim Potts,

Buckby, Jim Potts, John Nance, Mark Walker, Andrew and Liz Fotheringham, Ayo (RIP), Andrew Murray, Christine Melia and Barry Bycroft, Jim Buttery, Paul and Rachel Docherty, Colin and Lis Perchard. All of you or your ghosts know why you are here.

New Oxford area friends include James and Jo Bluemel, Eleanor and Bob, Ceilia, Hugh, Angus, Toby, Noreen and Adrian, Penelope and Piers Gardner-Chloros, Julie, Peter Strickland.

(l. to r.) Sarah & Josh, Rowan & Scarlett, Will & Dylan, Richard, Baz & Leo. Broadway. 2019

Photograph © Ian Cook

RICHARD WALKER spent part of his childhood in Ghana, read English at Oxford, and worked in Canada, Spain and Kuwait, before joining the British Council. Most of his subsequent professional life was spent travelling the world as a senior Director for the British Council. It brought him postings in Bangkok, New Delhi, Sao Paolo, Lagos, Cyprus, Athens, Brussels and Hong Kong. Now he divides his time between his home in Oxford, and the house and garden he and Lauren created by a Venetian town in the Peloponnese. Several of his stories and plays have been broadcast by the BBC, and in 1989 he published his first novel, *A Curious Child*. Innovative for being written from the perspective of a transgender person, this is also being republished by Amaurea Press in 2025. He was awarded an OBE in 1998 for Indo-British cultural relations.